TRACKING NUCLEAR PROLIFERATION

A Guide in Maps and Charts, 1995

Leonard S. Spector
Mark G. McDonough
with Evan S. Medeiros

A CARNEGIE ENDOWMENT BOOK

Tracking Nuclear Proliferation may be ordered from the Brookings Institution, Department 029, Washington, DC, 20042-0029, USA, Tel. 1/800-275-1447.

For permission to reproduce any part of *Tracking Nuclear Proliferation* for educational purposes, please contact the Nuclear Proliferation Project of the Carnegie Endowment (Tel. 202-862-7955). Any updated figures available may also be obtained on request.

Library of Congress Cataloging-in-Publication Data

Spector, Leonard S.
  Tracking nuclear proliferation : a guide in maps and charts
Leonard S. Spector, Mark G. McDonough
  p. cm.
Includes bibliographical references
ISBM: 0-87003-061-2
1. Nuclear weapons.   2. Nuclear weapons facilities—Maps.
3. Nuclear weapons—Charts, diagrams, etc.
I. McDonough, Mark G., 1953-   . II Title
U264.S635   1995
355.02'17'0223—dc20   95-13251
                                                  CIP

Tracking Nuclear Proliferation

Acknowledgments

Project Director: Leonard S. Spector
Senior Managing Editor: Mark G. McDonough
Associate Editor: Evan S. Medeiros
Contributing Editors: Tessie Topol, Noah Sachs

Portions of *Tracking Nuclear Proliferation: A Guide in Maps and Charts, 1995*, draw upon a periodic report prepared jointly by Leonard S. Spector and William C. Potter, *Nuclear Successor States of the Soviet Union: Nuclear Weapon and Sensitive Export Status Report* (Washington, DC: Carnegie Endowment for International Peace, and Monterey, CA: The Monterey Institute of International Studies, December 1994). Information concerning nuclear developments in the former Soviet Union, compiled by Dunbar Lockwood of the Arms Control Association, Washington, DC, and and by Thomas B. Cochran, Robert S. Norris, and Christopher Paine of the Natural Resources Defense Council, Washington, DC, also contributed importantly to this report.

David Kyd of the International Atomic Energy Agency was also of great assistance in providing authoritative information on that agency's safeguarding activities.

Valuable comments and information were also provided by a number of specialists, including David Albright, Joseph S. Bermudez, Jr., Stephen P. Cohen, Zachery Davis, David Kay, Alexander Pikayev, John Redick, Mitchell Reiss, and Henry Sokolski.

Michael V. O'Hare, Carnegie Endowment Director of Finance and Administration and Secretary, was supportive of this project from the start and steered the team toward the final title of the study. Valeriana Kallab, Carnegie Director of Publications, provided editorial, design, and production guidance. Kathleen A. Lynch edited the manuscript. Nuclear Non-Proliferation Project Administrative Assistant Sharon H. Pettie provided valuable support and assistance throughout the project; Carnegie Junior Fellows Brian Weinberger and Marcel Lettre also made useful contributions to the effort. Joan Van Den Berg designed the cover and basic book format for printing by Automated Graphic Systems.

The authors would like to express their appreciation to all of these colleagues for their important contributions. Responsibility for the final judgments made concerning the contents of this report of course rests with the authors.

The Project Director wishes to express special thanks to the Carnegie Corporation of New York and the Rockefeller Brothers Fund for making this publication possible through their programmatic support of the Carnegie Endowment's Nuclear Non-Proliferation Project.

Contents

1
INTRODUCTION

Introduction

This is the sixth in the Endowment's series on the spread of nuclear weapons, begun in 1984.[1] Through these reports, the Endowment has sought to increase public understanding of the status and process of nuclear proliferation and to promote informed discussion of this vital issue.

Building on the earlier reports, *Tracking Nuclear Proliferation: A Guide in Maps and Charts, 1995,* has adopted a new, condensed format in order to address more efficiently the rapidly changing and increasingly diverse international nuclear environment. The abbreviated format will also ease updating of the guide at shorter intervals than in the past.

The present survey consists of summaries of the nuclear activities of countries that currently or in the recent past have raised proliferation concerns, highlighting important recent developments. The summaries are followed by maps and charts detailing the nuclear infrastructure and, where applicable, the nuclear arsenals of these countries. Although the guide is condensed in comparison to earlier Endowment surveys, its focus has been broadened.

This 1995 guide begins with Russia and China, two nuclear-weapon states where current or impending political transitions may weaken central control over nuclear weapons, nuclear weapons materials, and/or nuclear exports. Such developments could lead to a global black market in sensitive nuclear goods that could greatly accelerate the rate of proliferation by other states desiring nuclear arms. At the same time, such clandestine trade could undermine the International Atomic Energy Agency (IAEA) inspections and supplier-country export controls that form the backbone of the international nuclear non-proliferation regime. In its most extreme form, the breakdown of central authority in Russia or China could lead to civil strife and even national fragmentation, raising a host of new proliferation dangers.[2]

The guide next examines a new class of potential proliferants, Belarus, Kazakhstan, and Ukraine, the successor states of the Soviet Union that, in addition to Russia, have Soviet nuclear weapons on their territory. None of these three states has asserted operational control over these weapons. All three, moreover, are in the process of transfering them to Russia and have become non-nuclear-weapon state parties to the Nuclear Non-Proliferation Treaty (NPT), which prohibits them from possessing or manufacturing nuclear arms and requires IAEA inspection of all their nuclear facilities. The report reviews the status of this denuclearization process, which will take a number of years to complete. In the case of Ukraine, where the palpable threat of fragmentation along regional lines has only recently diminished, the report also presents information on the geographic deployment of nuclear arms by region and administrative division. Finally, the report updates the nuclear programs of the regional powers that have acquired de facto nuclear arsenals or that have manifested an interest in acquiring nuclear weapons and taken significant steps to achieve this objective. As this region-by-region review indicates, in the past several years, a surprising number of states in this category have convincingly renounced their nuclear ambitions.

Indeed, the convincing renunciation of nuclear arms by potential proliferants is one of the most striking trends reflected in the survey. The roster of states in this category includes:

- South Africa, which has acknowledged building an undeclared—and now dismantled—nuclear arsenal of six weapons;
- Brazil, which has acknowledged pursuing a nuclear weapons program during the 1980s and had mastered the essential technologies for this effort;
- Argentina, which apparently pursued a nuclear weapons program in the late 1970s and early 1980s and had similarly mastered the essential technologies;
- Romania, which apparently initiated such a program in the 1980s under the Ceausescu

regime but had made considerably less technological progress;

- Algeria, whose secret acquisition of a large research reactor from China in the early 1980s was seen by many as a first step toward development of a nuclear weapons infrastructure;
- Ukraine, which during 1993 asserted administrative control over the nuclear weapons on its territory and a proprietary interest in them; and
- Belarus and Kazakhstan, which, though less fearful of Russian hegemony than Ukraine and thus less tempted to seize control of the nuclear weapons on their territory, might nonetheless have done so.

North Korea's signing of the October 1994 "Agreed Framework" with the United States may signal a similar nuclear renunciation. The agreement provides, among other measures, for an immediate, verified freeze of activities at the key North Korean facilities that are believed to support its nuclear weapons program; for the eventual dismantling of these facilities; and for eventual unfettered IAEA access to installations that will reveal the North's past nuclear activities. Finally, Iraq's involuntary denuclearization under UN Security Council Resolution 687 following the 1991 Gulf War has, at least temporarily, eliminated the threat of proliferation by this state.

Another positive trend has been the extraordinary reduction in the nuclear deployments of Russia and the United States, which have deactivated many hundreds of strategic nuclear weapons and thousands of tactical nuclear arms, while simultaneously dismantling thousands of nuclear warheads. In its coverage of Russian nuclear activities, the survey highlights changes in that country's nuclear arsenal.

A number of disturbing trends are also highlighted in the report. India, Israel, and Pakistan—three states that possess undeclared nuclear weapons or could deploy them rapidly in a crisis—have continued to reject new nuclear restraints, while gradually expanding their potential nuclear arsenals and/or production capabilities. Although Israel is engaged in a peace process that may eventually lead it to accept new non-proliferation controls as part of a broader regional settlement, relations between Pakistan and India remain seriously strained by tensions over Kashmir. Moreover, the apparent ability of both South Asian states to deploy short-range nuclear-capable ballistic missiles threatens to trigger an escalating nuclear arms race between them.

Also disturbing is Iran's effort to develop nuclear weapons. Although little information has become available on its activities in this regard, the United States remains deeply concerned over its

intentions. Highlighting this concern, then U.S. Director of Central Intelligence R. James Woolsey stated in September 1994:

> As threatening as this [Iran's] military program is, our biggest concern is in countering Iran's aggressive pursuit of development of weapons of mass destruction. Iran has turned to suppliers in both the East and West, using intermediaries to purchase technology clandestinely. We continue to pay close attention to Iranian efforts to purchase dual-use technology, technology which increases the difficulty we have in uncovering Iran's ultimate intentions and programs. . . .

> We pay particular attention to Iran's efforts to acquire nuclear and missile technology from the West in order to enable it to build its own nuclear weapons, despite being a signatory to the NPT. We believe that Iran is 8-10 years away from building such weapons, and that help from the outside will be critical in reaching this timetable. Iran has been particularly active in trying to purchase nuclear materials or technology clandestinely from Russian sources. Iran is also looking to purchase fully-fabricated nuclear weapons in order to accelerate sharply its timetable.[3]

Iraq, too, continues to pose an incipient proliferation threat. Although its nuclear weapons infrastructure was dismantled pursuant to Security Council Resolution 687 and although Iraq will remain under special long-term monitoring by the IAEA and the UN Special Commission on Iraq, it must be assumed that its desire for nuclear weapons remains strong and that it will exploit every opportunity to achieve this end. As in the case of Iran, the most practical means for Iraq to realize its nuclear ambitions would be through the acquisition of weapons-usable nuclear materials or nuclear weapons themselves from the former Soviet Union.

Indeed, ensuring the security of such matériel in the Soviet successor states has emerged as today's most serious proliferation challenge. The importance of this issue was underscored by the episodes of nuclear smuggling that came to light in Germany and Czechoslovakia during 1994. *Tracking Nuclear Proliferation* highlights this issue in its maps and charts indicating the many sites at which such nuclear arms and weapons-usable nuclear materials are being produced, stored, or used within the former Soviet Union.

A number of additional trends of importance to the field of non-proliferation could not be covered fully in this survey. Most important, perhaps, is the significant strengthening of the nuclear non-proliferation regime that has occurred in the past several years, a pattern that has included enhancements of IAEA safeguards, tightened supplier-state export controls, growing adherence to the NPT, and increased Security Council involvement in enforcing this pact. In addition, a number of global trends—especially the breakup of the Soviet Union, the end of the Cold War, and the spread of democracy and free-market economies—are having an important impact in containing proliferation. Future editions of *Tracking Nuclear Proliferation* will attempt to address such developments more fully. Finally, the future of the NPT is to be decided at the NPT Review and Extension Conference, to be held in New York in April-May 1995. The results of this meeting can be expected to have a profound impact on the future spread of nuclear arms.

Tracking Nuclear Proliferation is based on unclassified publications and on interviews with knowledgeable U.S. and foreign officials. Although the report attempts to reflect accurately the general consensus in official and scholarly circles about the nuclear status of the countries covered, there will inevitably be surprises ahead as new information becomes available on these issues.

NOTES

[1]The five predecessor volumes, all prepared at the Carnegie Endowment, are : Leonard S. Spector, *Nuclear Proliferation Today* (New York: Vintage Books, 1984); Leonard S. Spector, *The New Nuclear Nations* (New York: Vintage Books, 1985); Leonard S. Spector, *Going Nuclear* (Cambridge, MA: Ballinger Publishing Company, 1986); Leonard S. Spector, *The Undeclared Bomb* (Cambridge, MA: Ballinger Publishing Company, 1988); and Leonard S. Spector with Jacqueline R. Smith, *Nuclear Ambitions* (Boulder, CO: Westview Press, 1990).

[2]Fears of political disintegration in Russia eased during 1994 but were not completely dispelled. As recently as October 1993, a coup against President Boris Yeltsin was attempted by force of arms. The episode exposed deep fissures within the Russian polity and raised serious questions about the loyalty of many military units to the central government. Currently, the Chechen Republic is in open rebellion against Moscow, another reminder of Russia's potential fragility as a cohesive state.

China will undergo a difficult political transition when Deng Xiaoping passes from the scene. Although they represent a minority view, a number of China watchers believe the possibilities of civil turmoil and, conceivably, of national dissolution must be taken seriously. See references in note 1 of the China section of this report, p. 50.

[3]"Challenges to the Peace in the Middle East," Address of R. James Woolsey, DCI, to the Washington Institute for Near East Policy, Wye Plantation, MD, September 23, 1994, (revised version).

2

GLOBAL TRENDS
1995

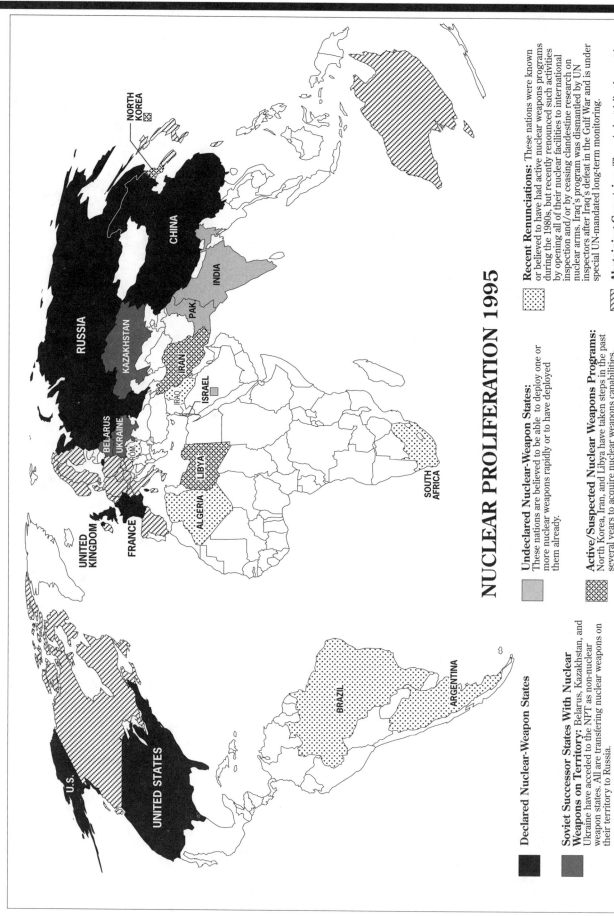

NUCLEAR PROLIFERATION 1995

Declared Nuclear-Weapon States

Soviet Successor States With Nuclear Weapons on Territory: Belarus, Kazakhstan, and Ukraine have acceded to the NPT as non-nuclear weapon states. All are transferring nuclear weapons on their territory to Russia.

Undeclared Nuclear-Weapon States: These nations are believed to be able to deploy one or more nuclear weapons rapidly or to have deployed them already.

Active/Suspected Nuclear Weapons Programs: North Korea, Iran, and Libya have taken steps in the past several years to acquire nuclear weapons capabilities.

Recent Renunciations: These nations were known or believed to have had active nuclear weapons programs during the 1980s, but recently renounced such activities by opening all of their nuclear facilities to international inspection and/or by ceasing clandestine research on nuclear arms. Iraq's program was dismantled by UN inspectors after Iraq's defeat in the Gulf War and is under special UN-mandated long-term monitoring.

Abstaining Countries: These industrialized countries have the technological base, but not thus far the desire, to develop nuclear weapons. A number have installations under international inspection that can produce weapons-grade nuclear material.

Carnegie Endowment for International Peace, *Tracking Nuclear Proliferation*, 1995.

NUCLEAR STATUS OF STATES, 1995

DECLARED NUCLEAR-WEAPON STATES
China, France, Russia, United Kingdom, United States: All have declared their nuclear status and are recognized under the Nuclear Non-Proliferation Treaty (NPT) as nuclear-weapon states because each detonated a nuclear test prior to Jan. 1, 1967. Estimated Nuclear Stockpiles: U.S., Strategic: 8,500/Tactical: 7,000; Russia, Str: 7,200/Tac: 6,000–13,000; United Kingdom, Str: 100/Tac: 100; France, Str: 482/Tac:0; China, Str: 284/Tac: 150.

SOVIET SUCCESSOR STATES WITH NUCLEAR WEAPONS ON TERRITORY
Belarus, Kazakhstan, Ukraine: All have joined the NPT as non-nuclear-weapon states and will place all of their nuclear activities under International Atomic Energy Agency (IAEA) inspection (excluding nuclear weapons still on their territory); all are transfering nuclear weapons to Russia; none is able to use remaining nuclear weapons independent of central command in Russia.

UNDECLARED NUCLEAR-WEAPON STATES
India, Israel, Pakistan: All are able to deploy nuclear weapons rapidly, but have not acknowledged possessing them. None is party to the NPT. Israeli arsenal probably 100+ devices; Indian arsenal probably 60+; Pakistani arsenal probably 15–25.

ACTIVE/SUSPECTED NUCLEAR WEAPONS PROGRAMS
Iran, Libya, North Korea: Nuclear weapons ambitions currently checked by international controls and technological constraints. Although these states are party to the NPT and have denied seeking nuclear weapons, their non-proliferation commitments are still considered suspect. North Korea closest; recently agreed to freeze and ultimately dismantle its nuclear weapons program under the October 1994 U.S.-North Korean ''Agreed Framework''; may have separated enough weapons-grade material for a nuclear device. Iran thought eight years from nuclear weapons, but could accelerate program if nuclear assets leak from former Soviet Union. Libya has extremely limited nuclear infrastructure.

RECENT RENUNCIATIONS
Algeria, Argentina, Brazil, Iraq, Romania, South Africa*: Were known or suspected to have secret nuclear weapons programs in the past, but recently abandoned these efforts by opening their nuclear facilities to international and/or regional inspection agencies, joining the NPT, and/or by terminating all research on nuclear arms. South Africa dismantled its program in the early 1990s and signed the NPT in 1991; the IAEA has verified complete dismantlement of all nuclear devices. Argentina and Brazil have both signed and ratified the Treaty of Tlatelolco and agreed to implement a system of comprehensive IAEA and bilateral inspections; on February 10, 1995, Argentina acceded to the NPT. Algeria acceded to the NPT in January 1995. Iraq's extensive nuclear program was dismantled by UN inspectors and is subject to special UN-mandated long-term monitoring. Romania, under the Ceausescu regime, apparently pursued a nuclear-weapons development program, which included experimental plutonium extraction not subject to IAEA monitoring. After Ceausescu's overthrow in 1989, the Iliescu government terminated the program.
*It has been reported that Saudi Arabia collaborated with Iraq in pursuing nuclear weapons during the 1980s, but this report has not been confirmed. Saudi Arabia joined the NPT in 1988. (See p. 127, note 4, for additional details.)

ABSTAINING COUNTRIES
Australia, Austria, Belgium, Canada, the Czech Republic, Denmark, Finland, Germany, Hungary, Ireland, Italy, Japan, Netherlands, Norway, Poland, Slovakia, South Korea, and Spain: All are industrialized nations that have the technical capacity but not the political desire to develop nuclear weapons. Almost all of these nations operate nuclear reactors that are under IAEA inspection, and several have stocks of weapons-usable nuclear material, also under IAEA monitoring.

3

THE INTERNATIONAL NUCLEAR NON-PROLIFERATION REGIME

The International Nuclear Non-Proliferation Regime

The Treaty on the Non-Proliferation of Nuclear Weapons (NPT) is the centerpiece of the global nuclear non-proliferation regime, a series of interlocking international treaties, bilateral undertakings, and multilateral inspections aimed at halting the spread of nuclear weapons. Other major elements of the regime are the International Atomic Energy Agency (IAEA) and two closely connected export control systems implemented by the key nuclear supplier countries (for details on these regime elements, see Appendices C and D).

*

The NPT, which was opened for signature in 1968 and entered into force in 1970, divides the countries of the world into two categories, "nuclear-weapon states" and "non-nuclear-weapon states." It defines the former category as those countries that detonated a nuclear explosion before 1967, namely the United States (first detonation in 1945), the Soviet Union (1949), Great Britain (1952), France (1960), and China (1964). Russia succeeded to the Soviet Union's status as a nuclear-weapon state under the treaty in 1992. The NPT treats all other countries as non-nuclear-weapon states. Under the pact:

- Non-nuclear-weapon states ratifying the Treaty pledge not to manufacture or receive nuclear explosives. (Both nuclear weapons and "peaceful nuclear explosives" are prohibited.)
- To verify that they are living up to this pledge, non-nuclear-weapon states also agree to accept IAEA safeguards on *all* their peaceful nuclear activities, an arrangement known as "full-scope safeguards."[1]

- All countries accepting the Treaty agree not to export nuclear equipment or material to non-nuclear-weapon states except under IAEA safeguards, and nuclear-weapon states agree not to assist non-nuclear-weapon states in obtaining nuclear weapons.
- All countries accepting the Treaty agree to facilitate the fullest possible sharing of peaceful nuclear technology.
- All countries accepting the Treaty agree to pursue negotiations in good faith to end the nuclear-arms race and to achieve nuclear disarmament under international control. (In practice, this applies to the nuclear-weapon states.)
- A party may withdraw from the Treaty on ninety days' notice if "extraordinary events related to the subject matter of the treaty" have "jeopardized its supreme interests."

All five nuclear-weapon states are parties to the NPT. The United States, Russia, and Great Britain are the Treaty's depositary states; China and France did not join until 1992. As of March 15, 1995, the Treaty had 169 non-nuclear-weapon state parties, for a total of 174 parties.

The NPT originally entered into force for twenty-five years, with periodic reviews of the Treaty occurring every five years. In May 1995, a majority of the parties to the pact must determine whether to extend the accord for a fixed term or terms, or indefinitely.

Among the states of proliferation concern today, India, Israel, and Pakistan are not parties to the pact. Each has nuclear installations not subject to IAEA safeguards that contribute to its respective nuclear weapons capability.[2] Iran, Iraq, and Libya are non-nuclear-weapon state parties to the Treaty, but their commitment to the accord is suspect because of their demonstrated interest in acquiring nuclear arms.[3]

North Korea became a party to the Treaty in 1985 but delayed more than six years before agreeing, in April 1992, to permit IAEA inspections of its nuclear activities. During that interval, it produced a quantity of plutonium that may be sufficient for one or two nuclear weapons. As of March 1995, it had not satisfactorily accounted for this material and was not in compliance with its IAEA safeguards obligations under the Treaty because of its refusal to allow the IAEA to permit an IAEA "special inspection" of two nuclear waste sites believed to contain information regarding past production of plutonium. Under an "Agreed Framework" signed with the United States in October 1994, North Korea has agreed to resolve these issues at a future date; in the meantime, it has accepted restrictions on its nuclear activities that go beyond its obligations under the NPT, including a freeze on the operation and construction of a number of sensitive facilities.

*

The IAEA is a second key element of the international non-proliferation regime. Founded in 1957, the Vienna-based IAEA is an international organization with 122 member countries. Its principal missions are to facilitate the use of nuclear energy for peaceful purposes and to implement a system of audits and on-site inspections, collectively known as "safeguards," to verify that nuclear facilities and materials are not being diverted for the production of nuclear explosives.

In addition to monitoring all peaceful nuclear activities in non-nuclear-weapon state parties to the NPT, the agency also monitors individual facilities in non-NPT parties at the request of these states. Thus, even though India, Israel, and Pakistan are not parties to the NPT, a number of nuclear facilities in each of these countries are subject to IAEA monitoring and cannot be used to support these nations' undeclared nuclear weapons programs.

Until 1991, in non-nuclear-weapon state parties to the NPT, the IAEA monitored only those facilities declared by the inspected country and did not seek out possible undeclared nuclear installations. After the 1991 Gulf War, however, it was learned that Iraq had secretly developed a network of undeclared nuclear facilities as part of an extensive nuclear weapons program. This led the IAEA in late 1991 to announce that it would begin to exercise its previously unused authority to conduct "special inspections," i.e., to demand access to undeclared sites where it suspected nuclear activities were being conducted.

The agency first attempted to conduct a special inspection in North Korea in 1992, but Pyongyang refused to comply with the IAEA's request, triggering a crisis that has yet to be fully resolved. However, the IAEA's new authority has indirectly provided added access for the agency in Iran. Because an IAEA demand for a special inspections carries the implied accusation that a country may be violating the NPT, Iran, anticipating that the agency might seek special inspections within its territory, has sought to avert the stigma associated with such inspections by agreeing to permit the IAEA to visit any location in Iran on request. The agency visited undeclared sites there in February 1992 and November 1993 but did not detect any activities in violation of Iran's NPT obligations.

*

Two informal coalitions of nations that voluntarily restrict the export of equipment and materials that could be used to develop nuclear weapons form the third major element of the non-proliferation regime.

Shortly after the NPT came into force in 1970, a number of Western and Soviet-bloc nuclear-supplier states began consultations concerning the procedures and standards that would apply to nuclear exports to non-nuclear-weapon states. The group, known as the NPT Exporters Committee (or the Zangger Committee, after its Swiss chairman), adopted a set of guidelines in August 1974, including a list of export items that would trigger the requirement for the application of IAEA safeguards in recipient states. These procedures and the "trigger list," updated in subsequent years, represent the first major agreement on uniform regulation of nuclear exports by actual and potential nuclear suppliers.

Following India's nuclear test in 1974, an overlapping group of supplier states—notably including France, which was not then a party to the NPT—met in London to elaborate export guidelines further. In January 1976, this group, which became known as the Nuclear Suppliers Group (NSG) or the London Suppliers Group, adopted guidelines similar to those of the NPT Exporters Committee, but which also extended to transfers of technology and included agreement to "exercise restraint" in the transfer of uranium-enrichment and plutonium-extraction equipment and facilities.

In April 1992, in the wake of the Gulf War, the NSG expanded its export control guidelines, which theretofore had covered only uniquely nuclear items, to cover sixty-five "dual-use" items, as well. The group also added as a requirement for future exports that recipient states accept IAEA inspection on all of their peaceful nuclear activities. This rule, previously adopted by only some NSG members, effectively precludes nuclear commerce by NSG member states with India, Israel, and Pakistan.

In addition to agreeing to such full-scope safeguards, all nations importing regulated items from NSG member states must promise to furnish adequate physical security for transfered nuclear materials and facilities; pledge not to export nuclear materials and technologies to other nations without the permission of the original exporting nation or without a pledge from the recipient nation to abide by these same rules; and promise not to use any imports to build nuclear explosives. (Similar rules—apart from the full-scope safeguards requirement—apply to exports regulated by the Zangger Committee, which continues to function, although it has been partially eclipsed by the Nuclear Suppliers Group, whose export controls have, in general, been more far-reaching.)

The members of the two supplier groups are listed in Appendix D.

NOTES

[1]The IAEA monitors only "peaceful" uses of nuclear energy to verify non-diversion to nuclear explosives. It does not monitor non-proscribed military uses of nuclear energy—i.e., the use of nuclear energy for submarine propulsion systems—and non-nuclear-weapon state NPT parties may request that nuclear materials be removed from IAEA monitoring for this purpose. To date, none of the states in this category possesses or is building nuclear submarines, and thus none has ever availed itself of this exception.

The IAEA verifies only activities involving the production or use of nuclear materials. The NPT makes no provision for verifying that non-nuclear-weapon state parties are not engaged in prohibited activities relating to the manufacture of nuclear weapons that do not involve nuclear materials, such as fabricating the non-nuclear components for nuclear arms.

[2]Brazil, which also has a substantial nuclear infrastructure and a past interest in acquiring nuclear arms, is also not a party to the NPT, but has accepted equivalent restrictions on its nuclear activities pursuant to the Treaty of Tlatelolco, which establishes a nuclear-weapon-free zone in Latin America and the Caribbean, and pursuant to bilateral agreements with Argentina.

[3]Iraq is also subject to a pervasive program of monitoring by the IAEA and the UN Special Commission on Iraq intended to eliminate its weapons of mass and certain missile capabilities. These arrangements are being implemented pursuant to UN Security Council resolutions adopted in the aftermath of the 1991 Persian Gulf War.

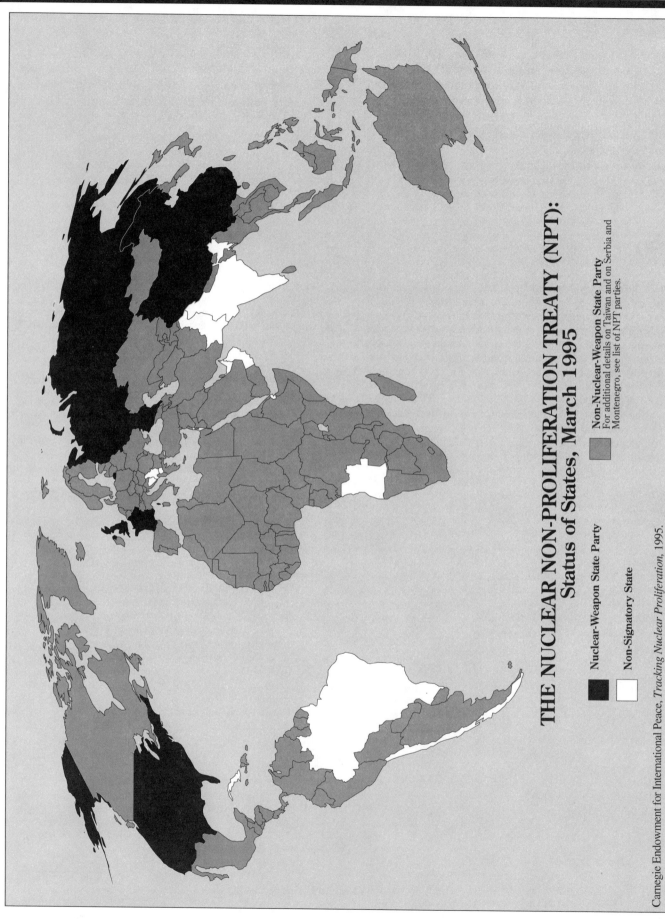

THE NUCLEAR NON-PROLIFERATION TREATY (NPT): Status of States, March 1995

Nuclear-Weapon State Party

Non-Signatory State

Non-Nuclear-Weapon State Party
For additional details on Taiwan and on Serbia and Montenegro, see list of NPT parties.

Carnegie Endowment for International Peace, *Tracking Nuclear Proliferation*, 1995.

States Party to the Nuclear Non-Proliferation Treaty (NPT) as of March 15, 1995[1,2]

COUNTRY	DATE SIGNED	DEPOSITED RATIFICATION	DEPOSITED ACCESSION
Afghanistan	7-01-68	2-04-70	
Albania			9-12-90
Algeria			1-12-95
Antigua & Barbuda			6-17-85
Argentina			2-10-95
Armenia			7-15-93
Australia	2-27-70	1-23-73	
Austria	7-01-68	6-27-69	
Azerbaijan			9-22-92
Bahamas			8-11-76
Bahrain			11-03-88
Bangladesh			8-31-79
Barbados	7-01-68	2-21-80	
Belarus			7-22-93
Belgium	8-20-68	5-02-75	
Belize			8-09-85
Benin	7-01-68	10-31-72	
Bhutan			5-23-85
Bolivia	7-01-68	5-26-70	
Bosnia & Herzegovina			8-15-94
Botswana	7-01-68	4-28-69	
Brunei			3-26-85
Bulgaria	7-01-68	9-05-69	
Burkino Faso	11-25-68	3-03-70	
Burundi			3-19-71
Cambodia			6-02-72
Cameroon	7-17-68	1-08-69	
Canada	7-23-68	1-08-69	
Cape Verde			10-24-79
Central African Republic			10-25-70
Chad	7-01-68	3-10-71	
China, People's Republic[N]			3-09-92
Colombia	7-01-68	4-08-86	
Congo			10-23-78
Costa Rica	7-01-68	3-03-70	
Côte d'Ivoire	7-01-68	3-06-73	
Croatia			6-29-92
Cyprus	7-01-68	2-10-70	
Czech Republic			1-01-93
Denmark	7-01-68	1-03-69	
Dominica			8-10-84
Dominican Republic	7-01-68	7-24-71	
Ecuador	7-09-68	3-07-69	
Egypt	7-01-68	2-26-81	
El Salvador	7-01-68	7-11-72	
Equatorial Guinea			11-01-84
Eritrea			3-03-95
Estonia			1-07-92
Ethiopia	9-05-68	2-05-70	
Fiji			7-14-72
Finland	7-01-68	2-05-69	
France[N]			8-03-92

COUNTRY	DATE SIGNED	DEPOSITED RATIFICATION	DEPOSITED ACCESSION
Gabon			2-19-74
Gambia	9-04-68	5-12-75	
Georgia			3-07-94
Germany,Federal Republic	11-28-69	5-02-75	
Ghana	7-01-68	5-04-70	
Greece	7-01-68	3-11-70	
Grenada			9-02-75
Guatemala	7-26-68	9-22-70	
Guinea			4-29-85
Guinea-Bissau			8-20-76
Guyana			10-19-93
Haiti	7-01-68	6-02-70	
Holy See			2-25-71
Honduras	7-01-68	5-16-73	
Hungary	7-01-68	5-27-69	
Iceland	7-01-68	7-18-69	
Indonesia	3-02-70	7-12-79	
Iran	7-01-68	2-02-70	
Iraq	7-01-68	10-29-69	
Ireland	7-01-68	7-01-68	
Italy	1-28-69	5-02-75	
Jamaica	4-14-69	3-05-70	
Japan	2-03-70	6-08-76	
Jordan	7-10-68	2-11-70	
Kazakhstan			2-14-94
Kenya	7-01-68	6-11-70	
Kiribati			4-18-85
Korea, North			12-12-85
Korea, South	7-01-68	4-23-75	
Kuwait	8-15-68	11-17-89	
Kyrgyzstan			7-05-94
Laos	7-01-68	2-20-70	
Latvia			1-31-92
Lebanon	7-01-68	7-15-70	
Lesotho	7-09-68	5-20-70	
Liberia	7-01-68	3-05-70	
Libya	7-18-68	5-26-75	
Liechtenstein			4-20-78
Lithuania			9-23-91
Luxembourg	8-14-68	5-02-75	
Madagascar	8-22-68	10-08-70	
Malawi			2-18-86
Malaysia	7-01-68	3-05-70	
Maldive Islands	9-11-68	4-07-70	
Mali	7-14-69	2-10-70	
Malta	4-17-69	2-06-70	
Marshall Islands			1-30-95
Mauritania			10-23-93
Mauritius	7-01-68	4-08-69	
Mexico	7-26-68	1-21-69	
Moldova			10-11-94
Monaco			3-13-95
Mongolia	7-01-68	5-14-69	

States Party to the NPT (cont'd.)

COUNTRY	DATE SIGNED	DEPOSITED RATIFICATION	DEPOSITED ACCESSION
Morocco	7-01-68	11-27-70	
Mozambique			9-04-90
Myanmar (Burma)			12-02-92
Namibia			10-02-92
Nauru			6-07-82
Nepal	7-01-68	1-05-70	
Netherlands	8-20-68	5-02-75	
New Zealand	7-01-68	9-10-69	
Nicaragua	7-01-68	3-06-73	
Niger			10-09-92
Nigeria	7-01-68	9-27-68	
Norway	7-01-68	2-05-69	
Panama	7-01-68	1-13-77	
Papua New Guinea			1-13-82
Paraguay	7-01-68	2-04-70	
Peru	7-01-68	3-03-70	
Philippines	7-01-68	10-05-72	
Poland	7-01-68	6-12-69	
Portugal			12-15-77
Qatar			4-03-89
Romania	7-01-68	2-04-70	
Russia*[N]	7-01-68	3-05-70	
Rwanda			5-20-75
Saint Kitts and Nevis			3-22-93
Saint Lucia			12-28-79
Saint Vincent & Grenadines			11-06-84
San Marino	7-01-68	8-10-70	
Sao Tome & Principe			7-20-83
Saudi Arabia			10-03-88
Senegal	7-01-68	12-17-70	
Seychelles			3-12-85
Sierra Leone			2-26-75
Singapore	2-05-70	3-10-76	
Slovakia			1-01-93
Slovenia			4-07-92
Solomon Islands			6-17-81
Somalia	7-01-68	3-05-70	
South Africa			7-10-91
Spain			11-05-87
Sri Lanka	7-01-68	3-05-79	
Sudan	12-24-68	10-31-73	
Suriname			6-30-76
Swaziland	6-24-69	12-11-69	
Sweden	8-19-68	1-09-70	
Switzerland	11-27-69	3-09-77	
Syria	7-01-68	9-24-69	
Taiwan[3]	7-01-68	1-27-70	
Tajikistan			1-17-95
Tanzania			5-31-91
Thailand			12-02-72
Togo	7-01-68	2-26-70	
Tonga			7-07-71
Trinidad and Tobago	8-20-68	10-30-86	

States Party to the NPT (cont'd.)

COUNTRY	DATE SIGNED	DEPOSITED RATIFICATION	DEPOSITED ACCESSION
Tunisia	7-01-68	2-26-70	
Turkey	1-28-69	4-17-80	
Turkmenistan			9-29-94
Tuvalu			1-19-79
Uganda			10-20-82
Ukraine			12-05-94
United Kingdom*N	7-01-68	11-27-68	
United States*N	7-01-68	3-05-70	
Uruguay	7-01-68	8-31-70	
Uzbekistan			5-02-92
Venezuela	7-01-68	9-25-75	
Vietnam			6-14-82
Western Samoa			3-17-75
Yemen	11-14-68	6-01-79	
Zaire	7-22-68	8-04-70	
Zambia			5-15-91
Zimbabwe			9-26-91

*Depositary states
N = Nuclear-weapon states

NOTES

1. Non-signatory states as of March 15, 1995, include Andorra, Angola, Brazil, Chile, Comoros, Cuba, Djibouti, India, Israel, Macedonia, Micronesia, Oman, Pakistan, Palau, United Arab Emirates, and Vanuatu.

2. Serbia and Montenegro claims NPT membership as the sole successor state to Yugoslavia. Its NPT status remains in dispute.

3. The United States recognizes the People's Republic of China as the sole legal government of China but regards Taiwan as bound by the terms of the NPT.

Sources: U.S. Arms Control and Disarmament Agency, "Signatories and Parties to the Treaty on the Non-proliferation of Nuclear Weapons," Fact Sheet, February 1, 1995 (updated on March 28, 1995); The Arms Control Association, Washington, D.C.

Treaty on the Non-Proliferation of Nuclear Weapons

Signed at Washington, London, and Moscow July 1, 1968

The States concluding this Treaty, hereinafter referred to as the "Parties to the Treaty,"

Considering the devastation that would be visited upon all mankind by a nuclear war and the consequent need to make every effort to avert the danger of such a war and to take measures to safeguard the security of peoples,

Believing that the proliferation of nuclear weapons would seriously enhance the danger of nuclear war,

In conformity with resolutions of the United Nations General Assembly calling for the conclusion of an agreement on the prevention of wider dissemination of nuclear weapons,

Undertaking to cooperate in facilitating the application of International Atomic Energy Agency safeguards on peaceful nuclear activities,

Expressing their support for research, development and other efforts to further the application, within the framework of the International Atomic Energy Agency safeguards system, of the principle of safeguarding effectively the flow of source and special fissionable materials by use of instruments and other techniques at certain strategic points,

Affirming the principle that the benefits of peaceful applications of nuclear technology, including any technological by-products which may be derived by nuclear-weapon States from the development of nuclear explosive devices, should be available for peaceful purposes to all Parties of the Treaty, whether nuclear-weapon or non-nuclear-weapon states,

Convinced that, in furtherance of this principle, all Parties to the Treaty are entitled to participate in the fullest possible exchange of scientific information for, and to contribute alone or in cooperation with other States to, the further development of the applications of atomic energy for peaceful purposes,

Declaring their intention to achieve at the earliest possible date the cessation of the nuclear arms race and to undertake effective measures in the direction of nuclear disarmament,

Urging the cooperation of all States in the attainment of this objective,

Recalling the determination expressed by the Parties to the 1963 Treaty banning nuclear weapons tests in the atmosphere, in outer space and under water in its Preamble to seek to achieve the discontinuance of all test explosions of nuclear weapons for all time and to continue negotiations to this end,

Desiring to further the easing of international tension and the strengthening of trust between States in order to facilitate the cessation of the manufacture of nuclear weapons, the liquidation of all their existing stockpiles, and the elimination from national arsenals of nuclear weapons and the means of their delivery pursuant to a treaty on general and complete disarmament under strict and effective international control,

Recalling that, in accordance with the Charter of the United Nations, States must refrain in their international relations from the threat or use of force against the territorial integrity or political independence of any State, or in any other manner inconsistent with the Purposes of the United Nations, and that the establishment and maintenance of international peace and security are to be promoted with the least diversion for armaments of the world's human and economic resources,

Have agreed as follows:

Article I

Each nuclear-weapon State Party to the Treaty undertakes not to transfer to any recipient whatsoever nuclear weapons or other nuclear explosive devices or control over such weapons or explosive devices directly, or indirectly; and not in any way to otherwise acquire nuclear weapons or other nuclear explosive devices, or control over such weapons or explosive devices.

Article II

Each non-nuclear-weapon State Party to the Treaty undertakes not to receive the transfer from any transferor whatsoever of nuclear weapons or other nuclear explosive devices or of control over such weapons or explosive devices directly, or indirectly; not to manufacture or otherwise acquire nuclear weapons or other nuclear explosive devices; and not to seek or receive any assistance in the manufacture of nuclear weapons or other nuclear explosive devices.

Article III

1. Each non-nuclear-weapon State Party to the Treaty undertakes to accept safeguards, as set forth in an agreement to be negotiated and concluded with the International Atomic Energy Agency in accordance with the Statute of the International Atomic Energy Agency and the Agency's safeguards system, for the exclusive purpose of verification of the fulfillment of its obligations assumed under this Treaty with a view to preventing diversion of nuclear energy from peaceful uses to nuclear weapons or other nuclear explosive devices. Procedures for the safeguards required by this article shall be followed with respect to source or special fissionable material whether it is being produced, processed or used in any principal nuclear facility or is outside any such facility. The safeguards required by this article shall be applied to all source or special fissionable material in all peaceful nuclear activities within the territory of such State, under its jurisdiction, or carried out under its control anywhere.

2. Each State Party to the Treaty undertakes not to provide: (a) source or special fissionable material, or (b) equipment or material especially designed or prepared for the processing, use or production of special fissionable material, to any non-nuclear-weapon State for peaceful purposes, unless the source or special fissionable material shall be subject to the safeguards required by this article.

3. The safeguards required by this article shall be implemented in a manner designed to comply with article IV of this Treaty, and to avoid hampering the economic or technological development of the Parties or international cooperation in the field of peaceful nuclear activities, including the international exchange of nuclear material and equipment for the processing, use or production of nuclear material for peaceful purposes in accordance with the provisions of this article and the principle of safeguarding set forth in the Preamble of the Treaty.

4. Non-nuclear-weapon States Party to the Treaty shall conclude agreements with the International Atomic Energy Agency to meet the requirements of this article either individually or together with other States in accordance with the Statute of the International Atomic Energy Agency. Negotiation of such agreements shall commence within 180 days from the original entry into force of this Treaty. For States depositing their instruments of ratification or accession after the 180-day period, negotiation of such agreements shall commence not later than the date of such deposit. Such agreements shall enter into force not later than eighteen months after the date of initiation of negotiations.

Article IV

1. Nothing in this Treaty shall be interpreted as affecting the inalienable right of all the Parties to the Treaty to develop research, production and use of nuclear energy for peaceful purposes without discrimination and in conformity with articles I and II of this Treaty.

2. All the Parties to the Treaty undertake to facilitate, and have the right to participate in, the fullest possible exchange of equipment, materials and scientific and technological information for the peaceful uses of nuclear energy. Parties to the Treaty in a position to do so shall also cooperate in contributing alone or together with other States or international organizations to the further development of the applications of nuclear energy for peaceful purposes, especially in the territories of non-nuclear-weapon States Party to the Treaty, with due consideration for the needs of the developing areas of the world.

Article V

Each party to the Treaty undertakes to take appropriate measures to ensure that, in accordance with this Treaty, under appropriate international observation and through appropriate international procedures, potential benefits from any peaceful applications of nuclear explosions will be made available to non-nuclear-weapon States Party to the Treaty on a nondiscriminatory basis and that the charge to such Parties for the explosive devices used will be as low as possible and exclude any charge for research and development. Non-nuclear-weapon States Party to the Treaty shall be able to obtain such benefits, pursuant to a special international agreement or agreements, through an appropriate international body with adequate representation of non-nuclear-weapon States. Negotiations on this subject shall commence as soon as possible after the Treaty enters into force. Non-nuclear-weapon States Party to the Treaty so desiring may also obtain such benefits pursuant to bilateral agreements.

Article VI

Each of the Parties to the Treaty undertakes to pursue negotiations in good faith on effective measures relating to cessation of the nuclear arms race at an early date and to nuclear disarmament, and on a treaty on general and complete disarmament under strict and effective international control.

Article VII

Nothing in this Treaty affects the right of any group of States to conclude regional treaties in order to assure the total absence of nuclear weapons in their respective territories.

Article VIII

1. Any Party to the Treaty may propose amendments to this Treaty. The text of any proposed amendment shall be submitted to the Depositary Governments which shall circulate it to all Parties to the Treaty. Thereupon, if requested to do so by one-third or more of the Parties to the Treaty, the Depositary Governments shall convene a conference, to which they shall invite all the Parties to the Treaty, to consider such an amendment.

2. Any amendment to this Treaty must be approved by a majority of the votes of all the Parties to the Treaty, including the votes of all nuclear-weapon States Party to the Treaty and all other Parties which, on the date the amendment is circulated, are members of the Board of Governors of the International Atomic Energy Agency. The amendment shall enter into force for each Party that deposits its instrument of ratification of the amendment upon the deposit of such instruments of ratification by a majority of all the Parties, including the instruments of ratification of all nuclear-weapon States Party to the Treaty and all other Parties which, on the date the amendment is circulated, are members of the Board of Governors of the International Atomic Energy Agency. Thereafter, it shall enter into force for any other Party upon the deposit of its instrument of ratification of the amendment.

3. Five years after the entry into force of this Treaty, a conference of Parties to the Treaty shall be held in Geneva, Switzerland, in order to review the operation of this Treaty with a view to assuring that the purposes of the Preamble and the provisions of the Treaty are being realized. At intervals of five years thereafter, a majority of the Parties to the Treaty may obtain, by submitting a proposal to this effect to the Depositary Governments, the convening of further conferences with the same objective of reviewing the operation of the Treaty.

Article IX

1. This Treaty shall be open to all States for signature. Any State which does not sign the Treaty before its entry into force in accordance with paragraph 3 of this article may accede to it at any time.

2. This Treaty shall be subject to ratification by signatory States. Instruments of ratification and instruments of accession shall be deposited with the Governments of the United States of America, the United Kingdom of Great Britain and Northern Ireland and the Union of Soviet Socialist Republics,[1] which are hereby designated the Depositary Governments.

3. This Treaty shall enter into force after its ratification by the States, the Governments of which are designated Depositaries of the Treaty, and forty other States signatory to this Treaty and the deposit of their instruments of ratification. For the purposes of this Treaty, a nuclear-weapon State is one which has manufactured and exploded a nuclear weapon or other nuclear explosive device prior to January 1, 1967.

4. For States whose instruments of ratification or accession are deposited subsequent to the entry into force of this Treaty, it shall enter into force on the date of the deposit of their instruments of ratification or accession.

5. The Depositary Governments shall promptly inform all signatory and acceding States of the date of each signature, the date of deposit of each instrument of ratification or of accession, the date of the entry into force of this Treaty, and the date of receipt of any requests for convening a conference or other notices.

6. This Treaty shall be registered by the Depositary Governments pursuant to article 102 of the Charter of the United Nations.

Article X

1. Each Party shall in exercising its national sovereignty have the right to withdraw from the Treaty if it decides that extraordinary events, related to the subject matter of this Treaty, have jeopardized the supreme interests of its country. It shall give notice of such withdrawal to all other Parties to the Treaty and to the

United Nations Security Council three months in advance. Such notice shall include a statement of the extraordinary events it regards as having jeopardized its supreme interests.

2. Twenty-five years after the entry into force of the Treaty, a conference shall be convened to decide whether the Treaty shall continue in force indefinitely, or shall be extended for an additional fixed period or periods. This decision shall be taken by a majority of the Parties to the Treaty.

Article XI

This Treaty, the English, Russian, French, Spanish and Chinese texts of which are equally authentic, shall be deposited in the archives of the Depositary Governments. Duly certified copies of this Treaty shall be transmitted by the Depositary Governments to the Governments of the signatory and acceding States.

IN WITNESS WHEREOF the undersigned, duly authorized, have signed this Treaty.

DONE in triplicate, at the cities of Washington, London, and Moscow, this first day of July one thousand nine hundred sixty-eight.

---

[1][*Editor's Note:* Russia has succeeded to the status of the U.S.S.R. as a Depositary Government.]

4

DECLARED NUCLEAR-WEAPON STATES WITH POTENTIAL FOR DOMESTIC INSTABILITY

Russia

Russia is the sole *de jure* nuclear power to emerge from the break-up of the Soviet Union in December 1991.[1] Although nuclear weapons were also located in Belarus, Kazakhstan, and Ukraine when the Soviet Union dissolved, Russia inherited the bulk of the Soviet nuclear arsenal and virtually all of its nuclear-weapons production infrastructure. More important, Russia inherited the Soviet nuclear command structure, including key codes needed to target and launch the Soviet strategic nuclear systems in Belarus, Kazakhstan, and Ukraine, and Russian military personnel controlled all tactical nuclear weapons there. This prevented the other three successor states from acquiring independent nuclear capabilities. Also contributing to Russia's acceptance as the sole nuclear successor to the Soviet Union was the desire of the United States and other powers to avert the creation of additional nuclear-weapon states, a development that would have introduced potential new nuclear threats and undermined the basic goal of the Non-Proliferation Treaty (NPT).[2]

Since late 1991, Russia has sought to retain control over all of the Soviet Union's nuclear arms and to have them transferred to Russian soil for redeployment or dismantling. The legal basis for the arrangements whereby Russia would become the custodian of these weapons was laid, initially, on December 21, 1991, at Alma-Ata (now Almaty), Kazakhstan, where leaders of eleven former Soviet republics signed a series of declarations establishing the Commonwealth of Independent States (CIS). In Article 6 of the Declaration on Nuclear Arms, a document signed only by the leaders of the four states with nuclear weapons on their territory, the four agreed that "[by] July 1, 1992, Belarus, Kazakhstan, and Ukraine will insure the withdrawal of tactical nuclear weapons to central factory premises for dismantling under joint supervision."[3,4] In addition, these three states agreed not to transfer nuclear weapons on their territory to others, but specified that this prohibition did not "stand in the way of transfering nuclear weapons from Belarus, Kazakhstan, and Ukraine to R.S.F.S.R. [Russia] with a view to destroying them"—a proviso that implicitly anticipated the future return of strategic nuclear weapons. Finally, Belarus and Ukraine (but not Kazakhstan) agreed to join the NPT as non-nuclear-weapon states (Article 5(i)).[5]

In a subsequent accord signed in Minsk on December 30, 1991, the leaders of the eleven CIS states agreed that a "decision on the need [to use nuclear weapons would be] made by the President of the Russian Federation in agreement with the heads of the Republic of Belarus, the Republic of Kazakhstan, and Ukraine, and in consultation with the heads of the other member states of the Commonwealth."[6] As a practical matter, however, control over the use of nuclear weapons remained under Russian authority. Arrangements for sharing authority in this area ended in June 1993, when Russia formally took full control over the use of all nuclear arms in the Soviet successor states.[7] In addition, in the Minsk agreement, Ukraine pledged that nuclear weapons on its territory would be dismantled by the end of 1994, with tactical nuclear weapons to be dismantled by July 1, 1992 (Article IV).[8]

This framework was further elaborated in the Lisbon Protocol to the Strategic Arms Reduction Treaty (START I), signed on May 23, 1992, by Belarus, Kazakhstan, Russia, and Ukraine. Through the Protocol, the four states agreed to participate jointly in the START I Treaty as successors to the former Soviet Union and to "implement the Treaty's limits and restrictions" (Article II of the Protocol). In addition, Belarus, Kazakhstan, and Ukraine agreed to "adhere to the Treaty on the Non-Proliferation of Nuclear weapons " as non-nuclear-weapon state parties "in the shortest possible time" (Article V of the Protocol).[9] In separate letters to President George Bush, each of the three also agreed to the elimination of all nuclear weapons—both strategic and tactical—on their territories within the seven-year START I implementation period. By this point, all tactical nuclear weapons had already been removed to Russia by the three states.[10]

START I, signed in Moscow by the United States and the Soviet Union on July 31, 1991, was the result of nine years of negotiations between the two superpowers. It was the first arms control treaty to mandate reductions of deployed strategic weapons as opposed to limitations on future deployments. Under the accord (as modified by the Lisbon Protocol to include Belarus, Kazakhstan, Russia, and Ukraine in lieu of the Soviet Union), the two sides will reduce their strategic nuclear forces to equal aggregate limits of 6,000 accountable warheads deployed on 1,600 strategic nuclear delivery vehicles (i.e., intercontinental ballistic missiles (ICBMs), submarine-launched ballistic missiles (SLBMs) and strategic bombers). Sublimits for warheads include the restriction that no more than 4,900 warheads may be deployed on ICBMs and SLBMs, and of this subtotal, no more than 1,100 warheads may be deployed mobile ICBMs and no more than 1,540 warheads on heavy ICBMs.[11]

The START I Treaty's entry into force was considerably delayed, however, after the Russian Supreme Soviet, in approving the ratification of the Treaty on November 4, 1992, attached the condition that Russia would not exchange instruments of ratification until after the three other Soviet-successor-states acceded to the NPT as non-nuclear-weapon states and carried out their other obligations under the Lisbon Protocol.[12]

In Belarus and Kazakhstan, taking these steps proved relatively uncontroversial. The Belarusian parliament ratified the START I Treaty on February 4, 1993, and Belarus formally acceded to the NPT on July 22, 1993. The parliament of Kazakhstan ratified START I on July 2, 1992, and Kazakhstan formally acceded to the NPT on February 14, 1994.[13]

In Ukraine, however, where tensions intensified with Russia over a number of issues in 1993, acceptance of START I and the NPT proved more contentious. The Ukrainian parliament, or Rada, approved ratification of the START I Treaty on November 18, 1993, but declared that a number of stiff conditions—which appeared likely to be unacceptable to Russia and the United States—would have to be met before ratification could be accomplished. Simultaneously, the Rada resolved that Ukraine was not bound by Article V of the Lisbon Protocol calling for quick accession to the NPT as a non-nuclear-weapon state.[14]

After extensive negotiations, on January 14, 1994, Ukrainian President Leonid Kravchuk, together with President Bill Clinton and Russian President Boris Yeltsin, signed the "Trilateral Statement" in which they agreed that all nuclear warheads would be transfered from the territory of Ukraine to Russia for the purpose of their subsequent dismantling in the shortest possible time. Ukraine would receive in exchange a number of political, economic, and security benefits. As a result of this understanding, on February 3, 1994, the Rada approved a two-part resolution which, first, instructed Kravchuk to exchange the instruments of ratification of the START I Treaty and, second, acknowledged that Article V of the Lisbon Protocol applied to Ukraine. The Rada also implicitly endorsed the Trilateral Statement but did not approve accession to the NPT.[15]

The Ukranian parliament took this step on November 16, 1994, but once again imposed conditions, making its accession to the Treaty contingent upon first receiving security guarantees by the nuclear states. Security guarantees in the form of a multilateral memorandum signed by the United Kingdom, the United States, and Russia were promised to Ukraine immediately prior to the November 16, 1994, parliamentary vote. At the Summit of the Conference on Security and Cooperation in Europe (CSCE), held in Budapest on December 5, 1994, the United Kingdom, the United States, and Russia provided this memorandum to Ukraine and initialed a document that also extended security guarantees to Kazakhstan and Belarus. France also provided security guarantees to Ukraine at the CSCE summit in a separate document. On the same occasion, Ukraine then presented its instruments of accession to the NPT.

This action, along with the earlier accessions by Belarus and Kazakhstan, satisfied Russia's conditions for ratifying the START I Treaty. Consequently, at the same meeting, the United States, Russia, Belarus, Kazakhstan, and Ukraine exchanged their START I Treaty instruments of ratification, finally bringing the Treaty into force.[16]

Earlier, on January 3, 1993, Presidents Bush and Yeltsin had signed in Moscow the follow-on, START II agreement, providing for even deeper cuts in strategic arsenals than START I. START II provides for the elimination of all multiple-warhead ICBMs and for a two-phase reduction of nuclear warheads deployed on strategic delivery vehicles. At the end of the first phase—seven years after entry into force of the START I Treaty—the United States and Russia may not deploy more than 3,800 to 4,250 warheads on delivery systems. In the second phase—by January 1, 2003 (or by December 31, 2000, if the United States is able to assist in financing the dismantlement and elimination of Russian nuclear weapons)—each of the two parties would reduce the overall total of deployed strategic warheads to between 3,000 and 3,500. This would represent a two-thirds reduction in strategic nuclear forces from peak Cold-War levels.[17] Because START II relied on the definitions, declarations, and verification provisions of START I, neither the United States Senate nor the Russian parliament would vote on ratification of START II until START I entered into force. As of March 1995, the U.S. Senate was considering the ratification of START II and approval was expected. Thereafter, the Treaty will be considered by Russia's parliament, the State Duma, where it may face greater opposition.

On January 14, 1994, Russia and the United States agreed that they would no longer target strategic missiles at one another. Great Britain joined this agreement on February 15, 1994. The agreement stipulates that strategic missiles under the command of the countries party to the agreement were to be detargeted no later than May 30, 1994. On September 2, 1994, Russia and China signed a similar detargeting agreement in which they pledged that they would no longer aim missiles at the other.[18]

Despite the delay in START I's entry into force, the United States and Russia have taken steps toward early deactivation of their strategic systems. In early March 1995, U.S. Secretary of Defense William Perry, in testimony before the Senate Foreign Relations Committee noted that the United States had "deactivated all of its forces to be eliminated under START I, by removing over 3,900 warheads from ballistic missiles and retiring heavy bombers to elimination facilities." In addition, he noted that the United States had "already eliminated about 290 missile launchers and over 230 heavy bombers, putting [the United States] below the first START I intermediate ceiling that will not come into effect until December 1997."[19] In an earlier speech Secretary Perry said that Russia had already removed 2,600 warheads from missiles and bomber bases; 750 missiles had been taken down from their launchers; and almost 600 launchers and bombers had been destroyed.[20]

In addition, Russia has concluded bilateral agreements with Belarus and Kazakhstan for the early deactivation and transfer of strategic systems to Russia. In the case of Belarus, forty-five single-warhead SS-25s and their warheads had been transferred to Russia by early December 1994.[21] All SS-25 missiles and their warheads are to be removed from Belarus by the end of July 1995. In Kazakhstan, as of December 1994, 810 warheads had been removed from their missiles: 440 from 44 SS-18 ICBMs and 370 from air-launched cruise missiles (ALCMs).[22] Approximately 632 of this total had been returned to Russia by March 1995, including all 370 ALCM warheads and presumably 260 SS-18 warheads. All 370 ALCMs and their associated strategic bombers had also been sent to Russia, and, according to some reports, twelve SS-18 missiles had been sent there as well.[23]

Ukraine's denuclearization process is guided by the "Trilateral Statement" noted earlier, which calls for a phased deactivation and transfer process. In the first phase, which was to be completed by mid-November 1994, all SS-24s on Ukrainian territory were to be deactivated. In fact, by early December 1994, not only had Ukraine deactivated all its SS-24s, but it had also deactivated 40 out of its 130 SS-19s. Second, the Trilateral Statement called for Ukraine to transfer at least 200 warheads from its SS-19s and SS-24s to Russia by mid-November.[24] By February 1995, it had transferred a total of 420 SS-24, SS-19, and heavy bomber warheads back to Russia.[25]

To assist denuclearization in Russia and the other former Soviet states with nuclear weapons, the United States is providing funds under the program for Cooperative Threat Reduction (CTR), also known as the "Nunn-Lugar" program, after its sponsors, Senators Sam Nunn (D-GA) and Richard Lugar (R-IN). By late February 1995, the United States had proposed $503 million for projects in Russia. Most of these projects, such as "Strategic Offensive Arms Elimination" (for example, missile silo elimination), are designed to reduce the strategic threat to the United States. Others, such as the project on "Material Protection, Control and Accounting" (i.e., accounting for weapons-usable nuclear materials), are designed to curb the proliferation risks associated with the drawdown of Russia's arsenal.[26] Three hundred million dollars of the funds authorized by Congress had actually been obligated to projects in Russia by February 1995.

The United States has agreed to purchase 500 metric tons of weapons-grade uranium from dismantled Russian nuclear weapons that is to be blended down to low-enriched uranium (LEU) suitable for use as nuclear power plant fuel. The LEU will be sold to the United States Enrichment Corporation for eventual use in nuclear power reactors. American inspectors will be allowed into Sverdlovsk-44 to verify that the HEU actually comes from dismantled warheads.[27]

A related initiative is the International Science and Technology Center (ISTC), a Moscow-based multilateral organization that provides peaceful employment opportunities to scientists and engineers in the Newly Independent States who were previously involved in work on weapons of mass destruction and missile technology.

The Center, which began operating in March 1994, was founded by the European Union, Japan, the Russian Federation, and the United States. In addition to the initial parties, Finland, Sweden, and Georgia are now members; Belarus, Armenia, Kazakhstan, and Canada have expressed their intentions of becoming members.[28]

Despite the progress in the denuclearization process, Russia has emerged as a serious nuclear proliferation concern because of fears that its current political and economic troubles may weaken central control over nuclear weapons, nuclear weapons materials, and/or nuclear exports. Such developments could lead to a global black market in sensitive nuclear goods that could greatly accelerate the rate of proliferation by other states desiring nuclear arms, while simultaneously undermining the International Atomic Energy Agency (IAEA) inspections and supplier-country export controls that form the backbone of the international nuclear non-proliferation regime.

During 1994, Russia's control over weapons-grade nuclear material has emerged as a particularly worrisome issue. In contrast to security arrangements for protecting deployed nuclear weapons, which are under exclusively military supervision and guarded by elite troops, security is thought to be relatively lax with respect to guarding weapons-grade nuclear materials. This is particularly true at research institutes run by civilian organizations, which are guarded by non-elite Ministry of Interior forces or local militia/police. Security applying to weapons-grade nuclear materials within the nuclear-weapons-production complex, under the control of the Ministry of Atomic Energy (MINATOM) and guarded by Interior Ministry forces, is thought to be better than at the research institutes, but weaker than that covering nuclear weapons.[29]

There have been several episodes confined to Russia involving the possible theft of weapons-grade materials including the "disappearance of an undisclosed quantity of highly enriched uranium (HEU) from the 'Luch' nuclear research facility at Podolsk, near Moscow," the "theft of three fuel rods containing HEU from a naval base in Murmansk" and a case mentioned by FBI Director Louis Freeh involving the possible theft of some two or more kilograms of HEU from St. Petersburg.[30]

More disturbing, during 1994, there were five instances involving the smuggling to Europe of weapons-usable materials that apparently originated in civilian research laboratories in Russia. German officials uncovered three distinct cases of the smuggling of weapons-grade plutonium: 6 grams of 99.75 percent Pu^{239} were confiscated in Tengen, on May

10; 300 grams were seized on August 10 in a Munich airport on a flight from Moscow; and just under 2 grams of plutonium were found in Bremen, on August 16.[31] In addition, there were two different seizures of HEU. One incident took place in Germany in mid-June 1994, when police in Landshut confiscated 800 milligrams of HEU enriched to 87.8 percent. The other incident occurred in Prague in mid-December 1994, when Czech police seized approximately 3 kilograms of HEU, the largest finding of weapons-grade nuclear material to date.[32]

In congressional testimony on June 27, 1994, former CIA Director R. James Woolsey said that Russian criminal organizations, which have established an extensive infrastructure consisting of front companies and international smuggling networks, may be facilitating the transfer and sale of nuclear materials, and possibly are also seeking to acquire nuclear weapons for the same purpose. He added that the target of opportunity for these organized crime groups could be "hostile states such as Iran, Iraq, Libya, and North Korea [which] may try to accelerate or enhance their own weapons development programs" through the acquisition of weapons-usable nuclear materials, complete nuclear weapons, or other weapons of mass destruction.[33]

Possible future political instability in Russia could further weaken controls over nuclear materials. Although fears that Russia might disintegrate have recently eased, as recently as October 1993, a coup against President Boris Yeltsin was attempted by force of arms. The episode exposed deep fissures within the Russian polity and raised serious questions about the loyalty of many military units to the central government.[34] In early 1995, moreover, the Chechen Republic was in open rebellion against Moscow, another reminder of Russia's potential fragility as a cohesive state.

Political instability could lead not only to weakened controls over key nuclear assets, but, in an extreme case, could also lead to the emergence of new splinter states with nuclear inheritances. If the political factions comprising the leadership of new entities managed to obtain custody of deployed nuclear weapons, their ability to assume operational control would depend on their capability to bypass sensing devices and/or coded switches that control access to the arming and fusing circuitry of the weapons. As one panel of experts has noted, the existence of such devices "cannot provide reassurance that these weapons would be useless to mutinous custodians or political factions who had prolonged possession of the weapons, especially if they had technical expertise."[35]

NOTES

[1]See "Message From Russian President Boris Yeltsin to Hans Blix, Director General of the International Atomic Energy Agency, January 17, 1992," *Tass*, January 17, 1992, in *FBIS-SOV*, January 21, 1992, p. 38.

In "The Written Statement by the Russian Side At the Signing of the Protocol To the START Treaty on 23 May 1992 in Lisbon," Russian Foreign Minister Andrei Kozyrev noted "that Russia as the successor state of the USSR is a Party to the Non-Proliferation Treaty and acts as a depositary state of this Treaty." See ("Documents," *Arms Control Today*, June 1992, p. 36; "'Nonnuclear' States Join," Moscow, *Itar-Tass*, May 24, 1992, in *FBIS-SOV-91-101*, May 26, 1992, p. 2.) Russia was also recognized as the largest and most powerful Soviet successor state, when it took the place of the Soviet Union as a permanent member of the UN Security Council on December 24, 1991.

[2]Under the NPT, states that have nuclear weapons on their territory but do not control them are considered non-nuclear-weapon states. Thus states where U.S. nuclear weapons have been deployed at various times (including Germany and South Korea) have held this status after joining the NPT.

[3]See "Texts of Accords by Former Soviet Republics Forming Commonwealth of Independent States," *Facts on File*, 1991, p. 972.

[4]See Eric Schmitt, "Soviet Nuclear Move Ahead of Schedule," *New York Times*, February 28, 1992. By May 7, 1992, both Belarus and Ukraine confirmed that the transfer of all tactical nuclear weapons to Russia was complete. Kazakhstan completed its transfer of tactical nuclear weapons by late January 1992. "Chronology of Commonwealth Security Issues," *Arms Control Today*, May 1992, p. 27.

[5]See "Texts of Accords by Former Soviet Republics Forming Commonwealth of Independent States," *Facts on File, op. cit.*

Ukraine did not ratify the Alma-Ata agreement, however. The accord, along with two other subsequent agreements—the "Agreement Between the Members States of the Commonwealth of Independent States on Strategic Forces," signed in Minsk on December 30, 1991, and an agreement by seven CIS states on command and control of conventional armies concluded on February 14, 1992, in Minsk—were later declared to be "invalid" by Ukraine's parliament. Ukraine ultimately accepted nuclear restraints comparable to those in the foregoing agreements, however, when, in 1994, it adopted the Lisbon Protocol to the Strategic Arms Reduction Treaty (START I), the "Trilateral Statement," the START I Treaty, and the NPT (all discussed in the text below). (Communication with official of the Ukrainian Embassy, February 1995.)

[6]See "Minsk Agreement on Strategic Forces, December 30, 1991," *Arms Control Today*, January/February 1992, p. 39.

[7]In June 1993, CIS joint command was abolished and in July 1993 Marshall Evgenii Shaposhnikov, the commander of the CIS nuclear forces, handed his set of launch codes to Russian Defense Minister Pavel Grachev, ending any pretense that several independent nations would control these nuclear forces. See *Radio Free Europe/Radio Liberty Daily Report*, July 23, 1993.

[8]As noted in note 5, however, Ukraine would not ratify the Minsk accord and later declared that it did not consider itself bound by its promise to return all nuclear arms to Russia.

[9]See "Documents: Protocol to the Treaty Between the United States of America and the Union of Soviet Socialist Republics on the Reduction and Limitation of Strategic Offensive Arms," *Arms Control Today*, June 1992, p. 33; "START I: Lisbon Protocol and the Nuclear Non-Proliferation Treaty," ACDA Fact Sheet, March 17, 1994.

[10]See note 4. Initially, these weapons were deployed at more than one hundred sites in Russia. Because of concerns over the stability of Russia's armed forces—highlighted in the refusal of certain units to follow orders during the early 1995 conflict to suppress the revolt in Chechnya—Washington urged the Russian government to consolidate these weapons in fewer locations with special security arrangements. Russia took such action in late 1994. (Interviews, Moscow, February 1995.)

[11]The START I Treaty was signed by President George Bush and Soviet President Mikhail Gorbachev on July 31, 1991, in Moscow. See "Strategic Arms Reduction Treaty (START): Analysis, Summary, Text," *Arms Control Today*, November 1991, p. 17; "START I: Lisbon Protocol and the Nuclear Non-Proliferation Treaty," ACDA Fact Sheet, March 17, 1994; "START I Entry Into Force and Security Assurances," ACDA Fact Sheet, December 5, 1994.

At the time of the signing of the Treaty, U.S strategic forces comprised an estimated total of 9,680 deployed warheads, 7,826 of which were deployed on ICBMs and SLBMs. Comparable figures for the Soviet Union were a total of 10,996 warheads, 10,181 of which were deployed on ballistic missiles. See International Institute for Strategic Studies, *The Military Balance 1990-1991* (London: International Institute for Strategic Studies, 1990), pp. 212-13.

[12]See "START I: Lisbon Protocol and the Nuclear Non-Proliferation Treaty," ACDA Fact Sheet, *op.cit.*

[13]*Ibid.*

[14]In addition, the Resolution of Ratification declared that only 36 percent of delivery vehicles and 42 percent of warheads deployed on Ukrainian territory would be subject to elimination. It also made elimination of the remaining delivery vehicles and warheads conditional on receiving aid to cover dismantlement costs, compensation for nuclear materials to be extracted from the warheads, and complex security guarantees. See "Parliament Ratifies START I Treaty, Lisbon Protocol," Moscow, *Interfax*, November 18, 1993, in *FBIS-SOV-93-222*, November 19, 1993, p. 45; "Supreme Council START I Ratification Resolution," Kiev, *UNIAR*, November 18, 1993, in *FBIS-SOV-93-222*, November 19, 1993, p. 45.

[15]For details see section on Ukraine in this report, p. 71ff.

[16]See "Text of Resolution Detailing NPT Reservations," *Kiev Radio Ukraine World Service in the Ukraine in FM-FBIS London UK*, November 16, 1994; "Ukraine Joins Treaty Curbing Nuclear Arms," *Washington Post*, November 17, 1994; "Ukraine Accedes to NPT Treaty," *United Press International*, December 5, 1994; "Remarks by President Clinton at Signing of Denuclearization Agreement," *Federal News Service*, December 5, 1994; "France Signs NPT Security Guarantee Document," Moscow, *Interfax*, December 5, 1994, in *FBIS-SOV-94-234*, December 6, 1994, p. 44; "START I Entry Into Force and Security Assurances," ACDA Fact Sheet, December 5, 1994; "START I Enters Into Force; Nuclear Arsenals to Be Reduced Dramatically," ACDA Press Release, December 5, 1994.

[17]See "START II: Analysis, Summary, Text," *Arms Control Today*, January/February 1993, p. 19; "Factfile: START II at a Glance," *Arms Control Today*, January/February 1993, p. 33;

"Strategic Arms Reduction Treaty II Chronology," ACDA Fact Sheet, January 6, 1993.

[18]See "Russian Missiles No Longer Targeted on U.S., UK," *Interfax*, May 30, 1994, in *FBIS-SOV-94-104*, May 30, 1994; *Radio Free Europe/Radio Liberty Daily Report*, September 5, 1994.

[19]"Testimony of U.S. Defense Secretary William Perry," before the Senate Foreign Relations Committee, March 1, 1995.

[20]Speech by U.S. Defense Secretary William Perry, American Legion, February 27, 1995.

[21]Dunbar Lockwood, "New Data From the Clinton Administration on the Status of Strategic Nuclear Weapons Deactivations," Memorandum, Arms Control Association, Washington, DC, December 7, 1994; unclassified CIA report, September 1994, as cited in "Nuclear Weapons Deactivation Continue in FSU," *Arms Control Today*, November 1994, p. 27; General Roland LaJoie, Deputy for Cooperative Threat Reduction to the Assistant to the Secretary of Defense for Atomic Energy, special briefing on the Cooperative Threat Reduction Program for the Senate Foreign Relations Committee, February 23, 1995.

[22]Dunbar Lockwood, "New Data From the Clinton Administration on the Status of Strategic Nuclear Weapons Deactivations," *op.cit.* Unclassified CIA report, September 1994, as cited in "Nuclear Weapons Deactivation Continue in FSU," *Arms Control Today*, op.cit.

[23]General Roland LaJoie, special briefing on the Cooperative Threat Reduction Program, *op.cit*; Dunbar Lockwood, "New Data From the Clinton Administration on the Status of Strategic Nuclear Weapons Deactivations," *op.cit.*; Unclassified CIA report, September 1994, as cited in "Nuclear Weapons Deactivation Continue in FSU," *op.cit.*

In congressional testimony in April 1994, Assistant Secretary of Defense Ashton Carter stated that "12 SS-18s and 120 warheads [had] been removed from silos in Kazakhstan, and the process of dismantling SS-18 silos" was expected to begin later in the year. See "Testimony of Dr. Ashton Carter, Assistant Secretary for Defense (International Security Policy)," before the Senate Armed Services Committee, April 28, 1994. (Press reports in February 1994 stated that the 12 SS-18s had already been sent to Russia for dismantlement. See *Radio Free Europe/Radio Liberty Daily Report*, February 14, 1994; "U.S. Reward Sought for Ceding A-Arms," *Washington Post*, February 14, 1994.) According to the September 1994 CIA report noted earlier, an additional 32 SS-18s had been deactivated as of that date. See "Nuclear Weapons Deactivations Continue in FSU," *Arms Control Today*, op.cit. See also General Roland LaJoie, special briefing on the Cooperative Threat Reduction Program, *op.cit.*

In May 1994 Russian press reports said that all nuclear warheads in Kazakhstan would be transfered to Russia by mid-1995 and all missile silos would be dismantled by mid-1997. (See *Radio Free Europe/Radio Liberty Daily Report*, May 4, 1994.) However, in his February 1995 briefing (cited earlier), General LaJoie projected that silo dismantlement would not be completed until the latter half of 1998.

[24]Although seven years was the original timetable for the transfer of all the warheads, a protocol signed by Ukraine's acting Prime Minister Yefim Zvyagilsky and Russian Prime Minister Victor Chernomyrdin on May 16, 1994, now obligates Ukraine to transfer its warheads within three years of the signing of the Trilateral Statement. See "Ukraine Pledges to Double Speed of Disarmament," *Reuters*, May 19, 1994.

[25]See General Roland LaJoie, special briefing on the Cooperative Threat Reduction Program, *op.cit.*

In congressional testimony in October 1994, Assistant Secretary of Defense Carter reported that there were 1,734 warheads in Ukraine prior to the initiation of the dismantlement process in January 1994, as opposed to 1,564 warheads as cited in the START I Memorandum of Understanding (MOU). See "Testimony of Assistant Secretary Carter," before the Senate Foreign Relations Committee, October 4, 1994.

[26]Other projects include the provision of secure railcars for transporting warheads and assistance in strengthening export control measures. See "CTR Programs by Country" and "CTR Obligations by Country/Project," Department of Defense, Office of Cooperative Threat Reduction, February 20, 1995.

[27]Thomas W. Lippman, "Russia Aims to Unload Its Uranium in the U.S.; Deal Moves Slowly Through Thorny Issues," *Washington Post*, August 5, 1992; and *Nuclear Fuel*, March 28, 1994, pp. 6-8.

[28]By December 1994, 94 project proposals had been approved, representing a total funding commitment of $48.5 million. These projects will sponsor more than 5,000 scientists for a period of about three years. Projects approved for funding include: Nuclear Waste Management and Disposal at Mayak NPA, Chelyabinsk, Russia; Conversion of Military Infrared Laser Technology for Dentistry; and New Fuel Elements for Water Cooled Power Reactors. See Joint Press Statement on International Science and Technology Center (Moscow: International Science and Technology Center, December 9, 1994); U.S. Department of State, Office of the Senior Coordinator for Nuclear Science and Science Centers, September 1994.

Japan and several European states are providing funds for disarmament and for the ISTC. Japan has pledged $17 million toward the ISTC and $79.99 million in aid to Russia for such purposes as fissile material storage, disposal of liquid rocket fuel, environmental restoration, and material control and accounting. France has signed agreements with Russia worth $98 million to supply radiation safety equipment, transport containers, and machine tools. The European Union has pledged $25 million toward the ISTC. See Leonard S. Spector and William C. Potter, *Nuclear Successor States of the Soviet Union: Nuclear Weapon and Sensitive Export Status Report* (Washington, DC: Carnegie Endowment for International Peace and Monterey, CA: Monterey Institute of International Studies, December 1994), pp. 26-29.

[29]The accuracy of this conclusion was confirmed by a Russian nuclear official in an interview with Leonard S. Spector in Moscow in May 1994. To underscore the point that the weakest security is at the research institutes, he stated that earlier in the year Gosatomnadzor (GAN)—Russia's Nuclear Regulatory Commission—had ordered certain activities at the All Union Research Institute for Non-Organic Substances in Moscow to shut down for six months because of lax arrangements for protecting a significant quantity of plutonium in the Institute's possession. See "Testimony of Leonard Spector," before the House Foreign Affairs Committee, Subcommittee on International Security, International Organizations, and Human Rights, June, 27, 1994.

[30]See "Testimony of William Potter," and "Testimony of Leonard Spector," before the House Foreign Affairs Committee, Subcommittee on International Security, International Organizations, and Human Rights, June, 27, 1994;

[31]Mark Hibbs, "Pu-239 Stolen From Russian Lab Was Weapons-Enriched in Centrifuge Plant," *Nuclear Fuel*, July 18, 1994, p. 1; "German Police Insist Stolen Plutonium Was Russian," *Reuters*, July 20, 1994; Ferdinand Protzman, "Germany Reaffirming Russian Origin of Seized Plutonium," *New York Times*, July 21, 1994; R. Jeffrey Smith and Steve Vogel,

"Agencies Hunt Black-Market Plutonium," *Washington Post*, July 23, 1994; Larry Thorson, "Germany—Nuclear Smuggling," *Associated Press*, August 11, 1994; Craig R. Whitney, "Germans Seize 3d Atom Sample, Smuggled by Plane From Russia," *New York Times*, August 14, 1994; David Ljunggren, "Russia Disowns Plutonium Seized in Germany," *Reuters*, August 15, 1994; Steve Coll, "Stolen Plutonium Tied to Arms Labs; German Scientists Trace Origin of Nuclear Materials to Russia," *Washington Post*, August 17, 1994; Craig R. Whitney, "Germans Seize More Weapons Material," *New York Times*, August 17, 1994; Rick Atkinson, "Officials Say Contraband Not a Threat," *Washington Post*, August 28, 1994; R. Jeffrey Smith, "Anti-Smuggling Effort Largely in Disarray," *Washington Post*, August 28, 1994. See also Mark Hibbs, "Plutonium, Politics, and Panic," *Bulletin of the Atomic Scientists*, November/December 1994, p. 24-31.

[32]Mark Hibbs, "German Police Find 800 Milligrams HEU, Say It May Be Sample of Larger Inventory," *Nuclear Fuel*, August 15, 1994, p. 1; "Czechs Hold Three Suspects After Seizing Uranium," *New York Times*, December 20, 1994; Michael R. Gordon, "Czech Cache of Nuclear Material Being Tested for Bomb Potential," *New York Times*, December 21, 1994; Rick Atkinson, "Prague Says Uranium Found in Czech Auto Could Trigger Bomb," *Washington Post*, December 21, 1994; Mark Hibbs, "Czech Find May Be Re-Enriched REPU to Fuel Naval Research Reactors," *Nuclear Fuel*, January 2, 1995, p. 12.

[33]"Testimony of R. James Woolsey," before the House Foreign Affairs Committee, Subcommittee on International Organizations, International Security and Human Rights, June 27, 1994.

[34]See Paul A. Goble, *Regions, Republics, and Russian Reform: Center-Periphery Relations in the Russian Federation* (Washington, DC: Carnegie Endowment for International Peace, 1994); Christine Wallich, *Fiscal Decentralization: Intergovernmental Relations in Russia* (Washington, DC: World Bank, 1992); Marie Mendras, "Existe-t-il un Etat Russe?" *Politique Etrangère*, Spring 1992, p. 25-34; Paul Goble, "The Coming Collapse of the Russian Federation," *NEFTE Compass*, January 1993, p. 2; Henry Huttenbach, "Can the Russian Federation Survive?" *Surviving Together*, Fall 1993, p. 8-10; Jessica Eve Stern, "Moscow Meltdown—Can Russia Survive?" *International Security*, Spring 1994, p. 40-65; Paul B. Henze, *Ethnic Dynamics and Dilemmas of the Russian Republic* (Santa Monica, CA: RAND, 1991); Emil Payin, "Russian Federation Facing Fate of USSR?" *KIARS Meeting Report* XI, August 1993, p.16; Sergei Beliaev, "Federalism: Tendencies in the New Equilibrium," *The Federalism Debate*, 1993.

[35]Kurt M. Campbell *et al.*, *Soviet Nuclear Fission: Control of the Nuclear Arsenal in a Disintegrating Soviet Union*, CSIA Studies in International Security, No. 1 (Cambridge, MA: Center for Science and International Affairs, Harvard University, November 1991), pp. 14-15.

During a prolonged period of civil strife components from dismantled nuclear weapons in storage—nuclear warheads, missile airframes, or ALCMs—would also be at risk of falling into the hands of parties not necessarily under central or regional control (for example, extremists, smugglers).

If a stored nuclear warhead came into the possession of such a party, the dangers would be great. Even if the warhead were equipped with sensing devices and/or coded switches or had been disabled by the removal of certain parts (for example, tritium reservoir, electronic firing units), its disassembly by suitably trained individuals could provide "valuable first-hand information on its design, materials, and components" or access to the fissionable core for use in another weapon. See U.S. Congress, Office of Technology Assessment, *Technologies Underlying Weapons of Mass Destruction*, OTA-BP-ISC-115 (Washington, DC: U.S. Government Printing Office, December 1993), p. 128.

It is also possible that a team with substantial technical expertise, with access to the weapon over an extended period, could recreate the missing parts and reactivate the weapon.

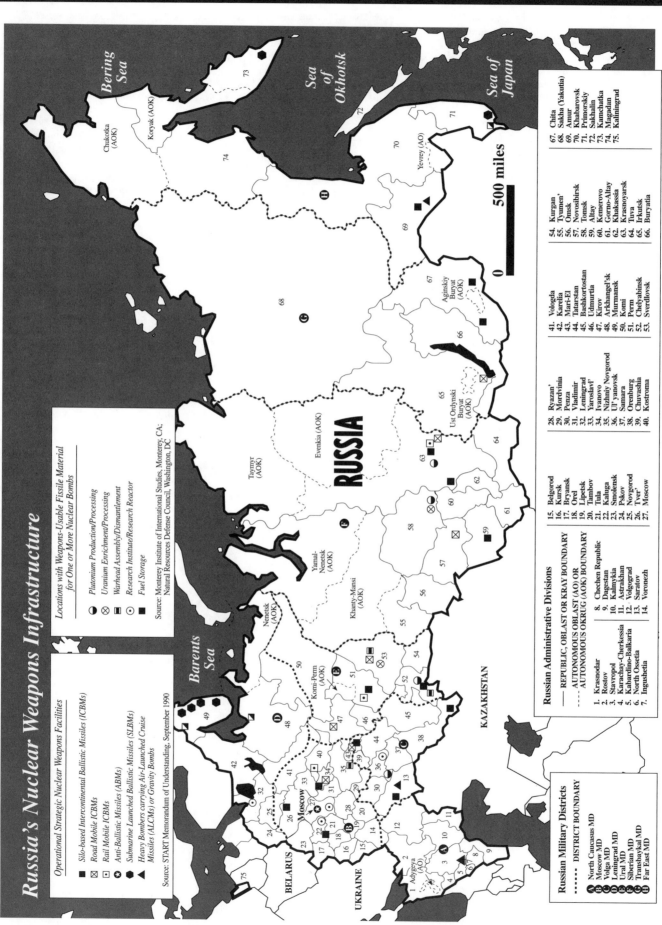

Russia's Nuclear Weapons Infrastructure

Operational Strategic Nuclear Weapons Facilities

- ■ Silo-based Intercontinental Ballistic Missiles (ICBMs)
- ⊠ Road Mobile ICBMs
- ⊡ Rail Mobile ICBMs
- ✪ Anti-Ballistic Missiles (ABMs)
- ⬡ Submarine Launched Ballistic Missiles (SLBMs)
- ▲ Heavy Bombers carrying Air-Launched Cruise Missiles (ALCMs) or Gravity Bombs

Source: START Memorandum of Understanding, September 1990

Locations with Weapons-Usable Fissile Material for One or More Nuclear Bombs

- ◐ Plutonium Production/Processing
- ⊗ Uranium Enrichment/Processing
- ⊞ Warhead Assembly/Dismantlement
- ⊙ Research Institute/Research Reactor
- ■ Fuel Storage

Source: Monterey Institute of International Studies, Monterey, CA; Natural Resources Defense Council, Washington, DC

Russian Military Districts

⸻ DISTRICT BOUNDARY

- Ⓐ North Caucasus MD
- Ⓑ Moscow MD
- Ⓒ Volga MD
- Ⓓ Ural MD
- Ⓔ Leningrad MD
- Ⓕ Siberian MD
- Ⓖ Transbaykal MD
- Ⓗ Far East MD

Russian Administrative Divisions

⸻ REPUBLIC, OBLAST OR KRAY BOUNDARY
--- AUTONOMOUS OBLAST (AO) OR AUTONOMOUS OKRUG (AOK) BOUNDARY

1. Krasnodar	8. Chechen Republic	15. Belgorod
2. Rostov	9. Dagestan	16. Kursk
3. Stavropol	10. Kalmykia	17. Bryansk
4. Karachay-Cherkessia	11. Astrakhan	18. Orel
5. Kabardino-Balkaria	12. Volgograd	19. Lipetsk
6. North Ossetia	13. Saratov	20. Tambov
7. Ingushetia	14. Voronezh	21. Tula

22. Kaluga	28. Ryazan'	41. Vologda	54. Kurgan	67. Chita
23. Smolensk	29. Mordvinia	42. Karelia	55. Tyumen'	68. Sakha (Yakutia)
24. Pskov	30. Penza	43. Mari-El	56. Omsk	69. Amur
25. Tver'	31. Vladimir	44. Tatarstan	57. Novosibirsk	70. Khabarovsk
26. Novgorod	32. Leningrad	45. Bashkortostan	58. Tomsk	71. Primorskiy
27. Moscow	33. Yaroslavl'	46. Udmurtia	59. Altay	72. Sakhalin
	34. Ivanovo	47. Kirov	60. Kemerovo	73. Kamchatka
	35. Nizhniy Novgorod	48. Arkhangel'sk	61. Gorno-Altay	74. Magadan
	36. Ul'yanovsk	49. Murmansk	62. Khakassia	75. Kaliningrad
	37. Samara	50. Komi	63. Krasnoyarsk	
	38. Orenburg	51. Perm'	64. Tuva	
	39. Chuvashia	52. Chelyabinsk	65. Irkutsk	
	40. Kostroma	53. Sverdlovsk	66. Buryatia	

Carnegie Endowment for International Peace, *Tracking Nuclear Proliferation*, 1995.

RUSSIA Chart 1: Nuclear Weapons Systems and Associated Warheads

TYPE[1]	WEAPONS SYSTEMS (START I MOU/Current)	WARHEADS (START I MOU/Current)	LOCATION (No. of Weapons Systems: START I MOU/Current)	COMMENTS
S T R A T E G I C W E A P O N S [2]				
ICBMs (Total)	1,064/app.756	4,278/app.3,787		
SS-11	326/0	326/0	Svobodnyy (60/NA)[3] Yasnaya (90/NA) Drovyanaya (50/NA) Krasnoyarsk (40/NA) Bershet (60/NA) Teykovo (26/NA)	All SS-11s have been deactivated.
SS-13	40/30	40/30	Yoshkar-Ola (40/30)	
SS-17	47/25	188/100	Vypolzovo (47/25)	Some SS-25s from Belarus reportedly are being sent to Vypolzovo to replace SS-17s that are being deactivated.[4]
SS-18	204/188	2,040/1,880	Uzhur (64/NA) Aleysk (30/NA) Kartaly (46/NA) Dombarovskiy (64/NA)	Twelve SS-18s have been transferred to Russia from Kazakhstan, but these have not been redeployed.[5] Although START I attributes 10 warheads to each SS-18, some may carry fewer.
SS-19	170/170	1,020/1,020	Tatishchevo (110/110) Kozel'sk (60/60)	
SS-24	43/46	430/460	Krasnoyarsk (12/NA) Tatishchevo (10/NA) Bershet (9/NA) Kostroma (12/NA)	Of the 46 SS-24s, 36 are rail-based and 10 are silo-based. The 36 rail-based SS-24s were removed from alert status under the October 1991 Gorbachev initiative.
SS-25	234/297[6]	234/297	Irkutsk (36/NA) Kansk (27/NA) Novosibirsk (27/NA) Yoshkar-Ola (18/NA) Nizhniy Tagil (45/NA) Yur'ya (45/NA) Teykovo (36/NA) Vypolzovo (0/NA)	Some of the SS-25s transferred to Russia from Belarus are being redeployed at Vypolzovo, Yoshkar-Ola, and Irkutsk.[7]
Air-launched cruise missiles and gravity bombs (Total)	176 + /870	176 + /870		
Long-range ALCMs	176/798	176/798	Mozdok (176/738) Engels (NA/60)	Sixty-two Bear H bombers are based at Mozdok (36 carrying up to 16 ALCMs each and 27 carrying up to 6 ALCMs each). Five Blackjack bombers (carrying up to 12 ALCMs) are based at Engels.[8, 9] Current bomber loadings are based on the START II MOU and more accurately reflect the actual carrying capacity of the bombers. The START I MOU undercounted this capacity.

TYPE[1]	WEAPONS SYSTEMS (START I MOU/Current)	WARHEADS (START I MOU/Current)	LOCATION (No. of Weapons Systems: START I MOU/Current)	COMMENTS
Gravity bombs and short-range ALCMS	–/72	–/72	Ukrainka (NA/72)	Current bomber loadings are based on the START II MOU.
Submarine-launched ballistic missiles (Total)[10]	940/680-728	2,804/2,544-2,592		
SS-N-6	192/16	192/16	Pavlovskoye (48/NA) Rybachiy (48/NA) Yagel'naya (96/NA)	One Yankee I submarine is in operation.[11]
SS-N-8	280/208[12]	280/208	Pavlovskoye (72/NA) Ribachiy (36/NA) Ostrovnoy (108/NA) Yagel'naya (64/NA)	Twelve Delta I submarines (carrying 12 SS-N-8s each) and 4 Delta II submarines (carrying 16 SS-N-8s each) are in operation.
SS-N-17	12/0	12/0	Yagel'naya (12/0)	The only submarine carrying SS-N-17s, a Yankee II submarine, is believed to have been decommissioned.[13]
SS-N-18	224/224	672/672	Rybachiy (144/144) Yagel'naya (48/48) Olenya (32/32)	
SS-N-20	120/120	1,200/1,200	Nerpich'ya (120/120)	
SS-N-23	112/112	448/448	Olenya (112/112)	
Strategic warheads in storage	NA	Proportion in storage vs proportion in dismantlement facilities not known.		As of late February 1995, 2,600 strategic warheads had been removed from missiles or bomber bases.[14]
Strategic warheads in dismantlement facilities	NA		Arzamas-16 Sverdlovsk-45 Zlatoust-36 Penza-19(?)	Russia has told the United States Department of Defense that it is dismantling between 2,000 and 3,000 warheads per year.[15] As of March 1, 1995, approximately 1,000 of the 1,500 strategic warheads removed from deployment in Kazakhstan, Belarus, and, Ukraine had been returned to Russia for dismantlement.[16]

TYPE	WEAPONS SYSTEMS	WARHEADS	LOCATION (No. of Weapons Systems)	COMMENTS
T A C T I C A L W E A P O N S				
Tactical nuclear weapons		Estimates of the total number of warheads on tactical nuclear weapons in Russia range from 6,000 to 13,000.[17] Proportion deployed vs. proportion held in storage or dismantlement facilities not known.	Tactical nuclear weapons have been withdrawn from submarines and surface ships.[18] Deployment sites for land-based tactical weapons and storage sites for all types of tactical weapons are located throughout Russia. The total number of such sites was reduced in 1994 to ehnance security.	Approximately 4,000 tactical nuclear weapons were withdrawn to Russia from Belarus, Kazakhstan, and Ukraine.[19]
Tactical warheads in storage	NA	Proportion deployed vs. proportion held in storage or dismantlement facilities not known.	In late 1994, the number of secure storage areas for tactical nuclear weapons was reduced; previously Russia was believed to have approximately 100 such storage locations.[20]	
Tactical warheads in dismantlement facilities	NA	Proportion deployed vs. proportion held in storage or dismantlement facilities not known.	Arzamas-16 Zlatoust-36 Sverdlovsk-45	Russia has told the United States Department of Defense that it is dismantling between 2,000 and 3,000 warheads per year.[21]
Anti-ballistic missiles	100	100	ABMs deployed within a 100 km radius of Moscow	

NOTES (Russia Chart 1)

1. The baseline figures for this chart are taken from the START I Memorandum of Understanding (MOU). Current as of September 1990, the MOU is an annex to the START I Treaty which details the numbers and locations of the strategic offensive forces of the United States and the Soviet Union as of that date. See "START-Related Facilities by Republic as Declared in MOU Data Exchange-Sept. 1, 1990," *Hearings on the START Treaty*, Committee on Foreign Relations, U.S. Senate, 102nd Cong., 2nd Sess., February 6, 1992, p. 497.

2. Information on current numbers of weapons and warheads has been compiled using the following sources: *The Military Balance 1994-1995 (*London: International Institute for Strategic Studies, 1994); *Jane's Defense Weekly*, March 27, 1993, p. 7; "Nuclear Notebook," *Bulletin of the Atomic*

Scientists, March/April 1994; A. Pikayev and A. Savelyev, "The USSR's Nuclear Might: On Land, At Sea, At Air," *Nezavisimaya Gazeta*, November 2, 1991; A. Arbatov, ed., *Nuclear Weapons and the Republic's Sovereignty*, 1992; unclassified CIA report, September 1994, as cited in "Nuclear Weapons Deactivations Continue in FSU," *Arms Control Today*, November 1994; Dunbar Lockwood, "New Data From the Clinton Administration on the Status of Strategic Nuclear Weapons Deactivations," Memorandum, Arms Control Association, Washington, DC, December 7, 1994. Where the above sources disagree, a range estimate is provided.

In a speech in late February 1995, U.S. Secretary of Defense William Perry said that Russia had already removed 2,600 warheads from missiles and bomber bases; 750 missiles had been taken down from their launchers; and almost

600 launchers and bombers had been destroyed. (Speech by U.S. Defense Secretary William Perry, American Legion, February 27, 1995. See also General Roland LaJoie, Deputy for Cooperative Threat Reduction to the Assistant to the Secretary of Defense for Atomic Energy, special briefing on the Cooperative Threat Reduction Program for the Senate Foreign Relations Committee, February 23, 1995.) Since he did not make clear, however, which missiles have had their warheads removed or which missiles had been removed from their launchers, it is impossible to determine the number and class of nuclear weapons that are deployed in Russia. The recent published sources listed above thus provide the best unclassified estimate of specific warhead and missile numbers.

3. "NA" designates not available. The current numbers of weapons systems located at specific sites in Russia are classified. The baseline 1990 START I MOU numbers are given in Russia Chart 1.

According to Russian television reports, 55 out of the 60 silos at Svobodnyy had been destroyed. See "Former ICBM Base to Launch Satellites," *Moscow Russian Television*, July 27, 1994, in *FBIS-SOV-94-148*, August 2, 1994.

4. *Izvestiya*, November 13, 1992, p. 1, as cited in "Belarus and Nuclear Weapons," February 2, 1994, *Research Brief from Radio Free Europe/Radio Liberty Research Institute*.

5. Press reports indicate that, as of September 1994, 22 SS-18s had been dismantled in Surovatikha near Nizhny Novgorod in Russia. Reports also suggest that a portion of the 22 dismantled SS-18s may have included those transferred to Russia from Kazakhstan. See Barbara Starr, "Perry Wants Speedier Russian Disarmament," *Jane's Defense Weekly*, October 1, 1994, p. 6; "Missile Destruction Process Outlined," August 20, 1994, in *FBIS-SOV-94-163,* August 23, 1994.

6. In addition to the 45 SS-25s transferred from Belarus, sources estimate that between 30 and 60 SS-25s have been deployed since the START MOU. Unclassified CIA report, September 1994, *op. cit.* lists 261. "Nuclear Notebook," *op. cit.* lists 405 SS-25s. Ralph Hallenbeck and Steve Bauer, "The Former Soviet Union," Read-Ahead Paper prepared for the ACDA Regional/Nonproliferation Workshop (McLean, VA: SAIC, April 12, 1994) lists 252 SS-25s.

7. *Izvestiya*, November 13, 1992, *op. cit.*; "SS-25 Topol Missiles Redeployed From Belarus to Russia," April 20, 1994, in *JPRS-TND-94-011*, May 16, 1994; "Withdrawal of SS-25 Missiles to Russia Redeployed," May 15, 1994, in *JPRS-TAC-94-005*, June 23, 1994.

8. "World's Air Forces," *Flight International*, August 1994, p. 29. See also Craig Covault, "Russia Launches Exercise of Composite Strike Force," *Aviation Week and Space Technology,* November 15, 1993, p. 51.

9. On February 2, 1995, Ukraine agreed to sell to Russia all of its 42 strategic bombers. Russian experts estimated

the value of the total bomber force at $75 million, but as of March 1995, the final figure of the sale had not yet been agreed upon. Russian officials noted that Ukraine plans to use this money to reduce its enormous energy debt to Russia. The deal, however, must be approved by each nation's government. See Anton Zhigulsky, "Future of Disputed Black Sea Fleet Remains Uncertain," *Defense News*, March 13-19, 1995, p. 8; "Russia Says Ukraine to Hand Over Strategic Bombers," *Reuters*, February 24, 1995.

10. Totals include only warhead-carrying SLBMs that are currently loaded or may be quickly loaded onto submarines.

11. Unclassified Naval Order of Battle, Office of Naval Intelligence, Department of the Navy, January 1994. This information was released in response to a Freedom of Information Act request filed by Josh Handler of Greenpeace. See also *Arms Control Association Fact Sheet*, Washington DC, November 1994.

12. Unclassified CIA report, September 1994, *op. cit.,* cites 208. Other sources give lower numbers. See "Nuclear Notebook," March/April 1994, *op. cit.*

Differences in SLBM figures may be caused by the exclusion or inclusion of SLBMs, depending on the operational status of certain Russian submarines. Russian press reports suggest that Russia maintains only one or two SSBNs on patrol at any time. Some analysts consider SSBNs that are not on patrol, such as those that are sitting in port, to be non-operational and therfore do not include the SLBMs loaded onto them in their calculations. The intelligence community, however, appears to account for SLBMs on all Russian submarines, regardless of their carrier's patrol status. See "No New Subs," *Aviation Week and Space Technology*, November 23, 1992.

13. *Military Forces in Transition* (Washington, DC: U.S. Department of Defense, 1991), p. 36.

14. Speech by U.S Secretary of Defense William Perry, American Legion, *op.cit.*; General Roland LaJoie, special briefing on the Cooperative Threat Reduction Program, *op.cit.*

15. "Testimony of Assistant Secretary of Defense Ashton Carter," before the Senate Armed Services Committee, April 28, 1994. These figures include the dismantlement of both strategic and tactical nuclear weapons.

16. "Testimony of U.S. Defense Secretary William Perry," before the Senate Foreign Relations Committee, March 1, 1995.

17. Deputy Defense Secretary John Deutch, U.S. Defense Department Briefing, September 22, 1994.

18. "Tactical Nuclear Arms Removed from Vessels," *ITAR-TASS*, February 4, 1994, in *FBIS-SOV-93-022*, February 4, 1994, p. 1.

19. Ashton Carter, April 28, 1994, *op. cit.*

20. "Testimony of Gloria Duffy, Deputy Assistant Secretary of Defense for Cooperative Threat Reduction," before the House Foreign Affairs Committee, Subcommittee on Europe and the Middle East, March 24, 1994.

Because of concerns over the stability of Russia's armed forces—highlighted in the refusal of certain units to follow orders during the conflict to suppress the revolt in Chechnya—Washington urged the Russian government to consolidate tactical nuclear weapons in fewer locations with special security arrangements. Russia took such action in late 1994. (Interviews, Moscow, February 1995.)

21. Ashton Carter, April 28, 1994, *op. cit.* These figures include the dismantlement of both tactical and strategic nuclear weapons.

As of spring 1993, half of the tactical nuclear weapons removed from Ukrainian territory had been dismantled. Russia is to pay $500 million to Ukraine in compensation for tactical nuclear warheads transfered to Russia in 1992. See "Interview with General Sergei Zelentsov and Colonel-General Vitali Yakovlev, former commander and current deputy commander of the Russian military's 12th Main Directorate, in charge of nuclear weapons, Moscow, May 1993," as cited in *Management and Disposition of Excess Weapons Plutonium* (Washington, DC: National Academy Press, 1994); "Ukraine Pledges to Double Speed of Disarmament," *Reuters*, May 19, 1994.

RUSSIA Chart 2: Locations with Separated Weapons-Usable (Fissile) Material Sufficient for One or More Nuclear Weapons[1]

LOCATION	ACTIVITY	PLUTONIUM	WEAPONS-USABLE URANIUM	IAEA SAFEGUARDS STATUS	COMMENTS
Arzamas-16 (Renamed: Kremlev)	Warhead design;warhead assembly/ dismantlement.	Yes	Yes	Unsafeguarded[2]	Small-scale warhead dismantlement only
Penza-19(?) (Renamed: Zarechnyy)	Warhead production; warhead assembly/ dismantlement.	Yes	Yes	Unsafeguarded	Uncertain whether facility handles weapons-grade nuclear materials.
Sverdlovsk-45 (Renamed: Lesnoy)	Warhead assembly/ dismantlement	Yes	Yes	Unsafeguarded	
Chelyabinsk-70 (Renamed: Snezhinsk)	Warhead design; fabrication of experimental and prototype warheads.	Yes	Yes	Unsafeguarded	Site of the All-Russian Scientific Research Institute of Technical Physics
Zlatoust-36 (Renamed: Trekhgornyy)	Warhead assembly/ dismantlement	Yes	Yes	Unsafeguarded	
Chelyabinsk-65[3] (Renamed: Ozersk)	Plutonium and tritium production reactors; spent fuel reprocessing; production of mixed-oxide (MOX) fuel pellets.	Yes	Presume	Unsafeguarded	All plutonium production reactors have been closed, but plutonium separation continues. Two isotope-production reactors, formerly and perhaps still used for the production of tritium, are operating.
Krasnoyarsk-26 (Renamed: Zheleznogorsk)	Spent fuel reprocessing	Yes		Unsafeguarded	Two of 3 plutonium production reactors have been closed. The reactor still in operation will be closed down by the year 2,000.[4] Separation activities continue.
Tomsk-7[5] (Renamed: Seversk)	Spent fuel reprocessing; production of plutonium (Pu) and uranium warhead components; storage of Pu triggers from dismantled warheads;[6] oxidation of HEU metal from dismantled warheads.[7]	Yes	Yes	Unsafeguarded	Three of 5 plutonium production reactors have been closed. The 2 reactors still in operation will be closed down by the year 2,000.[8] Separation activities continue.

LOCATION	ACTIVITY	PLUTONIUM	WEAPONS-USABLE URANIUM	IAEA SAFEGUARDS STATUS	COMMENTS
Sverdlovsk-44 (Renamed: Novouralsk)	Highly-enriched uranium (HEU) production; "blending down" of HEU from dismantled warheads into low-enriched uranium (LEU).[9]		Yes	Unsafeguarded	Although the USSR stopped production of HEU in 1989, HEU produced in the 1980s may still be stored at Sverdlovsk-44.[10]
Institute of Physics and Power Engineering (Obninsk)	Research reactor; research on weapons-grade materials.	Yes	Reactor fueled with app. 120 kg of HEU (90%)	Unsafeguarded	The research reactor has 150 kg of weapons-grade plutonium; the research facility has 750 kg of weapons-grade plutonium.[11]
Lenin Institute of Physics (St. Petersburg)	Research reactor		Reactor fueled with app. 20 kg of HEU	Unsafeguarded	
Bochvar All-Union Institute for Non-Organic Substances (Moscow)	Research reactor; research on weapons-grade materials.	Yes	Yes	Unsafeguarded	The Institute is involved in the handling and analyzing of MOX fuel. In early 1994, Gosatomnadzor (GAN)—Russia's Nuclear Regulatory Commission—ordered parts of this facility to shut down for six months because of its lax arrangements for protecting plutonium at the site.[12]
Kurchatov Institute (Moscow)	Research reactors; research on weapons-grade materials.		Research rectors fueled with a total of app. 5 kg of HEU and 4 kg of LEU.	Unsafeguarded	Other undisclosed quantities of weapons-grade material are present at the Institute.[13]
Luch Scientific Production Association (Podolsk)	Research and production of space-based nuclear reactors		Yes	Unsafeguarded	
Electrostal Machine-Building Plant	Fuel fabrication for propulsion, RMBK, VVER-440, fast breeder, and research reactors	Presumed	Yes	Unsafeguarded	
Severomorsk[14]	Fresh fuel storage for propulsion reactors		Yes	Unsafeguarded	

RUSSIA Chart 2 (cont'd.)

LOCATION	ACTIVITY	PLUTONIUM	WEAPONS-USABLE URANIUM	IAEA SAFEGUARDS STATUS	COMMENTS
Vladivostok	Fresh fuel storage for propulsion reactors		Yes	Unsafeguarded	See note 14.
Severodvinsk	Fresh fuel storage for propulsion reactors		Yes	Unsafeguarded	See note 14.
Scientific Research Institute for Atomic Reactors (Dmitrovgrad)	One fast-breeder reactor; research reactors; fabrication of mixed-oxide fuel elements	App. 350 kg of plutonium believed to be present	Research reactors fueled with a total of app. 25 kg of HEU	Unsafeguarded	Fast-breeder reactor fueled with plutonium and an unknown quantity of uranium enriched to 45%-90%.

NOTES (Russia Chart 2)

1. Weapons-usable fissile material includes uranium enriched to 90% or more in the isotope U-235 (referred to below as highly-enriched uranium, or HEU) and all forms of plutonium (Pu). About 15 kg of HEU or 5 kg of Pu are required for a nuclear weapon.

Principal sources for this table are William Potter, *Nuclear Profiles of the Soviet Successor States* (Monterey, CA: Monterey Institute for International Studies, 1993); Thomas B. Cochran and Robert S. Morris, *Russian/Soviet Nuclear Warhead Production, Nuclear Weapons Data Book Working Papers* (Washington, DC: Natural Resources Defense Council, 1993); interviews, Moscow, June and October 1994.

2. As a nuclear-weapon state party to the NPT, Russia is not required to place its nuclear facilities under International Atomic Energy Agency (IAEA) safeguards.

Under the NPT, Russia is prohibited from exporting nuclear equipment or material to any non-nuclear-weapon state unless the transfered items are subject to IAEA safeguards in the recipient state. Since Kazakhstan and Ukraine have not yet formally concluded safeguards agreements with the IAEA, continuing Russian exports of low-enriched uranium and fabricated nuclear fuel to these states constitute an infringement of this NPT requirement. In 1992, the Nuclear Suppliers Group, of which Russia is a member, agreed to withhold nuclear exports from states having any nuclear facilities not subject to IAEA safeguards. However, recognizing the unusual circumstances of the break-up of the Soviet Union, the Group agreed that the rule would not be applied to on-going supply commitments, such as those between Russia and a number of former Soviet republics.

3. Site of a fissile material storage center financed in large part by the United States. Ground-breaking took place in October 1994, and site preparation has begun.

4. An intergovernmental agreement signed by U.S. Vice President Albert Gore and Russian Prime Minister Viktor Chernomyrdin on June 23, 1994, obligates the Russian Federation to shut down, by the year 2,000 , the plutonium production reactor still operating in Krasnoyarsk. The agreement additionally provides that Russia will not use in nuclear weapons any plutonium produced by the production reactors after the agreement enters into force. Verification measures to assure compliance were to be developed over the next six months. See ''Vice President's Statement to the Press at the Signing Ceremony with Russian Prime Minister Chernomyrdin,'' Office of the Vice President, June 23, 1994.

5. Proposed site of a fissile material storage center. Japan has indicated that it may provide a portion of the financing for this project.

6. In a joint statement on March 16, 1994, the United States and Russia announced that they ''intend to conclude an agreement on the means of confirming the plutonium and highly enriched uranium inventories from nuclear disarmament.'' As of March 1995, experts on the two sides were working to develop appropriate measures that would be the basis of reciprocal inspections to verify these inventories, but no agreement had been reached to verify the number of dismantled warheads. (Interview with U.S. official, March 1995.) Earlier press reports had indicated that an agreement on verifying dismantled warheads had already been concluded. See Thomas L. Lippman, ''Accord Set on Nuclear Inspections,'' *Washington Post*, March 16, 1994.

7. The converted uranium will be sent to Sverdlovsk-44 for ''blending-down'' into low-enriched uranium. (See *Nuclear Fuel*, March 28, 1994.)

8. See note 4.

9. The United States has agreed to purchase 500 metric tons weapons-grade uranium from dismantled Russian nuclear weapons, which is to be blended down to low-enriched uranium (LEU) suitable for use as nuclear power plant fuel. (See Thomas W. Lippman, "Russia Aims to Unload Its Uranium in the U.S.; Deal Moves Slowly Through Thorny Issues," *Washington Post*, August 5, 1992.) The LEU will be sold to the United States Enrichment Corporation for eventual use in nuclear power reactors. American inspectors will be allowed into Sverdlovsk-44 to verify that the HEU actually comes from dismantled warheads. See *Nuclear Fuel*, March 28, 1994, pp. 6–8.

10. Three other sites, Kransnoyarsk-45, Tomsk-7, and Angarsk produce LEU for use as fuel for nuclear power plants. These facilities are capable of producing HEU but are believed not to have produced it in the past.

11. "Energy Conversion of Weapons Grade Plutonium," by V. M. Murogov, in *Nuclear Fuel Reprocessing, Storage and Usage of Power Plant and Weapons Grade Plutonium*, International Seminar, Moscow, December 14–16, 1992, p. 126.

12. "Testimony of Leonard S. Spector," before the House Foreign Affairs Committee, Subcommittee on International Security, International Organizations, and Human Rights, June 27, 1994.

13. "Kremlin Press Conference on Theft of Nuclear Materials with Senior Officials from the Kurchatov Institute," *Federal News Service Transcript* (S.8/23/3); interviews, Moscow, June and October 1994.

14. There are multiple storage sites for HEU in the form of fresh fuel for propulsion reactors in the Russian Northern and Pacific Fleets. These stocks are under custody of the Ministry of Shipbuilding and the Committee for the Defense Industry. See "Testimony of William C. Potter," before the House Foreign Affairs Committee, Subcommittee on International Security, International Organizations, and Human Rights, June 27, 1994.

RUSSIA Chart 3: Nuclear Weapons and Nuclear Power Infrastructure, by Administrative Division[1]

Note: Administrative divisions in bold italics contain nuclear weapons or quantities of weapons-usable nuclear material sufficient for one or more nuclear weapons.

ADMINISTRATIVE DIVISION	NUCLEAR WEAPONS/NUCLEAR FACILITIES
Adygeya	
Aginskiy Buryat	
Altay	ICBM base (*Aleysk*)
Amur	ICBM base (*Svobodnyy*), heavy bomber base (*Ukrainka*)
Arkhangel'sk	Submarine/surface ship propulsion reactors; SLBM storage, testing, and conversion/elimination. ICBM testing and training. Ballistic missile-equipped submarine production; SLBM loading. Fresh fuel storage (*Severodvinsk*)
Astrakhan	
Bashkortostan	
Belgorod	
Bryansk	
Buryatia	
Chelyabinsk	ICBM base (*Kartaly*). Nuclear weapons/nuclear warhead design. Research reactor (*Chelyabinsk-70*). Spent fuel reprocessing; 5 plutonium production reactors (shut down); MOX fuel fabrication (suspended); nuclear waste vitrification; tritium production reactors, proposed site of a fissile material storage center (all at *Chelyabinsk-65*). SLBM production.
Chita	ICBM bases (*Drovyanaya, Yasnaya*). Mining and processing of uranium ore (*Krasnokamensk*).
Chukotka	Four GBWR-12 power reactors (*Bilibino*, 44 MWe total, uranium enriched to 3.0-3.6%).
Chuvashia	
Dagestan	
Evenkia	
Gorno-Altay	
Chechen Republic	
Ingushetia	
Irkutsk	ICBM base (*Irkutsk*). Uranium enrichment (low-enriched uranium only) and uranium hexafluoride production (*Angarsk*).
Ivanovo	ICBM base (*Teykovo*)
Kabardino-Balkaria	
Kaliningrad	
Kalmykia	
Kaluga	ICBM base (*Kozel'sk*). Research reactor (*Obninsk*, 120 kg of HEU, enriched to 90%); ICBM training.
Kamchatka	Base for ballistic missile-equipped submarines (*Rybachiy*); submarine/surface ship propulsion reactors.
Karachay-Cherkessia	
Karelia	
Kemerovo	ICBM production
Khabarovsk	
Khakassia	

ADMINISTRATIVE DIVISION	NUCLEAR WEAPONS/NUCLEAR FACILITIES
Khanty-Mansi	
Kirov	ICBM base (*Yur'ya*)
Komi	
Komi-Perm	
Koryak	
Kostroma	ICBM base (*Kostroma*)
Krasnodar	ICBM training
Krasnoyarsk	ICBM bases (*Uzhur, Krasnoyarsk, Kansk*). Uranium enrichment, low only (*Krasnoyarsk-45*). Spent fuel reprocessing, plutonium production reactors (2 of 3 reactors shut down; the one reactor still in operation is to be shut down by the year 2000); uranium hexafluoride production, spent fuel storage (all at *Krasnoyarsk-26*). SLBM production.
Kurgan	
Kursk	Four RMBK-1000 power reactors (*Kursk*, 3,700 MWe total, uranium enriched to 2.4%); spent fuel storage.
Leningrad Oblast and City of St. Petersburg	Two research reactors (*St. Petersburg*, 20.4 kg total of uranium enriched to 90%); 4 RMBK-1000 power reactors (*Sosonovy Bor*, 3700 MWe total, uranium enriched to 2.4%).
Lipetsk	
Magadan	
Mari-El	ICBM bases (*Yoshkar-Ola*)
Mordovia	
Moscow Oblast and City of Moscow	Anti-ballistic missile bases; ICBM production and training; heavy bomber testing and training; fuel rod fabrication (*Electrostal Machine Building Plant*). Research reactors (*Kurchatov Institute*, substantial undisclosed quantities of weapons-grade materials; *Bochvar All-Union Institute for Non-Organic Substances,* undisclosed quantities of weapons-grade materials). Numerous nuclear research institutes.
Murmansk	Bases for ballistic missile-equipped submarines (*Nerpich'ya, Yagel'naya, Olen'ya, Ostrovnoy*); submarine/surface ship propulsion reactors; SLBM storage; 2 VVER-440 V-230 power reactors (*Polyarnye Zori*, 822 MWe total, uranium enriched to 3.6%); 2 VVER-440 V-213 power reactors (*Polyarnye Zori*, 822 MWe total, uranium enriched to 3.3%). Fresh fuel storage (*Severomorsk*)
Nenetsk	
Nizhniy Novgorod	Nuclear warhead assembly, dismantlement, and design (*Arzamas-16*). ICBM storage, no warheads (*Sarovatikha*).
North Ossetia	Heavy bomber base (*Mozdok*)
Novgorod	
Novosibirsk	ICBM base (*Novosibirsk*). Fuel rod and pellet fabrication (*Novosibirsk Chemical Concentrate Plant*). SLBM conversion/elimination.
Omsk	
Orel	
Orenburg	ICBM base (*Dombarovskiy*)
Penza	Nuclear warhead assembly/dismantlement; production of electronic components for warheads (*Penza-19*).
Perm	ICBM bases (*Bershet*); possible warhead production; ICBM training.
Primorskiy	Base for ballistic missile-equipped submarines (*Pavlovskoye*). Submarine/surface ship propulsion reactors; submarine reactor waste storage; SLBM conversion/elimination; fresh fuel storage (*Vladivostok*).

ADMINISTRATIVE DIVISION	NUCLEAR WEAPONS/NUCLEAR FACILITIES
Pskov	
Rostov	ICBM training and repair
Ryazan'	Heavy bomber training and repair
Sakha (Yakutia)	
Sakhalin	
Samara	Heavy bomber production
Saratov	ICBM base (*Tatishchevo*). Heavy bomber base (*Engels*). Heavy bomber conversion/elimination, 4 VVER-1000 reactors (*Balakovo*, 3800 MWe total, uranium enriched to 4.4%).
Smolensk	Three RMBK-1000 reactors (*Smolensk*, 2,775 MWe total, uranium enriched to 2%)
Stavropol	Uranium mining (mining location reportedly depleted)
Sverdlovsk	ICBM base (*Nizhniy Tagil*). Warhead assembly/dismantlement/storage (*Sverdlovsk-45*). Possible storage of weapons-grade uranium, "blending down" of weapons-grade uranium into low-enriched uranium (*Sverdlovsk-44*). Research reactor (*Yekaterinburg*, 1.7 kg of uranium enriched to 90%). One BN-600 fast-breeder reactor (*Beloyarsk*, 600 MWe, uranium enriched to 20-25%).
Tambov	
Taymyr	
Tatarstan	Heavy bomber production
Tomsk	Spent fuel reprocessing, uranium enrichment, plutonium production reactors (3 of 5 reactors shut down; those reactors still in operation are to be shut down by the year 2000). Production of plutonium and uranium warhead components; storage of plutonium triggers from dismantled warheads; oxidation of weapons-grade uranium metal from dismantled warheads; proposed site of fissile material storage center (all at *Tomsk-7*).
Tula	
Tuva	
Tver'	ICBM base (*Vypolzovo*); 2 VVER-1000 power reactors (*Kalinin*, 1,900 MWe total, uranium enriched to 3.3-4.4%); third unit nearly complete.
Tyumen'	
Udmurtia	ICBM storage, ICBM production
Ul'yanovsk	Mixed-oxide fuel production (*Dmitrovgrad*, 350 kg of plutonium present). Research reactors (*Dmitrovgrad*, 25 kg total of uranium enriched to 90%, 37 kg total of uranium enriched to 63%); 1 BOR-60 fast-breeder reactor (*Dmitrovgrad*, 11 MWe, initial core of uranium enriched up to 90%); 1 VK-50 power reactor (*Dmitrovgrad*, 50 MWe, uranium enriched to 1.5-2.0%). ICBM production.
Ust Ordynski Buryat	
Vladimir	
Volgograd	ICBM launcher production
Vologda	
Voronezh	Two VVER-440 V-179 power reactors (*Novovoronezh*, 770 MWe total, uranium enriched to 3.6%); 1 VVER-1000 V-187 power reactor (*Novovoronezh*, 950 MWe, uranium enriched to 4.4%).
Yamal-Nenetsk	
Yaroslavl'	
Yevrey	

NOTES (Russia Chart 3)

1. Principal sources for this table are William Potter, *Nuclear Profiles of the Soviet Successor States* (Monterey, CA.: Monterey Institute of International Studies, 1993); Thomas B. Cochran and Robert S. Norris, *Russian/Soviet Nuclear Warhead Production* (Washington, DC: Natural Resources Defense Council, 1993); START Memorandum of Understanding, September 1990. For references regarding the names of the administrative divisions, see Article 65, Constitution of Russia, *Rossiyskiye Vesti*, December 25, 1993, pp. I–III.

China

China has been a declared nuclear-weapon state since 1964, and its nuclear weapons program is not a target of international non-proliferation efforts. However, China continues to have a broad impact on the spread of nuclear arms and related delivery systems, affecting the nuclear policies and nuclear potential of many countries of proliferation concern. Specifically, China poses two distinct proliferation risks.

First, as China undergoes the profound economic and political changes expected to follow the death of its 90-year-old leader Deng Xiaoping, it is widely assumed that the central government's ability to manage national affairs will come under increasing challenge. This will greatly increase the possibility of unauthorized transfers of sensitive nuclear materials and technology and could conceivably result in fragmentation of the country's nuclear arsenal among competing factions or, in an extreme case, new splinter states.[1]

Second, China has directly contributed to proliferation by exporting a wide range of sensitive commodities that have assisted other states in pursuing suspect nuclear activities and missile development programs. On the nuclear front, China is understood to have given Pakistan the design for a nuclear weapon in the early 1980s, along with a quantity of highly enriched uranium for one or two nuclear devices. In addition, China may be helping Pakistan finish constructing a 50-70 MWt unsafeguarded plutonium production reactor at Khusab.[2] Such a facility, when coupled with Pakistan's unsafeguarded plutonium extraction facility at Chasma, would give Pakistan, for the first time, an unsafeguarded source of plutonium for use in nuclear weapons. In addition, China has sold two small research reactors and an experimental calutron to Iran and recently signed an agreement to build two 300 MWe power reactors in Iran, near Bushehr.[3] Fearing that any nuclear assistance to Iran could contribute to its efforts to acquire nuclear weapons, the United States has sought to impose an international embargo on all nuclear sales to Tehran. Western nuclear supplier countries are adhering to this quarantine (indeed Germany, at considerable cost, has refused to complete two partially built reactors on which construction began before the Iranian Revolution), but China has refused to implement the embargo.

With respect to missile exports, China has reportedly aided the missile programs of Pakistan, Iran, Libya, Syria, and possibly, North Korea. Of particular concern have been its transfers to Pakistan of complete missiles or key components for the short-range, nuclear-capable M-11. These transfers led the United States to impose sanctions against China and Pakistan in August 1993. The sanctions were lifted in October 1994, after China signed an agreement with the United States under which it accepted a ban on the sale of missiles inherently capable of carrying a 500 kg payload to a distance of 300 km or more—a ban that China agreed prohibited further exports of the M-11.[4]

Beyond China's activities directly linked to nuclear and missile proliferation, as a declared nuclear-weapon state and permanent member of the UN Security Council, Beijing's overall nuclear policies, its attitude toward non-proliferation and arms control, generally, and its participation in global proliferation regimes necessarily carry weight in the nuclear decision-making of many other states. Throughout the Cold War, China remained an outsider to most international arms control initiatives. It has never signed the 1963 partial Test Ban Treaty, and only became a member of the International Atomic Energy Agency in 1984. In 1992 it acceded to the Nuclear Non-Proliferation Treaty as a nuclear-weapon state. Most recently, China has declined to participate with the United States, Russia, France, and Great Britain in a moratorium on nuclear testing begun in October 1992 and has since conducted three nuclear tests. China has, however, repeatedly promised to sign a permanent nuclear test ban. More positively, China and the United States recently signed a statement pledging to work toward a multilateral convention banning the production of fissile materials for nuclear weapons.

NOTES

[1]*China in the Near Term*, (Washington, DC: Office of the Under Secretary of Defense (Policy), Office of Net Assessment, Summer 1994); Leonard S. Spector and Evan S. Medeiros, "China's Nuclear Question Mark," *Washington Post Outlook*, October 3, 1993; "China: In Deep Water," *The Economist*, September 25, 1993, p. 44; Peter Kien-hong Yo, "Regional Military Separatism in Communist China," *Global Affairs*, Spring 1993; Maria Hsia Chang, "China's Future: Regionalism, Federation, or Disintegration," *Studies in Comparative Communism*, September 1992.

[2]Interviews with U.S. officials, September 1994.

[3]See Mark Hibbs, "Bhutto May Finish Plutonium Reactor Without Agreement on Fissile Stocks," *Nucleonics Week*, October 6, 1994, p. 10; "China Goes Ahead With Nuclear Plants in Iran," *United Press International*, November 21, 1994.

[4]Elaine Sciolino, "U.S. and Chinese Reach Agreement on Missile Export," *New York Times*, October 5, 1994; Daniel Williams, "U.S. Deal With China Allows High-Tech Sales in Exchange for Pledge," *Washington Post*, October 5, 1994; William C. Potter and Harlan Jencks, eds., *The International Missile Bazaar* (Boulder, CO: Westview Press, 1994); interviews with U.S. officials, fall 1994.

China:
Map and Charts

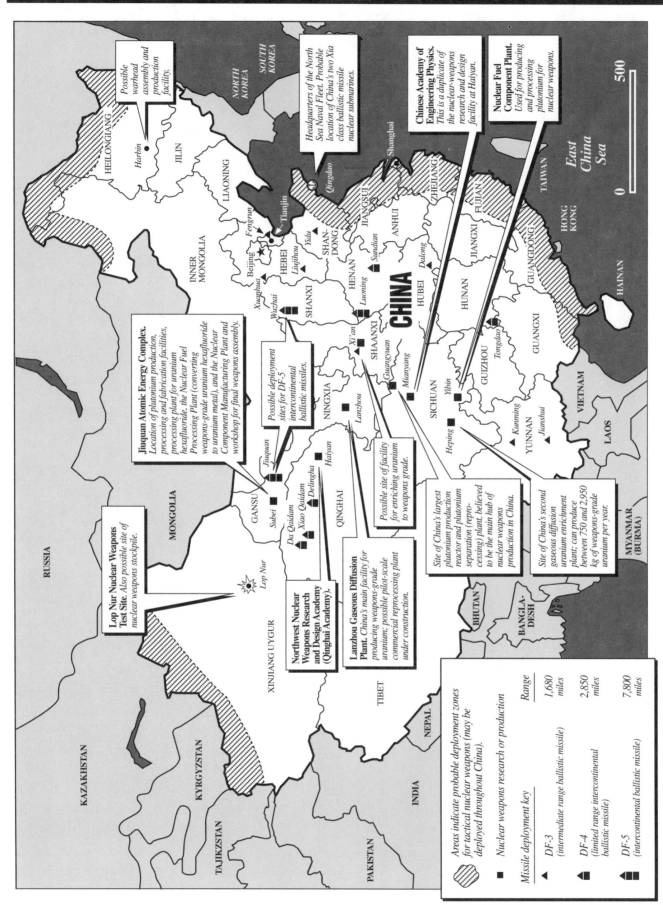

Possible warhead assembly and production facility.

Headquarters of the North Sea Naval Fleet. Probable location of China's two Xia class ballistic missile nuclear submarines.

Chinese Academy of Engineering Physics. This is a duplicate of the nuclear-weapons research and design facility at Haiyan.

Nuclear Fuel Component Plant. Used for producing and processing plutonium for nuclear weapons.

Jiuquan Atomic Energy Complex. Location of plutonium production, processing and fabrication facilities, processing plant for uranium hexafluoride, the Nuclear Fuel Processing Plant (converting weapons-grade uranium hexafluoride to uranium metal), and the Nuclear Component Manufacturing Plant and workshop for final weapons assembly.

Possible deployment sites for DF-5 intercontinental ballistic missiles.

Possible site of facility for enriching uranium to weapons grade.

Lop Nur Nuclear Weapons Test Site. Also possible site of nuclear weapons stockpile.

Northwest Nuclear Weapons Research and Design Academy (Qinghai Academy).

Lanzhou Gaseous Diffusion Plant. China's main facility for producing weapons-grade uranium; possible pilot-scale commercial reprocessing plant under construction.

Site of China's largest plutonium production reactor and plutonium separation (reprocessing) plant, believed to be the main hub of nuclear weapons production in China.

Site of China's second gaseous diffusion uranium enrichment plant; can produce between 750 and 2,950 kg of weapons-grade uranium per year.

Areas indicate probable deployment zones for tactical nuclear weapons (may be deployed throughout China).

Nuclear weapons research or production

Missile deployment key		Range
◀	DF-3 (intermediate range ballistic missile)	1,680 miles
◀◀	DF-4 (limited range intercontinental ballistic missile)	2,850 miles
◀◀◀	DF-5 (intercontinental ballistic missile)	7,800 miles

Carnegie Endowment for International Peace, *Tracking Nuclear Proliferation*, 1995.

Adapted from Robert S. Norris et al., *Nuclear Weapons Databook*, Vol. V, Natural Resources Defense Council, March 1994; and other sources.

CHINA Chart 1: Nuclear Weapons Systems[1]

TYPE	OPERATING PARAMETERS	NUMBER OF WEAPONS/ MISSILE LOCATIONS	COMMENTS
LAND-BASED MISSILES[2]			
Dong Feng-3(3A)/ CSS-2*	DF-3: 2,650 km/2,150 kg DF-3A: 2,800 km/2,159 kg Warhead: 1-3 Mt; 2 Mt	Total: 50 Fengrun, Xuanhua, Liujihou,Yidu, Xian, near Dalong, Jianshui, and around Kunming.	DF-3 was China's first indigenously produced missile. Extended range DF-3A produced in late 1980s. In 1987, 30 DF-3s sold to Saudi Arabia.
Dong Feng-4/CSS-3	4,750 km/2,200 kg Warhead: 3.3 Mt; 1-3 Mt	Total: 20 Xiao Qaidam, Da Qaidam, Delingha (all cave-based). Tongdao, Sundian (silo-based at both sites).	China's first missile capable of striking Moscow.
Dong Feng-5 (5A)/ CSS-4	DF-5: 12,000 km/3,200 kg DF-5A: 13,000 km/3,200 kg Warhead: 3.3 Mt; 4-5 Mt	Total: 4 Luoning (2 silos). Others possibly deployed as war reserves at Jiuquan and Wuzhai Centers.	China's first and only intercontinetal ballistic missile; identical airframe to CZ-2 space launch vehicle.
Dong Feng-21 (21A)/ CSS-6	DF-21: 1,700 km/600 kg DF-21A: 1,800 km/600 kg	Total: 36 Road-mobile, ''believed to be deployed in the northwest province of Qinghai and the southwest province of Yunan. . . .[allowing] coverage of northern India, most of the newly independent republics of Central Asia, most of Vietnam and large areas of Southeast Asia.''[3]	DF-21 is land-based version of JL-1 submarine launched ballistic missile (SLBM); China's first road-mobile, solid fuel missile.[4]
TACTICAL MISSILES			
Dong Feng-15/M-9/ CSST-600**	600 km/950 kg nuclear-capable; warhead yield unknown.	Unknown; may currently be deployed in Fujian province opposite to Taiwan.[5]	Solid fuel, road-mobile; DF-15 to be deployed by China's Second Artillery Corps; nuclear-capable. Some reports noted that DF-15 was given a conventional role.[6] The M-9 (export version of DF-15) may have been sold to Syria, Iran, or Libya.
Dong Feng-11/M-11/ CSS-7	300 km/500 kg; reportedly can carry 800 kg warhead to 290 km.[7]	Unknown	Solid fuel, road-mobile; built for export; likely sold to Pakistan and Iran; reportedly entered service with PLA in 1992.[8]

TYPE	OPERATING PARAMETERS	NUMBER OF WEAPONS/ MISSILE LOCATIONS	COMMENTS
S U B M A R I N E L A U N C H E D B A L L I S I T C M I S S I L E S [9] (S L B M)			
Julang-1/CSS-N-3***	1,700 km/600 kg one 200-300 Kt warhead	Total: 24 Deployed on two Daqingyu (Xia) class submarines, likely based at North Sea Naval Fleet in Qingdao; 12 JL-1's on each SSBN.	China's first submarine launched ballistic missile; solid fuel; sea-based version of DF-21 IRBM.

   * Dong Feng means "East Wind"; CSS is a U.S. designation for "Chinese Surface-to-Surface."

  ** The "M" family of missiles was developed exclusively for export; CSST is a U.S. designation for "Chinese Surface-to-Surface Tactical" missile.

*** Julang means "Giant Wave"; CSS-N is the U.S. designation for "Chinese Surface-to-Surface Naval."

NOTES (China Chart 1)

1. Principal sources include, John Wilson Lewis and Hua Di, "China's Ballistic Missile Program: Technologies Strategies and Goals," *International Security*, Fall 1992; Robert S. Norris, Andrew S. Burrows, and Richard W. Fieldhouse, *Nuclear Weapons Databook, Vol. V: British, French, and Chinese Weapons* (Washington, DC: Natural Resources Defense Council, 1994).

2. China is also developing three medium- and long-range ballistic missile systems: the DF-25, DF-31, and DF-41. These missile will replace currently deployed outdated models.

    The Dong Feng-25 (1,700 km/2,000 kg) is a land-mobile, solid fuel modification of the DF-31s first two stages. Initial operational capability planned for the mid-1990s.

    The Dong Feng-31 (8,000 km/700 kg) carries one 200-300 Kt warhead and is a solid fuel, land-mobile version of the JL-2 SLBM; initial operational capability planned for the mid-1990s.

    The Dong Feng-41 (12,000 km/800 kg) also carries one 200-300 Kt warhead and is a solid fuel replacement for the DF-5A ICBM; initial operational capability planned for the late 1990s.

3. "China Switches IRBM's to Conventional Role," *Jane's Defence Weekly*, January 29, 1994, p. 1.

4. One report noted that DF-21's nuclear warheads were replaced with conventional ones to be used in limited, local wars. (See "China Switches IRBMs to Conventional Role," *op. cit.*) The conclusions of this report are dubious since the 600 kg payload capacity of the DF-21(21A) would not permit it to deliver a very destructive conventional warhead, while such a payload capacity would be ideal for delivering a nuclear warhead.

5. One report noted that China recently redeployed an undisclosed number of M-9 missiles from Jiangxi province to Fujian province opposite Taiwan. However, the validity of this source is unclear. See "China Shifts Missiles," *Jane's Defence Weekly*, March 4, 1995, p. 4.

6. "China Switches IRBMs to Conventional Role," *op. cit.*

7. "China's M-11 is Revealed," *Jane's Defence Weekly*, April 9, 1988, p. 655.

8. Duncan Lennox, "Ballistic Missiles Hit New Heights," *Jane's Defence Weekly*, April 30, 1994, p. 24. The DF-15 may have entered service after successful test launches in 1989.

9. China is also developing a second generation submarine launched ballistic missile (SLBM) called the Julang-2 (JL-2). The JL-2 (8,000 km/700kg), a sea-based version of the DF-31, can carry up to one 200-300 Kt nuclear warhead. The JL-2 is scheduled to reach initial operational capability in the mid-1990s and is slated to replace the JL-1 SLBM.

CHINA Chart 2: Nuclear Weapons Infrastructure, by Military District[1]

Note: Military districts in bold italics contain nuclear weapons or quantities of weapons-usable nuclear materials sufficient for one or more nuclear weapons.

MILITARY DISTRICT	NUCLEAR WEAPONS/FISSILE MATERIAL PRODUCTION FACILITIES
Anhui	
Fujian	Possible coastal deployment of tactical nuclear weapons.
Guandong	Possible coastal deployment of tactical nuclear weapons.
Guangxi	Possible coastal deployment of tactical nuclear weapons.
Gansu	Site of Jiuquan Atomic Energy Complex (near Subei), includes complete plutonium production, processing, and fabrication works, uranium hexafluoride processing plant, Nuclear Fuel Processing Plant, Nuclear Component Manufacturing Plant, and Assembly Workshop; Lanzhou Gaseous Diffusion Plant (Lanzhou), main facility to enrich uranium and site of pilot-scale commercial plutonium reprocessing plant under construction[2]; possible deployment of DF-5A intercontinental ballistic missiles (ICBMs) as war reserves (Jiuquan Space Center).
Guizhou	
Hebei	DF-3 intermediate range ballistic missiles (IRBMs) reportedly deployed (Fengrun, Xuanhua, and near Liujihou).
Heilongiang	Possible warhead assembly and production facility (near Harbin); tactical nuclear weapons possibly deployed along northern border with Russia.
Henan	DF-5A ICBMs deployed in silos (Luoning); DF-4 limited range ICBMs deployed in silos (Sundian).
Hubei	DF-3 IRBMs reportedly based (near Dalong).
Hunan	DF-4 limited range ICBMs deployed in silos (Tungdao).
Inner Mongolia	Tactical nuclear weapons possibly deployed along northern border with Russia.
Jiangsui	Possible coastal deployment of tactical nuclear weapons.
Jiangxi	
Jilin	
Liaoning	
Ningxia	
Qinghai	Northwest Nuclear Weapons Research and Design Academy; DF-4 limited range ICBMs deployed in caves (Da Qaidam, Xiao Qaidam, and Delingha).
Shaanxi	Possible uranium enrichment plant[3] and DF-3 IRBM site (Xi'an).
Shandong	Probable coastal deployment of tactical nuclear weapons; headquarters of North Sea Naval Fleet (Qingdao) and probable location of two Xia-class ballistic missile submarines; also reported location of DF-3 missiles (near Yidu).
Shanxi	Possible deployment of DF-5A ICBMs as war reserves (Wuzhai Missile Test Center).
Sichuan	China's largest plutonium production reactor and reprocessing facility with 300-400 kg plutonium per year capacity (Guangyuan); Nuclear Fuel Component Plant used for producing and processing plutonium for nuclear weapons (Yibin); Chinese Academy of Engineering Physics (Mianyang), functions as duplicate nuclear weapons research and design facility and possible site of a nuclear weapon stockpile; location of second largest gaseous diffusion uranium enrichment plant with capacity of 750 kg to 2,950 kg of weapons-grade uranium per year (Heping).
Tibet	
Xinjiang Uygur	Lop Nur nuclear weapons test site; reported location of nuclear weapons stockpile; reported future site of plutonium reprocessing plant[4] (Lop Nur). Tactical nuclear weapons possibly deployed along northwest border.
Yunan	DF-3 IRBM's deployment (near Jinashui and around Kunming).
Zhejiang	Probable coastal deployment of tactical nuclear weapons and planned future site of civilian plutonium reprocessing plant.[5]

NOTES (China Chart 2)

1. The principal sources for this table include Robert S. Norris et al., *Nuclear Weapons Databook Volume V: British, French, and Chinese Nuclear Weapons* (Washington, DC: Natural Resources Defense Council, 1993); John Wilson Lewis and Hua Di, "China's Ballistic Missile Programs: Technologies, Strategies and Goals," *International Security*, Fall 1992.

2. The pilot-scale commerical reprocessing plant is projected to begin operation in 2000 with a capacity of 100 kg plutonium per day, utilizing a three-cycle Purex extraction process. China's experience designing, constructing, and operating this facility will be used as a model for building larger, full-scale reprocessing plants. See Kenton D. Lindberg, "The People's Republic of China: Fueling Tremendous Growth with Nuclear Power," *NUEXCO Review*, September 1993, p. 31; "Datafile: China," *Nuclear Engineering International*, October 1993, p. 22.

3. Kenton D. Lindberg, "The Peoples Republic of China: Fueling Tremendous Growth with Nuclear Power," *op. cit.*; see also "Datafile: China," *op. cit.*

4. Reportedly, the plant will extract plutonium and uranium from spent fuel and will include waste solidification and burial facilities. A larger plant is planned to be commisioned in 2010 and is expected to have excess reprocessing and burial capacity. See Kenton D. Lindberg, "The People's Republic of China: Fueling Tremendous Growth with Nuclear Power," *op. cit.*; "Datafile: China," *op. cit.*

5. This plant will be used to reprocess the spent fuel from the two power reactors at Qinshan and the two at Daya Bay. See Kenton D. Lindberg, "The Peoples Republic of China: Fueling Tremendous Growth with Nuclear Power," *op. cit.*; "Datafile: China," *op. cit.*

5
SOVIET SUCCESSOR STATES WITH NUCLEAR WEAPONS ON TERRITORY

Belarus

When the Soviet Union dissolved in December 1991, Belarus emerged as an independent state that retained eighty-one strategic nuclear warheads on its territory, deployed on eighty-one single-warhead, road-mobile SS-25 intercontinental ballistic missiles (ICBMs). In addition, 725 tactical nuclear weapons were deployed in Belarus.[1] Russia retained the command and control capabilities, including arming and launching codes, required to use all of these armaments. Nonetheless, there was widespread concern that Belarus might become a new nuclear-weapon state and deal a serious blow to international efforts to curb the spread of nuclear arms.

In large part because of its close ties to, and dependency upon, Russia, Belarus has moved purposefully to transfer its nuclear arms to its eastern neighbor and to accept firm non-proliferation commitments. Belarus took the first steps in this direction when it signed the Declaration on Nuclear Arms, on December 21, 1991, at Alma-Ata (now Almaty), Kazakhstan, along with Kazakhstan, Russia, and Ukraine. Under the Declaration, Belarus pledged to join the Nuclear Non-Proliferation Treaty (NPT) as a non-nuclear-weapon state (Article 5(i)) and to return to Russia all tactical nuclear weapons in Belarus by July 1, 1992 (Article 6). In addition, it agreed not to transfer nuclear weapons on its territory to others, but specified that this prohibition did not preclude transfers of nuclear arms to Russia (Articles 5(ii),(iii)), in anticipation of the ultimate return of all strategic nuclear weapons from Belarus to Russia.[2]

In a subsequent accord signed in Minsk on December 30, 1991, Belarus agreed, together with the ten other members of the Commonwealth of Independent States (CIS) that a "decision on the need [to use nuclear weapons would be] made by the President of the Russian Federation in agreement with the heads of the Republic of Belarus, the Republic of Kazakhstan, and Ukraine, and in consultation with the heads of the other member states of the Commonwealth."[3] (Arrangements for sharing authority in this area ended in June 1993, when Russia formally took full control over the use of all nuclear arms in the Soviet successor states.)

Finally, in the May 23, 1992, Lisbon Protocol to the START I Treaty, Belarus agreed to participate jointly in the Treaty with Kazakhstan, Russia, and Ukraine as successors to the former Soviet Union and to "implement the Treaty's limits and restrictions" (Article II of the Protocol). Belarus also agreed to "adhere to the Treaty on the Non-Proliferation of Nuclear Weapons (NPT)" as a non-nuclear-weapon state party "in the shortest possible time" (Article V of the Protocol) and, in a side letter to President George Bush, Belarus pledged to eliminate all nuclear weapons on its territory within the seven-year START I implementation period.[4] By this point all tactical nuclear weapons had been transferred to Russia.

The Belarusian parliament ratified the START I Treaty on February 4, 1993, and Belarus formally acceded to the NPT on July 22, 1993. All tactical nuclear weapons in Belarus were withdrawn to Russia by early April 1992, several months ahead of the schedule established under the agreement signed in Alma-Ata.[5] Forty-five single-warhead SS-25s and their warheads had been transferred to Russia by early December 1994, out of a total of eighty-one such systems.[6] Russian Strategic Missile Forces chief, Col. Vladimir Krivomazov, announced on March 15, 1995, that all SS-25 missiles and warheads will be withdrawn from Belarus by July 25, 1995.[7] All SS-25s, however, will remain under formal Russian jurisdiction and control until withdrawal is complete.

To assist Belarus in denuclearizing, the United States began a program of aid for Cooperative Threat Reduction (CTR) in 1992, also known as the "Nunn-Lugar" program, after Senators Sam Nunn (D-GA) and Richard Lugar (R-IN), who sponsored the legislation providing funding for the effort. As of December 1993, the United States and Belarus had proposed $66 million in CTR-related contracts for environmental restoration, the purchase of emergency response equipment, and defense conversion, including $6 million for the elimination of ICBMs and their launchers. On January 15, 1994, during a visit to Belarus, President Clinton promised an additional $25 million in CTR funds for Belarus. Japan has also signed framework agreements with Belarus to provide assistance for denuclearization and environmental clean-up and has pledged $8.37 million for those purposes.[8]

Belarus is currently negotiating a "full-scope" safeguards agreement with the International Atomic Energy Agency (IAEA) that would place IAEA safeguards on all of its nuclear activities. At present, no nuclear facilities in Belarus are safeguarded by the IAEA. Yet the danger of diversion of nuclear materials in Belarus is relatively low inasmuch as Belarus has little nuclear infrastructure apart from its nuclear weapons. It has no nuclear power plants, uranium enrichment facilities, or spent-fuel reprocessing facilities. Of greatest proliferation concern is the possibility that a complete nuclear weapon en route to Russia could be attacked, stolen, or diverted. An additional concern is the presence at the Institute of Power Engineering Problems, in Sosny, Minsk, of enough highly enriched uranium (HEU) to make one or two nuclear bombs.[9] Officials from the Belarus Nuclear and Radiation Safety Agency, which is responsible for safeguarding these facilities, have said that physical protection "is not up to international and IAEA Safeguards."[10]

Belarus has passed several laws relating to export control but, with strained resources and little experience in export control, its system remains inchoate. Sixteen million dollars of the U.S. CTR funding is committed toward improving the Belarusian export control system. However, Belarus is still not a member of the Nuclear Suppliers Group (NSG), nor does it adhere to the export control standards established by the NSG.

Because of its proximity to Russia and Western Europe, Belarus could unwittingly serve as a conduit for nuclear materials being smuggled out of Russia. In November 1993, Belarusian officials announced that they had prevented an attempt to smuggle uranium into Poland, but other smuggling attempts may have succeeded or may succeed in the future.[11]

NOTES

[1]The basic source for these figures, as well as for those in the chart that follows, is the START I Treaty Memorandum of Understanding (MOU). Current as of September 1990, the MOU is an annex to the START I Treaty that specifies the numbers and locations of the strategic forces of the United States and the Soviet Union as of that date. See "START-Related Facilities by Republic as Declared in MOU Data Exchange, Sept. 1, 1990," *Hearings on the START Treaty*, Committee on Foreign Relations, U.S. Senate, 102nd Cong., 2nd Sess., February 6, 1992, p. 496. See also General Roland LaJoie, special briefing on the Cooperative Threat Reduction Program for the Senate Foreign Relations Committee, February 23, 1995; Dunbar Lockwood, "New Data From the Clinton Administration on the Status of Strategic Nuclear Weapons Deactivations," Memorandum, Arms Control Association, Washington, DC, December 7, 1994; unclassified CIA report, September 1994, as cited in "Nuclear Weapons Deactivation Continue in FSU," *Arms Control Today*, November 1994, p. 27; Robert S. Norris, "The Nuclear Archipelago," *Arms Control Today*, January/February 1992, p. 25.

A total of 54 single-warhead road-mobile ICBMs were declared to be on Belarusian territory in the START I Memorandum of Understanding, but 27 additional SS-25s were subsequently deployed. See *Radio Free Europe/Radio Liberty Daily Report*, December 23, 1993, quoting a spokesman from the Belarusian defense ministry. See also "FSU Strategic Nuclear Weapons Outside Russia," Arms Control Association Fact Sheet, January 1994.

[2]See "Texts of Accords by Former Soviet Republics Forming Commonwealth of Independent States," *Facts on File*, 1991, p. 972.

[3]See "Minsk Agreement on Strategic Forces, December 30, 1991," *Arms Control Today*, January/February 1992, p. 39.

[4]See "Documents: Protocol to the Treaty Between The United States of America And the Union of Soviet Socialist Republics On the Reduction and Limitation Of Strategic Offensive Arms," *Arms Control Today*, June 1992, p. 33; "START I: Lisbon Protocol and the Nuclear Non-Proliferation Treaty," ACDA Fact Sheet, March 17, 1994.

[5]See Dunbar Lockwood, "Nuclear Weapon Developments," *SIPRI Yearbook* (Oxford, UK: Oxford University Press, 1994); "Chronology of Commonwealth Security Issues," *Arms Control Today*, May 1992, p. 27.

[6]General Roland LaJoie, special briefing on the Cooperative Threat Reduction Program, *op.cit.*; Dunbar Lockwood, "New Data From the Clinton Administration on the Status of Strategic Nuclear Weapons Deactivations," *op.cit.*; unclassified CIA report, September 1994, as cited in "Nuclear Weapons Deactivation Continue in FSU," *op.cit.*

[7]Col. Krivomazov noted that out of the remaining 36 SS-25s deployed in Belarus, 18 are currently stationed near Lida and the other 18 in Mozyr, near the border with Ukraine. Krivomazov also added that it would take until the end of 1995 to withdraw all the other equipment of the missile divisions. See Doug Clarke, "Russian Strategic Missiles Out of Belarus By July," *OMRI Daily Digest*, March 16, 1995; "Strategic Missiles Will Be Removed from Belarus by July 1995," *Interfax News Agency*, March 15, 1995.

[8]"CTR Programs by Country" and "CTR Obligations by Country/Project," Department of Defense, Office of Coopera-

tive Threat Reduction, February 1995; ''Four Ex-Soviet States Share Japanese Aid,'' *Defense News*, April 11–17, 1994. See also Naoaki Usui, ''Japan's Denuclearization Programs Take Off in Ex-USSR,'' *Nucleonics Week*, November 11, 1993, p. 12; Douglas Jehl, ''Clinton Promises Help for Belarus Before Changing Focus to Mideast,'' *New York Times*, January 16, 1994; *Radio Free Europe/Radio Liberty Daily Report*, January 17, 1994.

[9]See Leonard S. Spector and William C. Potter, *Nuclear Successor States of the Soviet Union: Nuclear Weapon and Sensitive Export Status Report* (Washington, DC: Carnegie Endowment for International Peace and Monterey, CA: Monterey Institute of International Studies, December 1994), p. 14; William Potter, *Nuclear Profiles of the Soviet Successor States* (Monterey, CA: Monterey Institute of International Studies, May 1993), p. 7; Mark Hibbs, ''U.S.–Ukraine Safeguards Proposal Protested as Dangerous Precedent,'' *Nucleonics Week*, October 28, 1993, p. 6.

[10]Mark Hibbs, ''U.S.–Ukraine Safeguards Proposal Protested as Dangerous Precedent,'' *Nucleonics Week, ibid.*

[11]William Scally, ''Key U.S. Senator Says Belarus Stopped Uranium-Smuggling Effort,'' *Reuters*, November 25, 1993.

LITHUANIA

LATVIA

RUSSIA

Vilnius ★

Lida ■

Institute for Power, Engineering Problems.
Critical assemblies with an inventory of 33-35 kg of weapons-grade (90% enriched) uranium; may be sufficient for one or two nuclear weapons.

Minsk ★

ICBM base with road-mobile SS-25s

Kolosovo ○

Lesnaya ○

BELARUS

Mozyr' ■

ICBM base with road-mobile SS-25s

UKRAINE

0   100 mi

○ *ICBM production, testing/training, conversion/elimination, or storage facilities; possible presence of ICBMs (but not ICBM warheads).*

Belarus is transferring its ICBMs and warheads to Russia; the process is expected to be completed by the end of July 1995.

As a party to the Nuclear Non-Proliferation Treaty, Belarus is negotiating an agreement with the IAEA to place all of its peaceful nuclear activities under IAEA inspection (nuclear weapons, which are not under Belarusian control, are excluded).

Carnegie Endowment for International Peace, *Tracking Nuclear Proliferation*, 1995.

Adapted from William Potter, *Nuclear Profiles of the Soviet Successor States*, 1993; and START Treaty Memorandum of Understanding, 1990.

BELARUS: Nuclear Infrastructure and Other Sites of Proliferation Concern

Note: Locations in bold italics contain nuclear weapons or quantities of weapons-usable nuclear material sufficient for one or more nuclear weapons

NAME/LOCATION OF FACILITY	TYPE/STATUS	IAEA SAFEGUARDS[1]
NUCLEAR-WEAPONS BASES AND SUPPORT FACILITIES		
Lida	ICBM base with 18 road-mobile SS-25s carrying 1 warhead each.[2] (Forty-five out of a reported total of 81 SS-25s deployed on Belarusian territory have been withdrawn to Russia.)	
Mozyr	ICBM base with 18 road-mobile SS-25s carrying 1 warhead each[3]	
Kolosovo	Storage facilities for 23 SS-11 ICBMs and 17 SS-19 launchers, all non-deployed	
Lesnaya	Conversion and elimination facilities for ICBMs	
NUCLEAR AND NUCLEAR-RELATED RESEARCH CENTERS		
Institute of Power, Engineering Problems, Sosny Misnk (formerly Institute of Atomic Energy)	Reactors, critical assemblies, and associated storage facility contain 33–35 kg of uranium enriched to 90%. (See research reactors and critical assemblies below.)[4]	
Scientific Research Institute of Nuclear Problems, Belarus State University, Minsk	Research-training facility	
RESEARCH REACTORS[5]		
IRT-M[6] (Institute of Power, Engineering Problems)	Pool IRT, HEU, 4–8 MWt; shut down in 1988.	No (pending)
Experimental reactor, Minsk	Operating	No (pending)
Critical Assembly No. 1, Minsk	Fast critical assembly (containing 234 kg of LEU); operating.	No (pending)
Critical Assembly No. 2, Minsk	Fast critical assembly (containing 15 kg of uranium enriched to 90%)	No (pending)

Abbreviations:

HEU	=	highly enriched uranium
LEU	=	low-enriched uranium
nat. U	=	natural uranium
MWe	=	millions of watts of electrical output
MWt	=	millions of watts of thermal output
KWt	=	thousands of watts of thermal output

NOTES (Belarus Chart)

1. As required by its adherence to the NPT, Belarus is negotiating a full-scope nuclear safeguards agreement with the International Atomic Energy Agency (IAEA) that will subject all nuclear materials and activities in Belarus to IAEA monitoring. (Nuclear weapons, which are not under Belarusian control, are excluded.)

2. According to a March 15, 1995, statement by Russian Strategic Forces chief, Col. Vladimir Krivomazov, out of the remaining 36 SS-25s located in Belarus, 18 are deployed near Lida. See Doug Clarke, "Russian Strategic Missiles Out of Belarus By July," *OMRI Daily Digest*, March 16, 1995; "Strategic Missiles Will Be Removed from Belarus by July 1995," *Interfax News Agency*, March 15, 1995. An additional three SS-25s were listed in the START I MOU as located in restricted areas of the base, presumably in non-deployed status.

3. According to the March 15, 1995 statement by Russian Strategic Forces chief, Col. Vladimir Krivomazov, of the remaining 36 SS-25s deployed in Belarus, 18 are located at Mozyr. See Doug Clarke, "Russian Strategic Missiles Out of Belarus By July," *op. cit.*; "Strategic Missiles Will Be Removed from Belarus by July 1995," *op. cit.* An additional three SS-25s were listed in the START I MOU as located in restricted areas of the base, presumably in non-deployed status.

4. Interview by William C. Potter with officials of the Institute of Power Engineering Problems, Minsk, June 1994, cited in Leonard S. Spector and William C. Potter, *Nuclear Successor States of the Soviet Union: Nuclear Weapon and Sensitive Export Status Report* (Washington, DC: Carnegie Endowment for International Peace and Monterey, CA: Monterey Institute of International Studies, December 1994), p. 14. See also "CIS Nonproliferation Database," (Monterey, CA: Monterey Institute of International Studies, January 1995).

5. In October 1993, Belarusian officials announced preliminary plans to build one or two VVER-type power reactors to help alleviate Belarus' chronic energy shortages. These plans may require parliamentary approval. See Mark Hibbs, "Energy Strapped Belarus Leans Towards VVER Project," *Nucleonics Week*, October 28, 1993, p. 1.

6. Reactor core contains up to 4 kg of U-235 enriched up to 90 percent. See William Potter, *Nuclear Profiles of the Soviet Successor States* (Monterey, CA: Monterey Institute of International Studies, 1993), p. 7; "CIS Nonproliferation Database," *op. cit.*

Spent Fuel Storage facilities at the Institute have an inventory of up to 100 kg of uranium "with initial enrichment in the range of 22–36 percent U-235 and an average burn-up of 30 percent U-235." See William Potter, *Nuclear Profiles of the Soviet Successor States, op. cit.* See also Mark Hibbs, "U.S.-Ukraine Safeguards Proposal Protested as Dangerous Precedent," *Nucleonics Week*, October 28, 1993, p. 6.

Fresh Fuel and Bulk Material Storage facilities at the Institute have an inventory of "6 kg of U-235 with enrichment level of 22–90 percent." See William Potter, *Nuclear Profiles of the Soviet Successor States, op. cit.*, p. 8.

Additional References

1992: Robert S. Norris, "The Soviet Nuclear Archipelago," *Arms Control Today*, January/February 1992, p. 24; "Chronology of Commonwealth Security Issues," *Arms Control Today*, May 1992, p. 27. **1993:** *Reuters,* "Belarus Approves First Arms-Limitation Pact," *New York Times*, February 5, 1993. **1994:** "Strategic Missiles Being Removed From Belarus," Embassy of the Republic of Belarus, March 21, 1994; "Statement by Dr. Ashton B. Carter, Assistant Secretary of Defense (International Security Policy)," before the Senate Armed Services Committee, April 28, 1994.

Kazakhstan

When the Soviet Union dissolved in December 1991, Kazakhstan emerged as an independent state that retained more than 1,400 strategic nuclear warheads on its territory and a still undisclosed number of tactical nuclear arms. The strategic warheads were deployed on 104 ten-warhead SS-18 intercontinental ballistic missiles (ICBMs) and on 370 single-warhead air-launched cruise missiles (ALCMs), the latter deliverable by Bear-H bombers.[1] Russia, however, retained the command and control capabilities, including arming and launching codes required to use these systems.[2]

In large part because of its close ties to, and dependency upon, Russia, Kazakhstan has moved deliberately to transfer its nuclear arms to its northern neighbor and to accept firm non-proliferation commitments. Kazakhstan took the first steps in this direction when, together with Belarus, Russia, and Ukraine, it signed the Declaration on Nuclear Arms, on December 21, 1991, at Alma-Ata (now Almaty), Kazakhstan. Under the Declaration, Kazakhstan was to return to Russia all tactical nuclear weapons on its territory by July 1, 1992 (Article 6). In addition, it agreed not to transfer nuclear weapons on its territory to others but specified that this prohibition did not preclude transfers of nuclear arms to Russia (Articles 5(ii),(iii)), in anticipation of the ultimate return of all strategic nuclear weapons from Kazakhstan to Russia.[3] (Unlike Belarus and Ukraine, however, Kazakhstan did not give a pledge in the Alma-Ata Declaration to join the Nuclear Non-Proliferation Treaty (NPT) as a non-nuclear-weapon state.)

In a subsequent accord signed in Minsk on December 30, 1991, Kazakhstan agreed, together with the ten other members of the Commonwealth of Independent States (CIS), that a "decision on the need [to use nuclear weapons would be] made by the President of the Russian Federation in agreement with the heads of the Republic of Belarus, the Republic of Kazakhstan, and Ukraine, and in consultation with the heads of the other member states of the Commonwealth."[4] (Arrangements for sharing authority in this area ended in June 1993, when Russia formally took full control over the use of all nuclear arms in the Soviet successor states.)

Finally, in the May 23, 1992, Lisbon Protocol to the START I Treaty, Kazakhstan agreed to participate jointly in the START I Treaty with Belarus, Russia, and Ukraine as successors to the former Soviet Union and to "implement the Treaty's limits and restrictions" (Article II of the Protocol). Kazakhstan also agreed to "adhere to the Treaty on the Non-Proliferation of Nuclear weapons (NPT)" as a non-nuclear-weapon state party "in the shortest possible time" (Article V of the Protocol)[5] and, in a side letter to President George Bush, Kazakhstan pledged to eliminate all nuclear weapons—both strategic and tactical—on its territory within the seven-year START I implementation period.

Kazakhstan's parliament ratified the START I Treaty on July 2, 1992, and approved Kazakhstan's accession to the NPT on December 13, 1993. Its NPT instrument of ratification was deposited on February 14, 1994.[6, 7]

In the meantime, all tactical nuclear weapons on Kazakh territory were withdrawn to Russia by late January 1992, some four months ahead of the schedule established under the Alma-Ata Declaration on Nuclear Arms.[8]

An agreement on the disposition of strategic nuclear weapons on Kazakh territory was reportedly reached soon afterward, at a March 28, 1994, summit between Russian President Boris Yeltsin and Kazakh President Nursultan Nazarbayev. According to the press reports, the agreement provided for the transfer to Russia of all strategic warheads within fourteen months and for the dismantlement of all missile silos within three years. This schedule was far more rapid than required under the Lisbon Protocol. There were no references to Kazakhstan's earlier demand that Russia provide compensation for the fissile material in the warheads of these strategic weapons and previously returned tactical weapons.[9]

As of December 1994, 810 of the warheads in Kazakhstan had been removed from their missiles: 440 from 44 SS-18 ICBMs and 370 from ALCMs.[10] By March 1995, approximately 632 of this total had been returned to Russia, including all 370 ALCM warheads and presumably 260 SS-18 warheads. All 370 ALCMs and their associated strategic bombers had also been sent to Russia, and, according to some reports, twelve SS-18 missiles had been sent there, as well.[11]

A separate issue concerns an undetonated nuclear device with a yield of approximately 0.4 Kt that is located at the Semipalatinsk nuclear test site in Kazakhstan. The nuclear device was to be used in a May 1991 physical irradiation experiment. To conduct the experiment, the bomb was buried in a 592-meter long tunnel approximately 130 m from the surface. In August 1991, the test range was closed, the test was never conducted, and the undetonated device was left buried in Degelen Mountain. During 1994, a joint Russian-Kazakh group began work to remove the nuclear device. It was estimated that the bomb would be recovered by the winter of 1994-1995. The device and associated equipment would become the property of Russia.[12]

On November 23, 1994, the U.S. government disclosed that approximately 600 kg of highly enriched uranium (HEU) had been stored at a uranium conversion (UO_2) and fuel pellet production facility at Ust-Kamenogorsk. The bulk of the material, which was stored under inadequate security arrangements, was in a form that could be directly used for weapons or that could easily be processed to make it suitable for nuclear arms.[13] The material was originally destined for use as fuel in Soviet naval reactors rather than in nuclear weapons.

To address the threat of diversion posed by the presence of the material, U.S. spokesmen stated that pursuant to arrangements with the government of Kazakhstan, and in consultation with the goverment of Russia, the material had been transported to the United States. There it was to be blended with non-weapons-grade uranium to produce fuel for nuclear power plants. Kazakhstan will reportedly receive several tens of million of dollars in U.S. economic assistance in return for relinquishing the material.[14] The disclosure of the storage of this material at Ust-Kamenogorsk highlighted the potential risk that may currently exist from the presence of weapons-usable nuclear material at locations outside Russia and at locations not directly connected to the production or storage of nuclear arms.

On July 26, 1994, Kazakhstan signed a safeguards agreement with the International Atomic Energy Agency (IAEA), which provides for IAEA inspection of all Kazakh nuclear activities (nuclear weapons still on Kazakh territory are excluded). This agreement will enter into force upon its ratification by the Kazakh parliament and Kazakhstan's subsequent deposit of official notification with the IAEA.[15]

Kazakhstan has only one civilian nuclear reactor, a fast-breeder reactor at Aktau. In 1993, Russia proposed the construction of an integrated fast-reactor complex at Aktau that would include two or three additional reactors and a spent-fuel reprocessing facility.[16] If this complex were built, Kazakhstan would acquire a plutonium-production capability. Kazakhstan also has a number of research reactors at the Institute of Nuclear Physics, in Almaty, and at the Baikal Test Facility, in Semipalatinsk. Although most of these reactors are fueled with low-enriched uranium (LEU), a significant amount of weapons-usable highly enriched uranium (at least 22 kg enriched to 90 percent) is located at the Baikal complex.[17]

Kazakhstan's efforts to regulate exports of nuclear goods are still in their formative stage. Almaty has adopted several laws relating to export control, including a provision that requires nuclear or dual-use materials to be placed under IAEA safeguards in the recipient country, and it is currently in negotiations to join the Nuclear Suppliers Group.[18]

U.S. disarmament assistance to Kazakhstan is being provided under the Cooperative Threat Reduction (CTR) program, also known as the ''Nunn-Lugar'' program, after its sponsors, Senators Sam Nunn (D-GA) and Richard Lugar (R-IN). As of March 1993, the United States had proposed $99.9 million in CTR-related contracts, the bulk of which were for the elimination of ICBMs and their silos. Disbursement of these funds followed Kazakhstan's accession to the NPT in February 1994. At this time, President Clinton also promised an additional $311 million in economic assistance to Kazakhstan. Japan has signed framework agreements with Kazakhstan to provide assistance for denuclearization and environmental clean-up and has pledged $11.43 million for those purposes.[19]

NOTES

[1]The basic source for these figures, as well as for those in the chart that follows, is the START I Treaty Memorandum of Understanding (MOU). Current as of September 1990, the MOU is an annex to the START I Treaty that specifies the numbers and locations of the strategic forces of the United States and the Soviet Union on that date. See "START-Related Facilities by Republic as Declared in MOU Data Exchange-Sept. 1, 1990," *Hearings on the START Treaty,* Committee on Foreign Relations, U.S. Senate, 102nd Cong., 2nd Sess., February 6, 1992, p. 496. See also General Roland LaJoie, Deputy for Cooperative Threat Reduction to the Assistant to the Secretary of Defense for Atomic Energy, special briefing on the Cooperative Threat Reduction Program for the Senate Foreign Relations Committee, February 23, 1995; Dunbar Lockwood, "New Data From the Clinton Administration on the Status of Strategic Nuclear Weapons Deactivations," Memorandum, Arms Control Association, Washington, DC, December 7, 1994; Unclassified CIA report, September 1994, as cited in "Nuclear Weapons Deactivation Continues in FSU," *Arms Control Today,* November 1994, p. 27.

[2]Russia also has "administrative control" over the ICBMs, i.e., Russia is responsible for the security of the missiles and the administration of the missile facilities. See Leonard S. Spector and William C. Potter, *Nuclear Successor States of the Soviet Union: Nuclear Weapon and Sensitive Export Status Report* (Washington, DC: The Carnegie Endowment for International Peace, and Monterey, CA: Monterey Institute of International Studies, December 1994), pp. 2, 6.

[3]See "Texts of Accords by Former Soviet Republics Forming Commonwealth of Independent States," *Facts on File,* 1991, p. 972.

[4]See "Minsk Agreement on Strategic Forces, December 30, 1991," *Arms Control Today,* January/February 1992, p. 39.

[5]"Documents: Protocol to the Treaty Between The United States of America And the Union of Soviet Socialist Republics On the Reduction and Limitation Of Strategic Offensive Arms," *Arms Control Today,* June 1992, p. 33; "START I: Lisbon Protocol and the Nuclear Non-Proliferation Treaty," ACDA Fact Sheet, March 17, 1994.

[6]See note 5.

[7]Inasmuch as Kazakhstan had never asserted control of any kind over the nuclear weapons on its territory, the strategic nuclear arms remaining there after Kazakhstan joined the NPT were deemed to be Russian arms for the purposes of the Treaty and their presence did not impair Kazakhstan's status as a non-nuclear-weapons state under the accord.

[8]See "Chronology of Commonwealth Security Issues," *Arms Control Today,* May 1992, p. 27.

[9]See *Radio Free Europe/Radio Liberty Daily Report,* May 4, 1994.

[10]Dunbar Lockwood, "New Data From the Clinton Administration on the Status of Strategic Nuclear Weapons Deactivations," *op. cit.;* unclassified CIA report, September 1994, as cited in "Nuclear Weapons Deactivation Continue in FSU," *Arms Control Today, op. cit.*

[11]General Roland LaJoie, special briefing on the Cooperative Threat Reduction Program, *op. cit*; Dunbar Lockwood, "New Data From the Clinton Administration on the Status of Strategic Nuclear Weapons Deactivations," *op. cit.*; unclassified CIA report, September 1994, as cited in "Nuclear Weapons Deactivation Continue in FSU," *op. cit.*

In congressional testimony in April 1994, Assistant Secretary of Defense Ashton Carter stated that "12 SS-18s and 120 warheads [had] been removed from silos in Kazakhstan, and the process of dismantling SS-18 silos" was expected to begin later in the year. See "Testimony of Dr. Ashton Carter, Assistant Secretary for Defense (International Security Policy)," before the Senate Armed Services Committee, April 28, 1994. (Press reports in February 1994 stated that the 12 SS-18s had already been sent to Russia for dismantlement. See *Radio Free Europe/ Radio Liberty Daily Report,* February 14, 1994; "U.S. Reward Sought for Ceding A-Arms," *Washington Post,* February 14, 1994.) According to the September 1994 CIA report noted earlier, an additional 32 SS-18s had been deactivated as of that date. See "Nuclear Weapons Deactivations Continue in FSU," *Arms Control Today, op. cit.* See also General Roland LaJoie, special briefing on the Cooperative Threat Reduction Program, *op. cit.*

In May 1994 Russian press reports said that all nuclear warheads in Kazakhstan would be transferred to Russia by mid-1995 and all missile silos would be dismantled by mid-1997. (See *Radio Free Europe/Radio Liberty Daily Report,* May 4, 1994.) However, in his February 1995 briefing (cited earlier), General LaJoie projected that silo dismantlement would not be completed until the latter half of 1998.

[12]See "Nuclear Bomb to be Removed from Kazakhstan Test Site," *Komsomolskaya Pravda,* May 13, 1994, in *FBIS-SOV-94-093,* May 13, 1994, pp. 13–14.

[13]Interviews with U.S. officials, December 1994.

[14]See R. Jeffrey Smith, "U.S. Takes Nuclear Fuel," *Washington Post,* November 23, 1994; Steven Erlanger, "Kazakhstan Thanks U.S. on Uranium," *New York Times,* November 25, 1994.

[15]Although the agreement has not yet entered into force, representatives of the IAEA have already begun "visiting" a number of facilities on an informal basis in preparation for the agreement's implementation once it becomes effective. See "Kazakhstani-IAEA Safeguards Agreement: Hans Blix in Almaty," *Sovety Kazakhstana,* August 19, 1994, in *JPRS-TND-94-016,* August 19, 1994, p. 54; "Nuclear Safeguards Pact Signed With IAEA," *Nuclear News,* September 1994, p. 92.

[16]See Mark Hibbs, "Russian Industry Seeks Pact for Kazakhstan FBR Complex," *Nucleonics Week,* December 16, 1993, p. 14.

[17]William Potter, *Nuclear Profiles of the Soviet Successor States* (Monterey, CA: Monterey Institute of International Studies, 1993), p. 19.

[18]For a more detailed analysis of Kazakhstan's export-control regime see *ibid.,* pp. 16–32, and B. Ayaganov, "Nuclear Export Controls in Kazakhstan," a paper prepared for the CIS Nonproliferation Project (Monterey, CA: Monterey Institute of International Studies, April 1993). See also Leonard S. Spector and William C. Potter, *Nuclear Successor States of the Soviet Union: Nuclear Weapon and Sensitive Export Status Report, op. cit.,* p. 33.

[19]"CTR Programs by Country" and "CTR Obligations by Country/Project," Department of Defense, Office of Cooperative Threat Reduction, February 1995; Leonard S. Spector and William C. Potter, *Nuclear Successor States of the Soviet Union: Nuclear Weapon and Sensitive Export Status Report, op. cit.,* p. 23; "Four Ex-Soviet States Share Japanese Aid," *Defense News,* April 11–17, 1994. See also Naoaki Usui, "Japan's Denuclearization Programs Take Off in Ex-USSR," *Nucleonics Week,* November 11, 1993, p. 12.

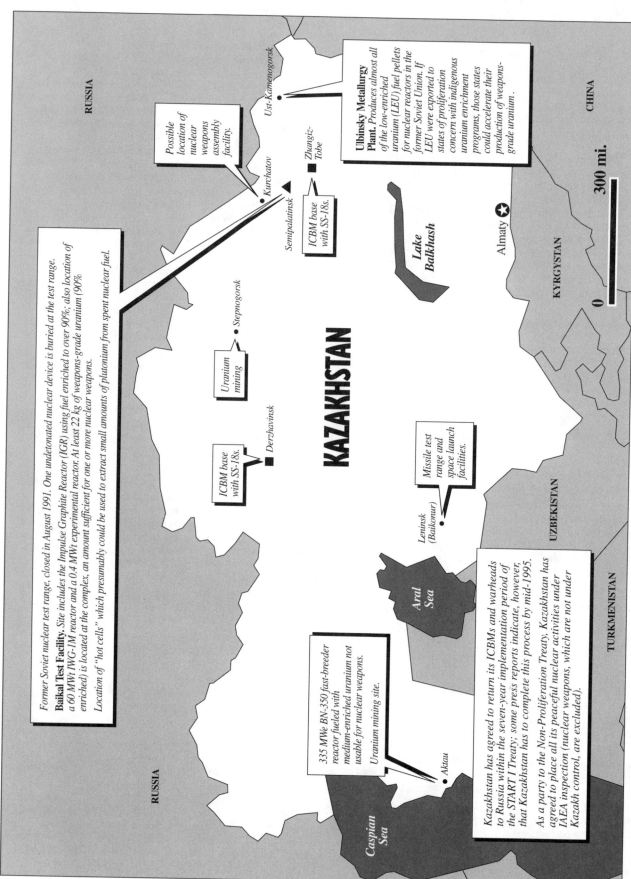

Former Soviet nuclear test range, closed in August 1991. One undetonated nuclear device is buried at the test range.

Baikal Test Facility. Site includes the Impulse Graphite Reactor (IGR) using fuel enriched to over 90%; also location of a 60 MWt IWG-1M reactor and a 0.4 MWt experimental reactor. At least 22 kg of weapons-grade uranium (90% enriched) is located at the complex, an amount sufficient for one or more nuclear weapons.

Location of "hot cells" which presumably could be used to extract small amounts of plutonium from spent nuclear fuel.

Possible location of nuclear weapons assembly facility.

Ulbinsky Metallurgy Plant. Produces almost all of the low-enriched uranium (LEU) fuel pellets for nuclear reactors in the former Soviet Union. If LEU were exported to states of proliferation concern with indigenous uranium enrichment programs, those states could accelerate their production of weapons-grade uranium.

ICBM base with SS-18s.

Uranium mining

ICBM base with SS-18s.

Missile test range and space launch facilities.

335 MWe BN-350 fast-breeder reactor fueled with medium-enriched uranium not usable for nuclear weapons. Uranium mining site.

Kazakhstan has agreed to return its ICBMs and warheads to Russia within the seven-year implementation period of the START I Treaty; some press reports indicate, however, that Kazakhstan has to complete this process by mid-1995.

As a party to the Non-Proliferation Treaty, Kazakhstan has agreed to place all its peaceful nuclear activities under IAEA inspection (nuclear weapons, which are not under Kazakh control, are excluded).

RUSSIA

CHINA

KAZAKHSTAN

KYRGYSTAN

UZBEKISTAN

TURKMENISTAN

Caspian Sea

Aral Sea

Lake Balkhash

Ust-Kamenogorsk

Kurchatov

Semipalatinsk

Zhangiz-Tobe

Stepnogorsk

Derzhavinsk

Almaty

Leninsk (Baikonur)

Aktau

0   300 mi.

Carnegie Endowment for International Peace, *Tracking Nuclear Proliferation,* 1995.

Adapted from William Potter, *Nuclear Profiles of the Soviet Successor States,* 1993.

KAZAKHSTAN: Nuclear Infrastructure and Other Sites of Proliferation Concern

Note: Locations in bold italics contain nuclear weapons or quantities of weapons-usable nuclear material sufficient for one or more nuclear weapons.

NAME/LOCATION OF FACILITY	TYPE/STATUS	IAEA SAFEGUARDS
NUCLEAR WEAPONS BASES AND SUPPORT FACILITIES		
Derzhavinsk	ICBM base with SS-18s carrying 10 warheads each. (Out of the total 104 MOU-specified SS-18s deployed on Kazakh territory, 12 have been removed from their silos and reportedly sent to Russia. An additional 32 have been deactivated.)[1]	
Zhangiz Tobe	ICBM base with SS-18s carrying 10 warheads each[2]	
Semipalatinsk	Former Soviet nuclear test range (closed in August 1991). One unexploded nuclear device with a yield of approximately 0.4 kiloton is buried at the test site. All strategic bombers and associated ALCMs in Kazakhstan have been moved to Russia.	
Leninsk (Baikonur)	Test range and space launch facilities; location of 4 SS-18s and 2 SS-19s; all non-deployed.	
Kurchatov (Semipalatinsk-21)	Facility with possible capability to assemble nuclear weapons components	
NUCLEAR AND NUCLEAR-RELATED RESEARCH CENTERS		
Institute of Nuclear Physics, Almaty	See research reactor and critical assembly, below	No (pending)
POWER REACTORS		
Aktau	BN-350 (sodium-cooled, fast-breeder), medium-enriched uranium, 335 MWe; shut down.[3]	No (pending)
RESEARCH REACTORS		
Almaty (Institute of Nuclear Physics)	WWR-K, 36% enriched uranium, 10 MWe; shut down?	No (pending)
Almaty	Critical assembly; operating.	No (pending)
IGR (Baikal Test Facility) Semipalatinsk	Graphite-moderated, water-cooled, HEU; operating.[4]	
IWG-1M, Semipalatinsk	60 MWt reactor; operating.	No (pending)
RA, Semipalatinsk	0.4 MWt experimental reactor	No (pending)
URANIUM PROCESSING		
Aktau	Uranium mining; operating.	N/A (Not applicable)
Stepnogorsk	Uranium mining; operating.[5]	N/A
Ulbinsky Metallurgy Plant Ust-Kamenogorsk	Uranium conversion (UO$_2$) and fuel pellet production facility.[6]	No (pending)

Abbreviations:

HEU = highly enriched uranium
MWe = millions of watts of electrical output
MWt = millions of watts of thermal output

NOTES (Kazakhstan Chart)

1. An additional three SS-18s were listed in the START I Treaty MOU as located at the Derzhavinsk maintenance facility in non-deployed status.

2. An additional two SS-18s were listed in the START I Treaty MOU as located at the Zhangiz-Tobe maintenance facility in non-deployed status (i.e., without warheads).

3. There are conflicting reports on the reactor's operational status. See "Fast Breeder Reactor Closed for Lack of Money," Moscow, *Ostankino Television First Channel Network*, June 28, 1994, in *FBIS-SOV-94-125*, June 29, 1994, p. 54; "CIS Nonproliferation Database" (Monterey, CA: Monterey Institute of International Studies, January 1995).

4. Weapons-grade uranium may also be stored at Semipalatinsk as a result of activities related to nuclear testing. According to Russian officials, the most sensitive materials and equipment at the site remain under Russian control and are to be removed to Russia. The nuclear materials involved will apparently not come under IAEA safeguards pursuant to the Kazakhstan-IAEA agreement.

5. Other sites that may be involved in uranium mining activities include: Aksuyek-Kiyakhty, Chiili, Koktas, Mirny, Shalygiya, Stepnoe, Tabackbulak, and Taukent.

6. This plant produces almost all of the LEU fuel pellets for nuclear reactors in the former Soviet Union. If LEU were exported to states of proliferation concern with indigenous uranium enrichment programs, those states could accelerate their production of weapons-grade uranium.

Additional References

1992: "Testimony by Robert Gates, Director of Central Intelligence and Gordon Oehler, Director of Central Intelligence Center for Non-Proliferation," Hearings on Non-Proliferation of Weapons of Mass Destruction and Regulatory Improvement Act of 1992, Committee on Banking, U.S. House of Representatives, 102nd Cong., 2nd Sess., May 8, 1992; *Arms Control Today*, June 1992, p. 34; "Nuclear Device Still Underground at Semipalatinsk," *FBIS-SOV-92-232*, December 2, 1992, p. 22. **1993:** *Jane's Defense Weekly*, March 27, 1993, p. 7; International Institute for Strategic Studies, *The Military Balance 1993-1994* (London: International Institute for Strategic Studies, October 1993), p. 99; R. Jeffrey Smith, "Kazakhstan Ratifies Nuclear Con-trol Pact, Will Get U.S. Aid," *Washington Post*, December 14, 1993; Richard L. Berke, "Prodded by Gore, Kazakhstan Signs Arms Accord," *New York Times*, December 14, 1993. **1994:** "FSU Strategic Weapons Outside Russia," *Arms Control Association Fact Sheet*, January 1994; "Unexploded Nuclear Device Left Under Semipalatinsk Site," *Krasnaya Zvezda*, January 14, 1994, in *JPRS-TND-94-004*, February 11, 1994; "Further on Terms of Kazakhstani-IAEA Safeguards Agreement," Moscow, *Segodnya*, July 28, 1994, in *FBIS-USR-94-085*, August 8, 1994, p. 100; R. Jeffrey Smith, "U.S. Takes Nuclear Fuel," *Washington Post*, November 23, 1994; Steven Erlanger, "Kazakhstan Thanks U.S. on Uranium," *New York Times*, November 25, 1994.

Ukraine

Following the break-up of the Soviet Union in December 1991, Ukraine emerged as an independent state with the world's third largest nuclear arsenal on its territory. This arsenal included: 176 Soviet intercontinental ballistic missiles (ICBMs) with a total of 1,240 warheads (46 ten-warhead SS-24s, armed with a total of 460 warheads, and 130 six-warhead SS-19s, armed with a total of 780 warheads); 21 Bear-H strategic bombers (carrying up to 16 air-launched cruise missiles (ALCMs) each) and 13 Blackjack strategic bombers (carrying up to 12 ALCMs each); and between 2,650 and 4,200 Soviet tactical nuclear weapons.[1]

Unlike Belarus and Kazakhstan, which have been on close terms with Russia since their independence and have moved steadily toward eliminating their nuclear arms, Ukraine has struggled to assert its independence from Moscow and, until early 1994, threatened to retain the nuclear weapons on its territory as part of its bid for autonomy. As a result, during 1992 and 1993, Ukraine's progress toward denuclearization was halting and erratic.

Ukraine's seeming ambivalence was reflected in its efforts to exercise increasing control over its nuclear legacy and in its reluctance, until 1994, to accept binding denuclearization and non-proliferation commitments.

Ukraine has never possessed the ability to launch or use any of these nuclear weapons without the agreement of Russia, which has always controlled the arming and targeting codes necessary to take such actions. Nevertheless, since independence, Kiev has asserted the right to block the use of these weapons. This was the first step in its efforts to establish a degree of control over the nuclear arms on its soil. In June 1992, Ukraine broadened its authority by asserting "administrative control" over these arms, effectively taking custody of them by replacing the Russian soldiers guarding them with Ukrainian forces.[2] In late 1992 and 1993, Ukraine also began to claim that it owned the components

of the warheads, as a means, *inter alia*, of establishing its right to receive compensation for the valuable plutonium and highly enriched uranium they contained. It also asserted ownership of the warheads' delivery vehicles. This increasing dilution of Russian nuclear authority coincided with a highly publicized debate within the Ukrainian parliament, or Rada, over whether the country should acquire nuclear weapons in order to ensure its security against what many Ukrainians perceived to be the growing threat of Russian hegemony.

In parallel with these actions, Ukraine signed but then backed away from a series of denuclearization and non-proliferation undertakings. In its declaration of independence of December 1, 1991, for example, Ukraine renounced the possession of nuclear weapons, but in 1992-1993, the Rada dissociated itself from this pledge.

Similarly, Ukraine pledged in the December 21, 1991, Declaration on Nuclear Arms signed in Alma-Ata with Belarus, Kazakhstan, and Russia to join the Nuclear Non-Proliferation Treaty (NPT) as a non-nuclear-weapon state (Article 5(i)) and to return to Russia all tactical nuclear weapons in Belarus by July 1, 1992 (Article 6). In addition, it agreed not to transfer nuclear weapons on its territory to others, but specified that this prohibition did not preclude transfers of nuclear arms to Russia (Articles 5(ii),(iii)), in anticipation of the ultimate return of all strategic nuclear weapons from Ukraine to Russia.[3] The Ukrainian Rada did not ratify this accord, however, and later claimed that it was not binding.

In the December 30, 1991, Minsk Agreement on Strategic Forces, Ukraine again made a series of nuclear pledges, promising that all nuclear weapons on its territory would be dismantled by the end of 1994 (with the dismantling of tactical nuclear weapons to be completed by July 1, 1992). The Minsk Agreement also stipulated that a "decision on the need [to use nuclear weapons would be] made by the president of the Russian Federation in agreement with the heads of the Republic of Belarus, the Republic of Kazakhstan, and Ukraine, and in consultation with the heads of the other member states of the Commonwealth.''[4] (Arrangements for sharing authority in this area ended in June 1993, when Russia formally took full control over the use of all nuclear arms in the Soviet successor states.) Once again, however, the Rada did not ratify the agreement, undercutting its validity.

Finally, on May 23, 1992, Leonid Kravchuk, Ukrainian president at that time, signed the Lisbon Protocol to the START I Treaty. Under the Protocol, Ukraine agreed to participate jointly in the START I Treaty with Belarus, Kazakhstan, and Russia, as successors to the former Soviet Union and to ''implement the Treaty's limits and restrictions'' (Article II of the Protocol). Ukraine also agreed to ''adhere to the Treaty on the Non-Proliferation of Nuclear Weapons (NPT)'' as a non-nuclear-weapon state party ''in the shortest possible time'' (Article V of the Protocol) and, in a side letter to President George Bush, President Kravchuk pledged to eliminate all nuclear weapons—both strategic and tactical—on Ukrainian territory within the seven-year START I implementation period.[5]

The Lisbon Protocol was never approved by the Rada. Nonetheless, on November 18, 1993, the Rada did ratify the START I Treaty, but attached a number of major qualifications and conditions. First it declared that only 36 percent of the strategic delivery vehicles and 42 percent of the strategic warheads deployed on Ukrainian territory would be subject to elimination (Article 6 of the Resolution of Ratification), allowing Ukraine to retain the remainder on its territory, contrary to previous presidential commitments. The Rada also made the elimination of the remaining delivery vehicles and warheads conditional on Ukraine's receiving aid to cover dismantlement costs, compensation for nuclear materials to be extracted from the warheads, and complex security guarantees. At the same time, the Rada resolved that Ukraine was not bound by Article V of the Lisbon Protocol calling for quick accession to the NPT and, by implication, the relinquishment of all nuclear weapons.[6]

Coming in the wake of Ukraine's growing exercise of control over the strategic nuclear arms still on its territory—all tactical nuclear weapons had been transferred to Russia by May 1992[7]—this new challenge by the Rada triggered a period of intensive negotiations among Ukraine, Russia, and the United States.

''Trilateral Statement.'' The result was the January 14, 1994, ''Trilateral Statement,'' signed by Presidents Leonid Kravchuk, Bill Clinton, and Boris Yeltsin, a major turning point that would lead to Ukraine's fulfillment of its denuclearization and non-proliferation pledges. Under the Trilateral Statement, over a seven-year period Ukraine is to transfer the approximately 1,800 warheads on Ukrainian soil to Russia, where highly enriched uranium from the warheads is to be extracted and blended down to low-enriched uranium. This material is then to be converted to fuel rods to be transferred to Ukraine for use in nuclear power reactors as compensation for its relinquishing the weapons-grade uranium in the strategic warheads. Ukraine will also receive (in addition to nuclear fuel) U.S. economic aid and U.S. technical assistance for the safe, secure dismantlement of its nuclear arms. Russia and the United States also promised to provide explicit security guarantees upon Ukraine's accession to the NPT. In one of several confidential side letters, Ukraine privately agreed to transfer all warheads on its territory to Russia within three years and, in addition, Russia promised to forgive large portions of Ukraine's debt for energy supplies as compensation for Ukraine's prior transfer of tactical nuclear weapons to Russia.[8]

In effect, the Trilateral Statement sought to satisfy the conditions attached by the Ukrainian Rada to its approval of the START I Treaty, and, on February 3, 1994, the Rada approved a two-part resolution which, first, instructed Kravchuck to exchange the instruments of ratification of the START I Treaty and, second, acknowledged that Article V of the Lisbon Protocol, calling for rapid adherence to the NPT as a non-nuclear-weapon state, applied to Ukraine. The Rada also implicitly endorsed the Trilateral Statement. It did not, however, approve accession to the NPT.[9]

Accelerated Transfer. During the remainder of 1994, the pace of Ukrainian denuclearization accelerated as Ukraine exceeded the initial phases of the deactivation and transfer process outlined in the Trilateral Statement. The Statement specified that, by mid-November 1994, all SS-24s on Ukrainian territory were to be deactivated. In fact, by early December 1994, not only had Ukraine deactivated all its SS-24s, but it had also deactivated 40 out of its 130 SS-19s. Second, the Trilateral Statement called for Ukraine to transfer at least 200 warheads from its SS-19s and SS-24s to Russia by mid-November.[10] Ukraine also exceeded this goal, transfering 360 warheads by that date, and, as of February 1995, it had transferred a total of 420 SS-24, SS-19, and heavy bomber warheads back to Russia.[11]

On November 16, 1994, the Rada took the next step to confirm its denuclearization commitments, approving Ukraine's accession to the NPT. Once again, however, it imposed a condition, making

Ukraine's accession contingent upon its first receiving security guarantees by the nuclear states. The condition was one that was then in the process of being satisfied, inasmuch as security guarantees in the form of a multilateral memorandum signed by the United Kingdom, the United States, and Russia were promised to Ukraine immediately prior to the November 16, 1994, parliamentary vote.

CSCE. At the Summit of the Conference on Security and Cooperation in Europe (CSCE), held in Budapest on December 5, 1994, the United Kingdom, the United States, and Russia provided this memorandum to Ukraine and also extended security guarantees to Kazakhstan and Belarus. France also provided security guarantees to Ukraine at the CSCE summit in a separate document. On the same occasion, Ukraine presented its instruments of accession to the NPT. This action, together with the earlier accessions by Belarus and Kazakhstan, satisfied Russia's conditions for exchanging the instruments of ratification for the START I Treaty. Consequently, at the same meeting, the United States, Russia, Belarus, Kazakhstan, and Ukraine exchanged their START I Treaty instruments of ratification, finally bringing the Treaty into force.[13]

Assistance. U.S. assistance for the safe, secure dismantlement (SSD) of Ukrainian nuclear weapons is provided for under the Cooperative Threat Reduction (CTR) program, also known as the "Nunn-Lugar" program, after its sponsors, Senators Sam Nunn (D-GA) and Richard Lugar (R-IN). On March 4, 1994, during the visit of President Kravchuk to Washington, President Clinton announced that the United States would nearly double its aid to Ukraine over the next year to $700 million. This amount included an increase in SSD-related funds to $350 million and an increase in conventional economic assistance from the $155 million announced in January 1994 to $350 million. However, the slow pace of disbursal of SSD-related funds—only $6-million by August 1994—became an issue in U.S.-Ukrainian relations in the summer of 1994. Japan has signed framework agreements with Ukraine to provide assistance for denuclearization and environmental clean-up and has pledged $17.08 million for those purposes.[14]

Nuclear Infrastructure. Ukraine's nuclear power program comprises five stations, each with a number of reactors either operating or under construction. These stations are located at Pripyat/Chornobyl, Neteshin, Kuznetsovsk, Kostantinovsk, and Energodar.[15]

The country's nuclear research base includes the Institute for Nuclear Research in Kiev, housing a 10 MWe research reactor reportedly out of operation, and the Defense Ministry's High Marines School at Sevastopol, which also has a research reactor that is out of service.

There are no reprocessing or uranium enrichments plants in Ukraine that would give it the capability to produce weapons-usable plutonium or highly enriched uranium (HEU). However, the Khar'kiv Physical-Technical Institute has in its possession up to 75 kg of weapons-grade HEU in bulk form enriched up to 90 percent.[16] Since this nuclear material is not yet under International Atomic Energy Agency (IAEA) safeguards, it could be of proliferation concern.

Also unsafeguarded are several heavy water production plants located in Dnepropetrovsk giving Ukraine the capability to produce about 250 metric tons of such material per year. Ukraine's export of heavy water to a country with unsafeguarded, plutonium-producing heavy water reactors (e.g., India) would enhance the recipient's potential to produce nuclear weapons.[17]

On September 28, 1994, Ukraine signed a full-scope safeguards agreement with the IAEA that provides for IAEA inspection of all Ukrainian nuclear activities. (Nuclear weapons still on Ukrainian territory are excluded.) The agreement will enter into force upon Ukraine's deposit of official notification with the IAEA.

Ukraine's domestic export control system for nuclear and nuclear-related technology and materials is in the process of development. As of early 1995, an Expert-Technical Committee under the Cabinet of Ministers was reviewing a draft of "Regulations on Procedures for the Export and Import of Nuclear Materials, Technology, Equipment, Facilities, Special Non-Nuclear Materials, Sources of Radiation and Isotopes."[18]

Ukraine has inherited much of the Soviet missile production industrial base, which it plans to utilize for the manufacture of space-launch systems for export. However, this infrastrucure also gives Ukraine the capability to produce or export ballistic missiles. Certain space equipment is already being produced at the Yuzhmash Plant, a former SS-18 production facility at Dnepropetrovsk. Moreover, a former SS-24 production plant at Pavlograd, which is also believed to be operating, may be engaged in similar research and development activities.[19] In a Memorandum of Understanding signed in Washington on May 13, 1994, Ukraine agreed to conduct its missile- and space-related exports according to the criteria and standards of the Missile Technology Control Regime (MCTR).[20] It is not, however, a formal member of the MCTR.

Political Instability. There has been concern within the U.S. intelligence community that Ukraine's acute economic crisis, separatist tendencies in Eastern Ukraine (particularly in the Crimea), and the unsettled state of Ukrainian politics could lead to civil strife and, conceivably, national fragmentation.[21] This could endanger control over nuclear weapons and/or nuclear facilities and undermine existing export controls. One scenario envisions Eastern Ukraine, with its large Russian population, electing to join the Russian Federation; or Crimea alone—with its strong pro-Russian leanings—could take this step. Under another scenario, should pro-Russian sentiment within the Ukrainian government intensify, the western portion of Ukraine might choose to secede. This break-away region containing provinces (oblasts) that were formerly part of Hungary, Poland, and Romania, would also likely include Khmel'nitskiy Oblast, where Ukrainian nationalism is strong. This would place the Khmel'nitskiy ICBM base in the hands of a new secessionist entity.

If the political factions comprising a new government managed to get custody of deployed ICBMs, their ability to assume operational control as a deterrent to Russia or as a way to intimidate the eastern regions would depend on their capability to bypass environmental sensing devices (ESDs) and/or coded switches, known as permissive action links (or PALs), that control access to the arming and fusing circuitry of the weapons. As one panel of experts has noted, the existence of PAL-type devices "cannot provide reassurance that these weapons would be useless to mutinous custodians or political factions who had prolonged possession of the weapons, especially if they had technical expertise."[22]

NOTES

[1]The basic source for these figures, as well as for those in the chart that follows, is the START I Memorandum of Understanding (MOU). Current as of September 1990, the MOU is an annex to the START I Treaty which specifies the numbers and locations of the strategic forces of the United States and Soviet Union as of that date. (See "START-Related Facilities by Republic as Declared in MOU Data Exchange-Sept. 1, 1990," Hearings on the START Treaty, the Committee on Foreign Relations, U.S. Senate, 102nd Cong., 2nd Sess., February 6, 1992, p. 495.) The START MOU under-counts the number of ALCMs heavy bombers can carry, attributing 8 to each bomber. The actual carrying capacities of the Blackjack and the Bear-H are 12 and 16 ALCMs respectively. See Dunbar Lockwood, "FSU Strategic Nuclear Weapons Outside Russia," Arms Control Association Fact Sheet, January 1994. See also General Roland LaJoie, Deputy for Cooperative Threat Reduction to the Assistant Secretary of Defense for Atomic Energy, special briefing on the Cooperative Threat Reduction Program for the Senate Foreign Relations Commitee, February 23, 1995; Dunbar Lockwood, "New Data From the Clinton Administration on the Status of Strategic Nuclear Weapons Deactivations," Memorandum, Arms Control Association, Washington, DC, December 7, 1994; Unclassified CIA report, September 1994, as cited in "Nuclear Weapons Deactivation Continue in FSU," Arms Control Today, November 1994, p. 27.

[2]In June 1992, the Ukrainian Defense Ministry established the Center for the Administrative Command and Control of the Troops of the Strategic Nuclear Forces, setting up a dual administrative structure with Russia for controlling the strategic nuclear forces. See "Ukraine Said Seeking Command of Nuclear Forces," Izvestiya, June 11, 1992, translated in FBIS-SOV, June 11, 1992, p. 2.

Ukrainian scientists also reportedly initiated work during 1992 on developing the capability to bypass the codes for using the nuclear weapons in Ukraine, but there are no indications that any such efforts have been successful.

Ukraine also exercises physical control over some of the strategic bombers on its territory.

[3]See "Texts of Accords by Former Soviet Republics Forming Commonwealth of Independent States," Facts on File, 1991, p. 972.

[4]See "Minsk Agreement on Strategic Forces, December 30, 1991," Arms Control Today, January/February 1992, p. 39.

[5]See "Documents: Protocol to the Treaty Between the United States of America and the Union of Soviet Socialist Republics on the Reduction and Limitation of Strategic Offensive Arms," Arms Control Today, June 1992, p. 33; "START I: Lisbon Protocol and the Nuclear Non-Proliferation Treaty," ACDA Fact Sheet, March 17, 1994.

[6]Arms Control Today, June 1992, p. 34; "Parliament Ratifies START I Treaty, Lisbon Protocol," Moscow, Interfax, November 18, 1993, in FBIS-SOV-93-222, November 19, 1993, p. 45; "Supreme Council START I Ratification Resolution," Kiev, UNIAR, November 18, 1993, in FBIS-SOV-93-222, November 19, 1993, p. 45.

[7]See "U.S. Confident on Soviet A-Weapons," New York Times, December 16, 1991; "57 Percent of Arms Removed," Komsomolskaya Pravda, March 26, 1992, in FBIS-SOV, March 26, 1992, pp. 3-4; "Chronology of Commonwealth Security Issues," Arms Control Today, May 1992, p. 27.

[8]Dunbar Lockwood, "U.S. Reaches Understanding with Ukraine, Russia on Denuclearization," Arms Control Today, January-February 1994, pp. 19-20.

The confidential side agreement to the Trilateral Statement that stipulated the three-year timetable for warhead withdrawal from Ukraine was formalized by Ukraine's acting Prime Minister Yefim Zvyagilsky and Russian Prime Minister Victor Chernomyrdin on May 16, 1994. See "Ukraine Pledges to Double Speed of Disarmament," Reuters, May 19, 1994.

[9]John W. R. Lepingwell, "Ukrainian Parliament Removes START-1 Conditions," Radio Free Europe/Radio Liberty Research Report, February 25, 1994, p. 37.

[10]On February 2, 1995, Ukraine agreed to sell to Russia all of its strategic bombers. Russian experts estimated the value of the total bomber force at $75 million. As of mid-March 1995,

however, the final figure of the sale had not yet been agreed upon. Russian officials noted that Ukriane plans to use this money to reduce its enormous energy debt to Russia. The deal, however, must be approved by each nation's government. See Anton Zhigulsky, "Future of Disputed Black Sea Fleet Remains Uncertain," *Defense News*, March 13-19, 1995, p. 8; "Russia Says Ukraine to Hand Over Strategic Bombers," *Reuters*, February 24, 1995.

[11]General Roland LaJoie, special briefing on the Cooperative Threat Reduction Program, *op. cit.*

In congressional testimony in October 1994, Assistant Secretary of Defense Carter reported that there were 1,734 warheads in Ukraine prior to the initiation of the dismantlement process in January 1994, as opposed to 1,564 warheads as cited in the START I Memorandum of Understanding (MOU). See "Testimony of Assistant Secretary Carter," before the Senate Foreign Relations Committee, October 4, 1994.

[12]See "Text of Resolution Detailing NPT Reservations," *Kiev Radio Ukraine World Service in the Ukraine in FM FBIS London UK*, November 16, 1994; "Ukraine Joins Treaty Curbing Nuclear Arms," *Washington Post*, November 17, 1994; "Ukraine Accedes to NPT Treaty," *United Press International*, December 5, 1994; "Remarks by President Clinton at Signing of Denuclearization Agreement," *Federal News Service*, December 5, 1994; "France Signs NPT Security Guarantee Document," Moscow, *Interfax*, December 5, 1994, in *FBIS-SOV-94-234*, December 6, 1994, p. 44.

[13]"CTR Programs by Country" and "CTR Obligations by Country/Project," Department of Defense, Office of Cooperative Threat Reduction, February 1995; Leonard S. Spector and William C. Potter, *Nuclear Successor States of the Soviet Union: Nuclear-Weapon and Sensitive Export Status Report* (Washington, DC: Carnegie Endowment for International Peace and, Monterey, CA: Monterey Institute of International Studies, December 1994) p. 24; "Four Ex-Soviet States Share Japanese Aid," *Defense News*, April 11–17, 1994. See also Naoaki Usui, "Japan's Denuclearization Programs Take Off in Ex-USSR," *Nucleonics Week*, November 11, 1993, p. 12.

[14]See William Potter, *Nuclear Profiles of the Soviet Successor States* (Monterey, CA: Monterey Institute of International Studies, 1993), p. 83; See also "CIS Nonproliferation Database," (Monterey, CA: Monterey Institute of International Studies, January 1995).

[15]Leonard S. Spector and William C. Potter, *Nuclear Successor States of the Soviet Union: Nuclear-Weapon and Sensitive Export Status Report, op. cit.*, p. 18.

[16]Mark Hibbs, "Nonproliferation Policy on Hold, Kiev's Heavy Water at Issue," *Nuclear Fuel*, August 17, 1992, p. 8.

[17]Leonard S. Spector and William C. Potter, *Nuclear Successor States of the Soviet Union: Nuclear-Weapon and Sensitive Export Status Report, op. cit.*, p. 37.

[18]U.S. Congress, Office of Technology Assessment, *Technologies Underlying Weapons of Mass Destruction*, OTA-BP-ISC-115 (Washington, DC: U.S. Government Printing Office, December 1993), p. 12; "Perry Visits Strategic Missile Unit," Moscow, *Itar-Tass*, March 22, 1994, in *FBIS-SOV-94-056*, March 23, 1994, p. 27; "Implementation of Lisbon Protocol," *Hearings on the START Treaty*, Committee on Foreign Relations, U.S. Senate, 102nd Cong., 2nd Sess., June 23, 1992, p. 199.

As a result of the break-up of the Soviet Union's armed forces, Ukraine has also inherited a number of advanced strike aircraft that could be modified to carry nuclear weapons. They include the MiG-29 Fulcrum, Su-24 Fencer, Tu-22/26 Blinder, and MiG-27 Flogger D. See International Institute for Strategic Studies, *The Military Balance 1993–1994* (London: International Institute for Strategic Studies, October 1993), p. 91; Office of Technology Assessment, *Technologies Underlying Weapons of Mass Destruction, op. cit.*, pp. 235, 243.

[19]The MCTR restricts exports of missiles and related technology with respect to systems able to deliver weapons of mass destruction to a distance of more than 300 km. (See Appendix E of this report.)

[20]Daniel Williams and R. Jeffrey Smith, "U.S. Intelligence Sees Economic Plight Leading to Breakup of Ukraine," *Washington Post*, January 25, 1994; Tim Weiner, "C.I.A. Head Surveys World's Hot Spots," *New York Times*, January 26, 1994; "Testimony by CIA Director James Woolsey," before the Senate Select Intelligence Committee, January 25, 1994.

[21]Kurt M. Campbell *et al., Soviet Nuclear Fission: Control of the Nuclear Arsenal in a Disintegrating Soviet Union*, CSIA Studies in International Security, No. 1 (Cambridge, MA: Center for Science and International Affairs, Harvard University, November 1991), pp. 14-15.

During a prolonged period of civil strife components from dismantled nuclear weapons still stored in Ukraine—nuclear warheads, missile airframes, or ALCMs—would be at risk of falling into the hands of parties not necessarily under central or regional control (e.g., extremists, smugglers). If a stored nuclear warhead came into the possession of such a party, the dangers would be great. Even if the warhead was equipped with PALs or had been disabled by the removal of certain parts (e.g., tritium reservoir, electronic firing units), its disassembly by suitably trained individuals could provide "valuable first-hand information on its design, materials, and components" or access to the fissionable core for use in another weapon. (See U.S. Congress, Office of Technology Assessment, *Technologies Underlying Weapons of Mass Destruction, op. cit.*, p. 128.) It is also possible that a team with substantial technical expertise, with access to the weapon over an extended period, could recreate the missing parts and reactivate the weapon.

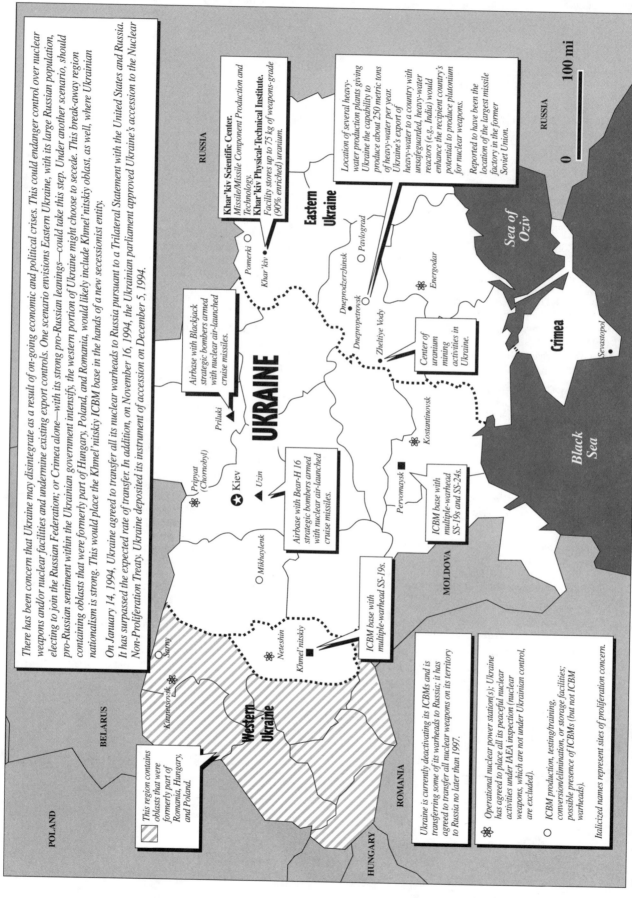

There has been concern that Ukraine may disintegrate as a result of on-going economic and political crises. This could endanger control over nuclear weapons and/or nuclear facilities and undermine existing export controls. One scenario envisions Eastern Ukraine, with its large Russian population, electing to join the Russian Federation; or Crimea alone—with its strong pro-Russian leanings—could take this step. Under another scenario, should pro-Russian sentiment within the Ukrainian government intensify, the western portion of Ukraine might choose to secede. This break-away region containing oblasts that were formerly part of Hungary, Poland, and Romania, would likely include Khmel'nitskiy oblast, as well, where Ukrainian nationalism is strong. This would place the Khmel'nitskiy ICBM base in the hands of a new secessionist entity.

On January 14, 1994, Ukraine agreed to transfer all its nuclear warheads to Russia pursuant to a Trilateral Statement with the United States and Russia. It has surpassed the expected rate of transfer: In addition, on November 16, 1994, the Ukrainian parliament approved Ukraine's accession to the Nuclear Non-Proliferation Treaty. Ukraine deposited its instrument of accession on December 5, 1994.

POLAND

BELARUS

Kuznetsovsk

Sarny

This region contains oblasts that were formerly part of Romania, Hungary, and Poland.

Western Ukraine

Neteshin

Khmel'nitsky

ICBM base with multiple-warhead SS-19s.

ROMANIA

HUNGARY

Mikhaylenk

Pripyat (Chornobyl)

★ Kiev

▲ Uzin

Airbase with Bear-H 16 strategic bombers armed with nuclear air-launched cruise missiles.

Priluki

Airbase with Blackjack strategic bombers armed with nuclear air-launched cruise missiles.

UKRAINE

Pervomaysk

ICBM base with multiple-warhead SS-19s and SS-24s.

Kostantinovsk

Center of uranium mining activities in Ukraine.

Zheltiye Vody

Dnepropetrovsk

Dneprozerzhinsk

Pavlograd

Energodar

Pomerki ○

Khar'kiv ●

Khar'kiv Scientific Center. *Missile/Missile Component Production and Technology:* **Khar'kiv Physical-Technical Institute.** *Facility stores up to 75 kg of weapons-grade (90% enriched) uranium.*

Eastern Ukraine

RUSSIA

Location of several heavy-water production plants giving Ukraine the capability to produce about 250 metric tons of heavy-water per year. Ukraine's export of heavy-water to a country with unsafeguarded, heavy-water reactors (e.g., India) would enhance the recipient country's potential to produce plutonium for nuclear weapons.

Reported to have been the location of the largest missile factory in the former Soviet Union.

MOLDOVA

Ukraine is currently deactivating its ICBMs and is transferring some of its warheads to Russia; it has agreed to transfer all nuclear weapons on its territory to Russia no later than 1997.

✳ Operational nuclear power station(s); Ukraine has agreed to place all its peaceful nuclear activities under IAEA inspection (nuclear weapons, which are not under Ukrainian control, are excluded).

○ ICBM production, testing/training, conversion/elimination, or storage facilities; possible presence of ICBMs (but not ICBM warheads).

Italicized names represent sites of proliferation concern.

Crimea

Sevastopol ●

Black Sea

Sea of Oziv

RUSSIA

0   100 mi

Carnegie Endowment for International Peace, Tracking Nuclear Proliferation, 1995.

Adapted from William Potter, *Nuclear Profiles of the Soviet Successor States*, 1993; and START Treaty Memorandum of Understanding, 1990.

UKRAINE: Nuclear Infrastructure and Other Sites of Proliferation Concern

Note: Locations in bold italics contain nuclear weapons or quantities of weapons-usable nuclear material sufficient for one or more nuclear weapons.

NAME/LOCATION OF FACILITY	TYPE/STATUS	IAEA SAFEGUARDS
NUCLEAR-WEAPONS BASES AND SUPPORT FACILITIES		
Pervomaysk	Intercontinental ballistic missile (ICBM) base with SS-19s carrying 6 warheads each. (Forty out of the total 130 MOU-specified SS-19s deployed on Ukrainian territory have been deactivated.)[1,2] Also base of silo-based SS-24s carrying 10 warheads each. (All of the 46 MOU-specified SS-24s have been deactivated.)	
Khmel'nitskiy	ICBM base with SS-19s carrying 6 warheads each[3]	
Uzin	Air base with 21 Bear-H(16)s strategic bombers capable of carrying up to 16 air-launched cruise missiles (ALCMs) each; all bombers being sold back to Russia[4]	
Priluki	Air base with 19 Blackjack strategic bombers capable of carrying up to 12 ALCMs each; all bombers sold to Russia[5]	
Mikhaylenk	Storage facility for ICBMs housing 4 SS-11s, 14 SS-17s and 46 SS-19s; all non-deployed (minus warheads).	
Pavlograd Mechanical Plant, Pavlograd	Former production facility for SS-24s[6]	
Yuzhmash Plant (formerly Southern Machine Building Plant), Dnepropetrovsk	Former production facility for SS-18s[7]	
Pomerki	Training facility for SS-18s	
Sarny	Conversion and elimination facility for ICBMs	
Belaya Taerkov	Repair facilities for heavy bombers and former heavy bombers	
Uzin	Storage, conversion, and elimination facilities for heavy bombers	
NUCLEAR AND NUCLEAR-RELATED RESEARCH CENTERS		
Khar'kiv Scientific Center, Khar'kiv	May have been engaged in work to bypass Russian-held codes for lauching nuclear weapons on Ukrainian territory.	
Khar'kiv Physical-Technical Institute	Facility stores up to 75 kg of HEU in bulk form enriched up to 90 percent.	No (pending)
Institute of Nuclear Research, Kiev	Site of research reactor (see below)	No (pending)
POWER REACTORS[8]		
Chornobyl, Units 1 and 3 Pripyat[9]	RBMK, LEU, 925 MWe; operating.	No (pending)
Chornobyl, Unit 2	RBMK, LEU, 925 MWe; shut-down; possible restart.	No (pending)
Khmel'nitskiy Unit 1, Neteshin	VVER-1000, LEU, 950 MWe; operating.[10]	No (pending)
Khmel'nitskiy Unit 2	VVER-1000, LEU, 950 MWe; under construction.	No (pending)

UKRAINE (cont'd.)

NAME/LOCATION OF FACILITY	TYPE/STATUS	IAEA SAFEGUARDS
Rovno Units 1, 2 and 3 Kuznetsovsk	VVER-440, LEU, 361 MWe; operating	No (pending)
Rovno Unit 4	VVER-1000, LEU, 950 MWe; under construction.	No (pending)
South Ukraine Units 1, 2 and 3 Kostantinovsk	VVER-1000, LEU, 950 MWe; operating.[11]	No (pending)
Zaporozhye Units 1, 2, 3, 4 and 5 Energodar	VVER-1000, LEU, 950 MWe; operating.	No (pending)
Zaporozhye Unit 6	VVER-1000, LEU, 950 MWe; under construction.[12]	No (pending)
RESEARCH REACTORS		
WWR-M (Institute of Nuclear Research), Kiev	Tank WWR, 36% enriched uranium, 10 MWE; shut down.[13]	No (pending)
Sevastopol	Tank WWR, LEU, 200 KWt; operating?	No (pending)
Sevastopol	Subcritical assembly, 36% enriched uranium; operating.	No (pending)
URANIUM PROCESSING		
Kirovograd Oblast	Uranium mining; operating.	N/A (Not applicable)
Krivoy Rog Oblast	Uranium mining; operating.	N/A
Zheltiye Vody	Uranium milling; operating.	N/A
Dneprodzerzhinsk	Uranium milling; operating.	N/A
Zheltiye Vody	Uranium conversion (UO_2); operating.[14]	No (pending)
HEAVY WATER PRODUCTION		
Dnepropetrovsk		No[15] (pending)

Abbreviations:

HEU = highly enriched uranium
LEU = low-enriched uranium
nat. U = natural uranium
MWe = millions of watts of electrical output
MWt = millions of watts of thermal output
KWt = thousands of watts of thermal output

NOTES (Ukraine Chart)

1. When the START MOU was originally signed in September 1990, an additional four SS-19s were listed as located at the Pervomaysk maintenance facility.

2. The warheads from the deactivation process are believed to be stored at facilities close to the Pervomaysk base, prior to their shipment to Russia.

3. An additional 11 SS-19s, listed in the MOU as non-deployed (minus warheads), were located at the Khmel'nitskiy maintenance facility when the MOU was originally signed.

Press reports indicate that construction has begun on a strategic missile dismantlement facility in Dnepropetrovsk, Ukraine. The plant will start "neutralizing" SS-19 rocket motors and fuel tanks in October 1995 at a rate of three rockets per month. The United States has contributed funds to this $63 million project. See *Radio Free Europe/Radio Liberty*, November 15, 1994, p. 5.

4. The MOU lists one Bear-A strategic bomber and one Bear-B strategic bomber as stored at the base. For accounting purposes under the Treaty both bombers are considered deployed. They are equipped for nuclear armaments other than ALCMs (i.e., gravity bombs). However, a senior Clinton administration official said on January 14, 1994, that there are no gravity bombs in Ukraine. See "Background Briefing by Senior Administration Officials; Topic: Documents Signed by Heads of State," *Federal News Service Transcript*, January 14, 1994, p. 8.

All ALCMs are believed to be in storage at or near airfields where associated bombers are based, with their warheads presumably stored in separate locations. The cassettes containing the software for the guidance systems of these ALCMs have reportedly been returned to Russia.

Ukraine's Ministry of Defense recently agreed to sell to Russia all 42 strategic bombers on its territory. Russian experts estimated the value of the total bomber force at $75 million, but, as of mid-March 1995, the final figure was pending. Russian officials noted that Ukraine plans to use this money to reduce its enormous energy debt to Russia. The deal, however, must be approved by each nation's government. "Russia Says Ukraine to Hand Over Strategic Bombers," *Reuters*, February 24, 1995; Anton Zhigulsky, "Future of Disputed Black Sea Fleet Remains Uncertain," *Defense News*, March 13-19, 1995, p. 8.

5. The MOU lists 13 Blackjack bombers at Priluki, but, according to the Arms Control Association, Washington, DC, 19 such aircraft are deployed at that base.

6. This plant is part of the missile production industrial base Ukraine inherited from the Soviet Union. Ukraine now plans to use this plant for the manufacture of space-launch systems for export and, possibly, for the production and/or export of ballistic missiles. The plant is believed to have the capability to do repair work on SS-24s or produce other types of boosters.

7. This facility is already producing certain space equipment.

8. On October 21, 1993, the Ukrainian parliament cancelled a resolution adopted in 1990 to close the Chornobyl nuclear power station by the end of 1993 and to impose a moratorium on the construction of new power reactors.

However, following an IAEA assessment that "international levels of safety are not being met at" Chornobyl, the Ukrainian government agreed in principle, in early 1994, to shut down the station at "the earliest possible date."

The October 1993 parliamentary vote will allow the completion of three VVER-1000 power reactors, one at Energodar in 1994 (Zaporozhye-6), one at Kuznetsovsk in 1995 (Rovno-4), and one at Neteshin in 1995–96 (Khmel'nitskiy-2). Three other units have been slated for completion in the longer term, presumably two additional units at Neteshin and one unit at Kostantinovsk. See Ann MacLachlan, "Ukraine Deputies Vote to Keep Chornobyl Open, Finish VVERs," *Nucleonics Week*, October 28, 1993, p. 1; Ann MacLachlan, "IAEA Sounds Alarm on Chornobyl Safety Level," *Nucleonics Week*, April 7, 1994, p. 1; Robert Seely, "Agency Finds Serious Safety Problems at Chornobyl Reactor," *Washington Post*, April 1, 1994; John H. Cushman, Jr., "Ukraine to Close Chornobyl Plant," *New York Times*, April 10, 1994.

As part of an international initiative to help Ukraine shut down the Chornobyl reactors, the G-7 (comprised of the world's seven leading industrial nations) agreed on July 9, 1994, to provide $200 million in grants to Ukraine. This was in addition to $620 million in assistance and loans pledged by the European Union two weeks earlier. Under the plan, a portion of the funds would be used to complete the aforementioned three VVER-1000s to compensate for the loss of the generating capacity of the Chornobyl complex. While the new Ukrainian government has accepted, in principle, the G-7 plan, a timetable for the plan's implementation is not yet in place. See Ann MacLachlan, "G-7 Partners Agree on Assistance to Help Ukraine Close Chornobyl," *Nucleonics Week*, July 14, 1994, p. 1; Ann MacLachlan, "Ukraine Government Change Augurs More Delay in Chornobyl Closure," *Nucleonics Week*, July 21, 1994, p. 8; Ann MacLachlan, "Ukraine Accepts G-7 Chornobyl Aid but Time, Price Remain Uncertain," *Nucleonics Week*, October 20, 1994, p. 7.

9. Chornobyl Unit 4 was the site of a catastrophic accident in April 1986.

10. Khmel'nitskiy Units 3 and 4 could be completed by July 1999 and June 2000, respectively, if sufficient resources became available. This is the view expressed in an U.S. interagency report entitled *U.S./Ukraine Evaluation of Energy Options to Replace the Chornobyl Nuclear Plant*. See Dave Airozo, "Efficiency and Renewables Touted as Answer to Ukraine Power Needs," *Nucleonics Week*, July 7, 1994, p. 4.

11. Construction of South Ukraine Unit 4 appears to have been postponed indefinitely.

12. In a referendum conducted as part of the Ukrainian national election on July 26, 1994, more than 90 percent of local voters in the Nikopol district, where Zaporozhye-6 is being built, voted against completion of the plant even though it is 95 percent finished. Mark Hibbs, "Local Voters Reject Plans to Finish Zaporozhe-6 VVER," *Nucleonics Week*, June 30, 1994, p. 9.

13. Reactor may contain up to 4 kg of U^{235} with fuel enriched up to 36 percent.

14. Additional uranium conversion activities may be taking place at Verkhnedneprovsky Mining and Chemical Works.

15. Production of heavy water may also be taking place at the aforementioned uranium milling facility at Dneprodzerzhinsk.

Additional References

1993: Mark Hibbs, "U.S.-Ukraine Safeguards Proposal Protested As Dangerous Precedent," *Nucleonics Week*, October 28, 1993, p. 6; *Radio Free Europe/Radio Liberty Daily Report*, November 11, 1993; Rostislav Khotin, "Ukraine Ratifies START-1 But Sets Own Arms Timetable," *Reuters*, November 18, 1993; Alexander Tkachenko, "Kravchuk Says Ukraine Must Disarm Fully," *Reuters*, November 19, 1993; Robert Burns, "U.S.-Ukraine Nuclear," *Associated Press*, November 20, 1993; Ron Popeski, "Ukrainian President Keeps Distance from Parliament," *Reuters*, November 21, 1993; *Radio Free Europe/Radio Liberty Daily Report*, December 22, 1993. **1994:** *Reuters,* "Ukraine Says Its A-Arms Are Being Handled Safely," *Washington Post*, January 7, 1994; Ann Devroy, "Pact Reached to Dismantle Ukraine's Nuclear Force," *Washington Post*, January 11, 1994; R.W. Apple Jr., "Ukraine Gives In On Surrendering Its Nuclear Arms," *New York Times*, January 11, 1994; Daniel Williams, "U.S. Secured Ukraine Arms Pact By Shifting Negotiating Tactics," *Washington Post*, January 15, 1994; *Radio Free Europe/Radio Liberty Daily Report*, February 1, 1994; *Radio Free Europe/Radio Liberty Daily Report*, February 2, 1994; Robert Seely, "A-Arms Pacts Approved in Ukraine," *Washington Post*, February 4, 1994; Steven Greenhouse, "Clinton Vows to Improve Relations With Ukraine," *New York Times*, March 5, 1994; Thomas W. Lippman, "Clinton Increases Aid, Support to Ukraine," *Washington Post*, March ·5, 1994; Robert Seely, "Perry Offers More Money to Ukraine," *Washington Post*, March 22, 1994; "Perry Visits Strategic Missile Unit," *Itar-Tass*, March 22, 1994, in *FBIS-SOV-94-056*, March 23, 1994, p. 27; Robert Seely, "Perry Stops at Ukraine's Deadliest Missile Facilities," *Washington Post*, March 23, 1994; "Ukraine Disarmament Expected to Continue," *New York Times*, March 23, 1994; "Resolution of the Verkhovna Rada [Parliament] of Ukraine Regarding Article V of the Lisbon Protocol to the START I Treaty, 3 February 1994," *PPNN Newsbrief*, First Quarter 1994, p. 17; "Statement by Dr. Ashton B. Carter, Assistant Secretary of Defense (International Security Policy)," before the Senate Armed Services Committee, April 28, 1994; "Ukraine Deactivates Most SS-24 Nuclear Missiles," *Reuters*, May 4, 1994; "Kravchuk Says Nuclear Disarmament Program on Schedule," *Itar-Tass*, May 13, 1994, in *FBIS-SOV-94-094*, May 16, 1994; "Ukraine Said Ready to Speed Nuclear Disarmament," *Reuters*, May 19, 1994; Douglas Jehl, "Ukraine Hints It Won't Close Nuclear Plants at Chornobyl," *New York Times*, June 12, 1994; "Agreement With IAEA on Nuclear Materials," Moscow, *Interfax*, July 5, 1994, in *FBIS-SOV-94-129*, July 6, 1994, p. 36; Dave Airozo, "Efficiency and Renewables Touted as Answer to Ukraine Power Needs," *Nucleonics Week*, July 7, 1994, p. 4; Carol Giacomo, "U.S. Aims to Convince Ukraine on Nuclear Pact," *Reuters*, August 3, 1994; Liam McDowall, "Ukraine-U.S.," *Associated Press*, August 10, 1994; "U.S. Officials Promise Speedy Disarmament Aid," *Reuters*, August 11, 1994; "Ukrainian Pledges Arms Pact Approval," *Reuters*, August 20, 1994; "Ukraine to Take Time Over Signing NPT Treaty—Deputy," *Reuters*, September 1, 1994; Ron Popeski, "Ukraine Foreign Minister for Better Russia Ties," *Reuters*, September 3, 1994; Lida Poletz, "Parliament Chairman Questions NPT for Ukraine," *Reuters*, September 15, 1994; "Ukraine Agrees to Close Chornobyl Nuclear Plant-EU Diplomats," *Reuters*, October 4, 1994; Lida Poletz, "Kuchma Presents Nuclear Pact to Parliament," *Reuters*, October 5, 1994; "Ukraine Parliament Head Unclear on Nuclear Pact," *Reuters*, October 6, 1994; *Radio Free Europe/Radio Liberty*, November 15, 1994, p.5.

6

EASTERN EUROPE

Romania

Romania ratified the Nuclear Non-Proliferation Treaty (NPT) on February 4, 1970, pledging not to manufacture nuclear weapons and agreeing to place all of its nuclear materials and facilities under International Atomic Energy Agency (IAEA) safeguards. However, in April and May 1989 the communist leader of Romania, Nicolae Ceausescu, stated that, from the standpoint of technical competence, his country had the ''ability to manufacture nuclear weapons.'' Two months later, Romanian officials reiterated that the country possessed this capability, adding that it would soon be able to manufacture medium-range missiles as well.[1]

Following the overthrow of the Ceausescu regime in December 1989, the new democratic government of Ion Iliescu initially dissociated itself from these nuclear-weapons-related statements. However, in April 1992, a vessel containing 470 ml of a mysterious nuclear substance was discovered at the Nuclear Research Institute (ICN) in Pitesti. Analysis showed the material to be nuclear waste from plutonium separation. Theodor Stolojan, who was then Prime Minister, reported the discovery to the IAEA and invited the agency to conduct a special inspection or ''visit'' of Romania's nuclear program. As a result, in June 1992, IAEA Director General Hans Blix told the agency's Board of Governors that in December 1985, Romania's (Communist) government had violated the country's safe-guards agreement with the IAEA by separating about 100 mg of plutonium from irradiated uranium in a laboratory-scale experiment. According to one report, the experiment was intended to serve as the basis of setting up a production capacity of 1 kg of plutonium a year. The same report noted that, during or after the 1992 special IAEA visit, IAEA officials told the Stolojan government that they had been aware of Ceausescu's clandestine nuclear weapons program all along.[2]

A 1993 report in a Romanian newspaper quoted the former head of Romania's Department of Foreign Intelligence and sources close to the Romanian Intelligence Service as saying that during the Ceausescu era secret planning took place for developing a medium-range missile with nuclear warheads. This report added that, in 1968–1970, ''Ceausescu had ordered the establishment of a large espionage network intended to obtain the documentation necessary for production of the nuclear weapon [sic].'' The purpose of manufacturing such weapons was to ''intimidate both the NATO [North Atlantic Treaty Organization] adversaries and those that were members of the Warsaw Pact'' and to sell them to countries in the Middle East.[3]

U.S. officials familiar with the Romanian case have confirmed the existence of a nuclear weapons program under Ceausescu, but have declined to provide additional details.[4]

NOTES

[1]See ''SPIEGEL Reports Missile Aid to Romania,'' Hamburg, *Der Spiegel*, May 8, 1989, in *FBIS-WEU-89*, May 8, 1989, p. 8; Henry Kamm, ''Hungarian Accuses Rumania of Military Threats,'' *New York Times*, July 11, 1989; ''Past Attempt to Produce Plutonium Disclosed,'' Bucharest, *Rompres*, May 25, 1993, in *FBIS-EEU-93-100*, May 26, 1993, p. 25; ''Romania Planned Atom Bomb,'' *Reuters*, May 26, 1993.

[2]See ''Past Attempt to Produce Plutonium Disclosed,'' Bucharest, *Rompres*, May 25, 1993, *op. cit.*; ''Romania Planned Atom Bomb,'' *Reuters*, *op. cit.*; Ann MacLachlan, ''Romania Produced Unsafeguarded Pu, Blix Tells IAEA Board of Governors,'' *Nuclear Fuel*, June 22, 1992, p. 16.

[3]See ''Ceausescu Effort to Build Nuclear Bomb Reported,'' Bucharest, *Evenimentul Zilei*, May 10, 1993, in *FBIS-EEU-93-092*, May 14, 1993, p. 14.

[4]Interviews, December 1994.

POLAND

0   100 mi

SLOVAKIA

UKRAINE

HUNGARY

Uranium mining ■ Botusana
                ■ Crucea

MOLDOVA

Uranium mining
                    Avram   ● Cluj
                    Iancu
                    ■

ROMANIA

Location of heavy-water production
plant intended to support the operation
of the Cernavoda power station.

Uranium milling; also
location of UO$_2$ powder
fabrication plant, subject
to IAEA inspection.

Brasov ■

Uranium mining

        ■ Dobrei
          South

        ■ Drobeta Turnu   ■ Pitesti
          Severin

★
Belgrade

SERBIA

Bucharest
★

Cernavoda ■

**Black
Sea**

Nuclear Research Institute (ICN).
Location of "hot cells" which
presumably could be used to extract
small amounts of plutonium from spent
nuclear fuel. In 1985, the then-
Communist government separated about
100 milligrams of plutonium,
presumably at this site, as part of a
nuclear-weapons research and
development effort.
Also site of fuel fabrication plant, subject
to IAEA inspection.

BULGARIA

Cernavoda nuclear power
station comprising five 700
MWe heavy-water reactors,
under construction. First unit
to enter service in 1995. All
facilities subject to IAEA
inspection after completion.

GREECE

TURKEY

Carnegie Endowment for International Peace, Tracking Nuclear Proliferation, 1995.

ROMANIA: Nuclear Infrastructure

NAME/LOCATION OF FACILITY	TYPE/STATUS	IAEA SAFEGUARDS
P O W E R R E A C T O R S		
Cernavoda I	Heavy water, natural U, 700 MWe; under construction; projected criticality in 1995.	IAEA (planned)
Cernavoda II	Heavy water, natural U, 700 MWe; under construction; projected completion in 1997.	IAEA (planned)
Cernavoda III[1]	Heavy water, natural U, 700 MWe; under construction; projected completion in 2001.	IAEA (planned)
R E S E A R C H R E A C T O R S		
Triga II (Nuclear Research Institute (ICN)), Pitesti	LEU, 14 MWt materials testing reactor; operating.[2]	IAEA
VVR-S (Units I and II) Magurele	Operating	IAEA
R E P R O C E S S I N G (P L U T O N I U M E X T R A C T I O N)		
ICN, Pitesti	Laboratory-scale hot cells	No[3]
U R A N I U M P R O C E S S I N G		
Avram Iancu, Apuseni mountains; Dobrei South, Banat mountains; Botusana and Crucea, Eastern Carpathians	Uranium mining; operating.	N/A (Not applicable)
Feldioara, Brasov	Uranium milling/Operating	N/A
Feldioara	UO$_2$ powder fabrication plant; operating.	IAEA
Romfuel, Pitesti	Fuel fabrication plant; operating.	IAEA
H E A V Y W A T E R P R O D U C T I O N		
ROMAG, Drobeta Turnu Severin[4]	Operating partially	No

Abbreviations:

HEU	=	highly enriched uranium
LEU	=	low-enriched uranium
nat. U	=	natural uranium
MWe	=	millions of watts of electrical output
MWt	=	millions of watts of thermal output
KWt	=	thousands of watts of thermal output

NOTES (Romania Chart)

1. Cernavoda Units IV and V are slated for completion "after 2001." See "Datafile: Romania," *Nuclear Engineering International*, August 1993, p. 52.

2. Originally rated at 40 MWt, the TRIGA reactor at Pitetsi was the largest of its type in the world. Supplied by the United States, it was fueled with U.S.-origin, weapons-usable HEU throughout the Ceausescu era. Although the facility was under IAEA monitoring from the time it began operating, Romania would have been able to use the unit's HEU fuel to fabricate a nuclear weapon had it been prepared to violate the IAEA safeguards covering the facility. (During the mid-1980s, Romania did, in fact, violate IAEA rules on a smaller scale by separating a small quantity of plutonium without notifying the agency (see Romania text) and, reportedly, by clandestinely shipping a quantity of heavy water to India, again without notifying the IAEA.)

Between 1989 and 1991, the reactor was shut down because the United States was no longer prepared to supply HEU fuel for the facility. After Romania agreed to convert the reactor to low-enriched uranium (LEU) fuel (not usable for nuclear arms), Washington approved the transfer of five LEU fuel elements for the plant. As part of an overall agreement on the final disposition of Romania's highly enriched uranium fuel for the reactor, the U.S. Department of Energy has agreed to convert 14 highly enriched fuel elements owned by the Romanian government to 14 low-enriched elements. See "U.S. and Romania Agree on Use of Low Enriched Uranium for Research Reactor," *DOE News*, November 8, 1991.

3. The 100 mg of plutonium that were separated in 1985 in violation of Romania's safeguards agreement with the IAEA presumably were extracted at these hot cells.

4. This plant reportedly has produced about 120–160 tons of heavy water out of the 500 tons needed to run the first unit of the Cernavoda nuclear power station when it becomes operational in 1995. However, three of the four production units of the heavy water plant were shut down in 1994 for safety checks. To meet the projected deficit in heavy water production, Romanian authorities in charge of the nuclear power program, in September 1994, signed a contract with India's department of atomic energy for the import of 350 tons of heavy water. There is considerable irony in this purchase, inasmuch as during the mid-1980s, Romania is believed to have transfered heavy water to India clandestinely, in violation of Romania's safeguards commitments. At the time, India lacked sufficient heavy water to operate three unsafeguarded reactors that it was about to bring on line. At least one of these, the Dhruva reactor at the Bhabha Atomic Research Center, was intended to produce plutonium for India's nuclear weapons program. See "Romania to Import 350 Tonnes of Indian Heavy Water," *Reuters*, September 23, 1994.

Additional References

1993: IAEA, *The Annual Report for 1992* (Vienna: IAEA, July 1993), pp. 158, 159, 160; OECD Nuclear Energy Agency and International Atomic Energy Agency, *Uranium* (Paris: OECD, 1993), pp. 207–212; "Datafile: Romania," *Nuclear Engineering International*, August 1993, p. 52; "Romania Producing Nuclear Fuel," *Radio Free Europe/Radio Liberty Daily Report*, February 3, 1993. **1995:** Communication with IAEA, January 1995.

7

SOUTH ASIA AND
EAST ASIA

India

India, which is not party to the Nuclear Non-Proliferation Treaty (NPT), demonstrated a nuclear-weapons capability by detonating a nuclear device in May 1974, its only nuclear test to date. In April 1994, the U.S. State Department submitted a report to the U.S. Congress projecting that India "could assemble a limited number of nuclear weapons in a relatively short timeframe" and that it possessed "combat aircraft that could be modified to deliver nuclear weapons in a crisis." The report also noted continued testing, over the preceding year, of two nuclear-capable, surface-to-surface ballistic missiles—the Prithvi and the Agni—with approximate ranges of 150–250 km and 2,500 km, respectively. In September 1994, Indian officials said that the Prithvi would be ready for serial production and deployment by mid-1995. However, the Agni program may have been suspended as of March 1994, according to Indian press reports.[1] India possesses a sizeable air force and deploys several advanced fighter-bombers that would be suitable for the delivery of nuclear weapons, including the British-French Jaguar and the Soviet-supplied MiG-23 and MiG-27. India could also use Soviet MiG-29 and French Mirage-2000 fighters for nuclear delivery missions.[2] India has not acknowledged possessing nuclear weapons, however.

According to conservative estimates of India's nuclear weapons potential, published in 1992, India at that time had enough plutonium not subject to International Atomic Energy Agency (IAEA) inspection for nearly sixty nuclear bombs, and by 1995, was projected to have enough plutonium for as many as eighty.[3] India also possesses the ability to enrich uranium, which could add to its stocks of weapons-usable material. The capabilities of its two enrichment facilities, at the Bhabha Atomic Research Center and Rattehalli, have not been disclosed; neither is subject to IAEA monitoring.

Peaceful Uses. During the 1950s and early 1960s, with assistance from Canada and the United States, India built a large research reactor and an associated plutonium separation plant at the Bhabha Atomic Research Center. India pledged to use the facility solely for peaceful purposes but it was not subject to IAEA inspections. Until the mid-1960s, India's public stance was one of unequivocally rejecting nuclear arms. In late 1964, however, shortly after China's first nuclear test and at time when India's defeat in its 1962 border war with China was still vivid, India quietly launched a program to develop nuclear explosives, ostensibly for peaceful purposes, such as civil excavation. At the time, the United States and the Soviet Union were experimenting with such uses of nuclear explosives, which are identical to nuclear weapons in all important respects.

India's refusal to join the NPT in 1968 permitted it to continue to accumulate plutonium at the Bhabha Atomic Research Center, without IAEA monitoring, and work on the design of nuclear explosives continued. When India conducted its nuclear test in 1974, it declared that it had tested a "peaceful nuclear explosion" and thus had not violated its agreements with Canada and the United States. Canada, rejecting this rationalization, shortly terminated all nuclear commerce with India, while the United States tightened controls on the use of the two nuclear power reactors at Tarapur, which it had sold to India in 1963.[4]

External Threat. India did not conduct additional nuclear tests and, although China's nuclear arsenal greatly expanded during the 1970s, India did not deploy a nuclear deterrent force to counter this threat. As Pakistan's bid to acquire nuclear arms became increasingly apparent in the late 1970s and early 1980s, however, India became increasingly alarmed and adopted the stance that, although it did not want to develop nuclear arms, it would take this step if Pakistan did so. Simultaneously, India significantly expanded its plutonium production capabilities. By the late 1980s, when it became clear that Pakistan could deploy several weapons, it was generally assumed that India had quietly acted to meet this challenge by preparing a readily deployable nuclear force, of perhaps several dozen weapons.

By this point, India was also working on the two nuclear-capable missiles noted earlier, the short-range Prithvi, apparently intended for use against Pakistan, and the intermediate-range Agni, apparently intended for use against China. India's decision in 1994 to halt work on the latter missile, while it continued to prepare for deployment of the former, suggests that at present New Delhi considers its most urgent nuclear challenge to come from Pakistan. India nonetheless remains concerned about the nuclear threat from China, and for this reason New Delhi has rejected numerous Pakistani proposals for bilateral non-proliferation arrangements that would obligate it to restrict or relinquish its current nuclear weapons capabilities. India and Pakistan have, however, adopted a number of more limited confidence-building measures intended to reduce the threat of conflict. These are described more fully in the Pakistan section of this report.

Over the past decade, Indo-Pakistani relations have been marked by cycles of tension, as New Delhi has accused Islamabad of supporting militant separatist movements in the Indian states of Punjab and Kashmir. In the winter of 1986–1987, and again in the spring of 1990, it was widely feared that India and Pakistan might go to war. By the time of the latter crisis, both India and Pakistan presumably possessed the ability to deploy nuclear weapons quickly, triggering concerns that, if war erupted, it might lead to a nuclear confrontation.[5] Frictions over Kashmir are continuing.[6]

Confidence Building. In recent years, the United States has gradually changed its non-proliferation policy toward India. From the time of India's 1974 test until the mid-1980s, U.S. policy focused predominantly on gaining New Delhi's acceptance of IAEA inspection on all of its nuclear program. As this goal appeared increasingly distant during the Bush and Clinton administrations, U.S. policy shifted toward efforts to reduce tensions and avert the risk of conflict between India and Pakistan by promoting confidence-building measures and political accommodation. Washington has also sought to persuade both states to cap their nuclear and missile capabilities as an initial step toward their ultimate elimination.[7]

NOTES

[1]See U.S. State Department, ''Report to Congress: Update on Progress Toward Regional Nonproliferation in South Asia,'' April 1994; ''Testimony of Robert Gates,'' before the Committee on Governmental Affairs, U.S. Senate, January 15, 1992; ''India to Deploy Missile by Next Year,'' *United Press International*, September 20, 1994.

The report to Congress was required under legislation adopted in 1992.

[2]International Institute for Strategic Studies, *The Military Balance 1994–1995* (London: International Institute for Strategic Studies, 1994), p. 155.

[3]See David Albright, Frans Berkhout, and William Walker, *World Inventories of Plutonium and Highly Enriched Uranium*, (Stockholm: SIPRI, 1992), pp. 160–161.

In placing nuclear materials and facilities under IAEA inspection, nations undertake not to use them for nuclear explosives. Normally a state would be legally free to use materials and facilities that are not under such IAEA safeguards for nuclear arms, assuming that the country involved had not had accepted other restrictions on their use.

The estimates of the plutonium available to India for use in nuclear weapons include the high quality plutonium not subject to IAEA inspection that India has produced at each of its two principal unsafeguarded research reactors (the Cirus and Dhruva reactors at the Bhabha Atomic Research Center) and at four unsafeguarded nuclear power reactors (Madras I and II and Narora I and II) during their respective start-up phase of operations. These estimates are conservative, however, because in the interim since they were made, India has begun to operate two additional nuclear power reactors not subject to IAEA inspections (Kakrapar I and II), which have also produced high-quality plutonium during their start-up—a period when fuel remains in the reactor more briefly than during normal operations, producing plutonium with a lower proportion of the isotopes that complicate nuclear weapons manufacture. Moreover, the estimates exclude the possibility that India may have chosen to operate some or all of these six power reactors *after* start-up in a mode that would maximize the production of high-quality plutonium, a step India could have taken by refueling the units more frequently than would normally be the case for the production of electricity. It may be added that even if India refueled these power reactors at normal rates, the lower quality plutonium produced in the reactors could also be used in nuclear arms, if India chose to use it.

India's ability to separate unsafeguarded power reactor plutonium is constrained only by the current capacity of its reprocessing facilities.

[4]Subsequent controversies involving the Tarapur reactors are described in the notes pertaining to the reactors in the chart that appears later in this section.

[5]If India and Pakistan had gone to war over Kashmir in 1990, it would have been the first major military conflict in history between two states with ready access to nuclear arms. If significant hostilities had appeared imminent, moreover, there is good reason to believe that both sides would have readied their nuclear arms, Pakistan to protect against a pre-emptive attack by superior Indian nuclear and/or conventional forces and India to protect against being placed at a disadvantage by

a nuclear-ready Pakistan. One report asserted that during the 1990 crisis the two states in fact came to the nuclear brink as Pakistan loaded nuclear weapons on U.S.-made F-16 strike aircraft. See Seymour M. Hersh, "On the Nuclear Edge," *New Yorker*, March 29, 1993, p. 86; Douglas Jehl, "Assertion India and Pakistan Faced Nuclear War Is Doubted," *New York Times*, March 23, 1993.

[6]Edward A. Gargan, "Indian Troops Are Blamed as Kashmir Violence Rises," *New York Times*, April 18, 1993; John F. Burns, "Rebels in Kashmir and Indian Army Ready for a Long Fight," *New York Times*, May 16, 1994; John F. Burns, "India Lengthens Emergency Powers in Kashmir," *New York Times*, August 9, 1994; Molly Moore and John Ward Anderson, "Warfare Intensifies in Kashmir," *Washington Post*, October 4, 1994.

[7]Since India's 1974 test, Washington has never backed up its non-proliferation diplomacy *vis-à-vis* India with significant sanctions—in contrast to the considerably harsher measures the United States imposed on Pakistan in an unsuccessful attempt to head off its development of nuclear arms (see Pakistan chapter). In late 1992, the U.S. Congress added new provisions to the Foreign Assistance Act (Section 620F), encouraging the president to pursue regional nuclear non-proliferation initiatives in South Asia and requiring him to submit twice-yearly reports, beginning in April 1993, on the nuclear weapon and ballistic missile programs in China, India, and Pakistan. Among other issues, the president is to determine whether any of these states possesses a nuclear explosive device. While not imposing sanctions, the legislation for the first time specifically treated India on a par with Pakistan as a proliferation concern.

In May 1992, the United States imposed limited trade sanctions against the Indian Space Research Organization (ISRO) and the Russian space agency, Glavkosmos, over a proposed sale to India of cryogenic rocket engines and related manufacturing technology. The United States argued that this sale was in violation of Missile Technology Control Regime (MTCR) guidelines, which Russia had agreed to enforce. These sanctions were lifted after a compromise was reached in July 1993, when Russia agreed, in a formal written pledge, to adhere to the export standards of the MTCR, and, with respect to the sale to India, agreed to transfer only completed cryogenic engines but not related manufacturing technology. See Gerald F. Seib, "Tranfer of Russian Missile Technology to India Leads to U.S. Trade Sanctions," *Wall Street Journal*, May 12, 1992, p. A5; "Official Reaction to U.S. Space Ban Viewed," in *JPRS-TND* June 10, 1992; R. Jeffrey Smith and Daniel Williams, "U.S. Russia Settle Dispute on Selling Rocket Engines, Technology to India," *Washington Post*, July 17, 1993; "Glavkosmos Works Out New Rocket Contract with India," Moscow, *RIA*, January 9, 1994, in *JPRS-TND*, January 31, 1994.

TAJIKISTAN

Kashmir
(disputed)

CHINA

AFGHAN.

PAKISTAN

Nangal

Narora I and II nuclear power
reactors: not subject to IAEA
inspection and therefore available
to produce plutonium for nuclear
weapons.

Nuclear test site

New
Delhi ★

INDIA

Narora

NEPAL

Uranium mining area

BHUTAN

Pokaran

Kota

Kakrapar I and II
nuclear power
reactors: not subject
to IAEA inspection
and therefore
available to
produce plutonium
for nuclear
weapons.

Jaduguda

BANGLADESH

Calcutta ●
Talcher

BURMA

Hazira
Baroda
Kakrapar
Tarapur
Trombay
Bombay
Thal Vaishet

*Arabian
Sea*

Large plutonium
extraction plant: not
under IAEA
inspection when
processing fuel from
Madras and Narora
reactors; presumed to
support nuclear
weapons program.
Two U.S.-supplied
electric power reactors
(under IAEA
inspection).

Hyderabad
Kaiga
Manuguru

Madras ●
Rattehalli

Kalpakkam
Tuticorin

*Bay of
Bengal*

Bhabha Atomic Research Center (BARC).
*Principal location of India's presumed nuclear
weapons program—including research, plutonium
production using Dhruva and Cirus research
reactors, and associated plutonium extraction
plant (none subject to IAEA inspection).*
*Pilot scale uranium enrichment plant: not subject
to IAEA inspection.*

Indira Gandhi Atomic Research Center.
*Site of Fast, Breeder Test Reactor (FBTR) and
associated pilot-scale plutonium extraction
plant.*
*Also location of Madras I and II nuclear
power reactors: not subject to IAEA inspection
and therefore available to produce plutonium
for nuclear weapons.*

SRI
LANKA

Pilot-scale uranium
enrichment plant: not
subject to IAEA
inspection.

Koodankulam

Indian Ocean

Italicized names represent
nuclear-related sites. See chart.

0   500

MILES

Carnegie Endowment for International Peace, *Tracking Nuclear Proliferation,* 1995.

INDIA: Nuclear Infrastructure

NAME/LOCATION OF FACILITY	TYPE/STATUS	IAEA SAFEGUARDS
P O W E R R E A C T O R S		
Tarapur I	Light-water, LEU, 150 MWe; operating.	Yes[1]
Tarpur II	Light-water, LEU, 150 MWe; operating.	Yes
Tarapur III	Heavy-water, natural U, 500 MWe; site preparation.	No
Tarapur IV	Heavy-water, natural U, 500 MWe; site preparation.	No
Rajasthan I Kota	Heavy-water, natural U, 207 MWe; operating.	Yes
Rajasthan II	Heavy-water, natural U, 207 MWe; operating.	Yes
Rajasthan III Kota	Heavy-water, natural U, 220 MWe; under construction.	No
Rajasthan IV	Heavy-water, natural U, 220 MWe; under construction.	No
Madras I Kalpakkam	Heavy-water, natural U, 220 MWe; operating.	No
Madras II	Heavy-water, natural U, 220 MWe; operating.	No
Narora I	Heavy-water, natural U, 220 MWe; operating.	No
Narora II	Heavy-water, natural U, 220 MWe; operating.	No
Kakrapar I	Heavy-water, natural U, 220 MWe; operating.	No
Kakrapar II	Heavy-water, natural U, 220 MWe; commissioned.	No
Kaiga I Karnataka	Heavy-water, natural U, 220 MWe; under construction.	No
Kaiga II	Heavy-water, natural U, 220 MWe; under construction.	No
Koodankulam I	Light-water, LEU, 500 MWe; site preparation.	No
Koodankulam II	Light-water, LEU, 500 MWe; site preparation.	No
R E S E A R C H R E A C T O R S		
Apsara Trombay	Light-water, medium-enriched uranium, 1MWt; operating.	No
Cirus Trombay	Heavy-water, natural U, 40 MWt; operating.	No
Zerlina Trombay	Heavy-water, variable fuel, 400 Wt; decommissioned.	No
Purnima II Trombay	Uranium-233, .005 KWt; dismantled.	No
Purnima III Trombay	Uranium-233, 30 KWt; operating.	No
Kamini Kalpakkam	Uranium-233, 30 KWt; operating.	No
Dhruva Trombay	Heavy-water, natural U, 100 MWt; operating.	No
Fast Breeder Test Reactor (FBTR), Kalpakkam	Plutonium and natural U, 15 MWe; operating.	No
U R A N I U M E N R I C H M E N T		
Tombay	Pilot-scale ultracentrifuge plant; operating.	No
Rattehalli	Pilot-scale ultracentrifuge plant; operating.	No

INDIA (cont'd.)

NAME/LOCATION OF FACILITY	TYPE/STATUS	IAEA SAFEGUARDS
REPROCESSING (PLUTONIUM EXTRACTION)		
Trombay	Medium-scale; operating.	No
Tarapur	Large-scale; operating.	Only when safeguarded fuel is present
Kalpakkam	Laboratory-scale; operating.	No
Kalpakkam	Large-scale; under construction.	No
Kalpakkam	Fast-reeder fuel reprocessing plant; under construction.[2]	No
URANIUM PROCESSING		
Jaduguda	Mining and milling; operating.	(Not applicable)
Hyderabad	Uranium purification (UO_2); operating.	No
Hyderabad	Fuel fabrication; operating.	Partial
Trombay	Uranium conversion (UF_6); operating.	No
Trombay	Fuel fabrication; operating.	No
Tarapur	Mixed uranium-plutonium oxide (MOX) fuel fabrication; operating.	Only when safeguarded fuel is present
HEAVY WATER PRODUCTION[3]		
Nangal	Operating	No
Baroda	Intermittent operation	No
Tuticorin	Operating	No
Talcher	Operating	No
Kota	Operating	No
Thal-Vaishet	Operating	No
Manuguru	Operating	No
Hazira	Operating	No

Abbreviations:

HEU	=	highly enriched uranium
LEU	=	low-enriched uranium
nat. U	=	natural uranium
MWe	=	millions of watts of electrical output
MWt	=	millions of watts of thermal output
KWt	=	thousands of watts of thermal output

NOTES (India Chart)

1. In February 1994, India agreed to place the spent fuel from the U.S.-supplied Tarapur I and II reactors under International Atomic Energy Agency (IAEA) safeguards in perpetuity, following the expiration of the Indo-U.S. nuclear cooperation agreement covering the transfer of the reactors. That agreement had provided for IAEA safeguards to be applied to the plants and all of the plutonium-bearing fuel produced in them during the agreement's 30-year duration, triggering a dispute about whether IAEA monitoring was to continue thereafter.

Indian officials have indicated that India would like to reprocess the reactor's spent fuel at the Tarapur reprocessing facility under IAEA monitoring to produce plutonium for mixed oxide (plutonium-uranium) fuel (MOX), which would then be used to refuel the two reactors. In this context, the IAEA reportedly is expanding its presence at the reprocessing plant. However, India and the United States differ on whether India must obtain U.S. approval before it reprocesses the fuel, with Washington insisting on the need for such consent. The United States argues that such approval was required under the terms of the Indo-U.S. agreement for cooperation and that U.S. approval rights did not lapse with the expiration of that accord. India insists that the United States had granted its approval in the late 1960s and that, in any event, the approval rights expired with the overall agreement. See Mark Hibbs, "Tarapur Negotiations Deadlocked; U.S. Seeks 'Broader Solution,'" *Nuclear Fuel*, January 3, 1994, p. 10; Mark Hibbs, "Safeguards Deal on TAPS BWRs Left Consent Issue Unresolved," *Nucleonics Week*, March 10, 1994, p. 7.

Throughout much of 1994 the future fuel supply for the reactors remained in doubt. Neither the United States, which ended low-enriched uranium fuel shipments to the plants in 1982, nor France, which served as a substitute fuel supplier from 1982 to 1993, when the overall nuclear cooperation Indo-U.S. agreement expired, was prepared to supply the facility in the future. They and other members of the Nuclear Suppliers Group (NSG) (including Western Europe, Japan, and Russia) have agreed not to make nuclear transfers to states, such as India, that are not among the five nuclear-weapon states recognized by the NPT and which continue to operate nuclear facilities not subject to IAEA inspection. Although the reactors could operate on MOX fuel instead of low-enriched uranium, India lacks sufficient capacity to fabricate mixed oxide fuel for the reactors.

In January 1995, India announced that China, which is not a member of the NSG, would supply the low-enriched uranium fuel for the reactors. (See Krishnan Guruswamy, "India-Nuclear," *Associated Press*, January 7, 1995; "India Buying Chinese Uranium," *Washington Post*, January 8, 1995.) The development came as a surprise given the strategic rivalry between the two countries and the fact that India considers itself under a nuclear threat from China.

In February 1994, Indian officials also gave indications that India may be willing to apply IAEA safeguards at the currently unsafeguarded Kalpakkam reprocessing facility, as part of a safeguards "package deal" with the United States, but, as of early 1995, India had not agreed to these new restrictions. See Mark Hibbs, "India May Apply IAEA Safeguards on Future Plutonium Separation," *Nuclear Fuel*, February 14, 1994, p. 9.

2. Neel Patri, "India Might Take Another Look at Plans to Expand Heavy Water Plant," *Nuclear Fuel*, May 9, 1994, p. 14.

3. For many years the output of these facilities has been far below their design capabilities, necessitating clandestine imports of heavy water during the 1980s. Recently output has increased, and in April 1994 India signed a contract for the export of 100 tons of heavy water to South Korea. Another contract was signed in September 1994 with Romania for the export of 350 tons of heavy water to that country. See Leonard S. Spector with Jacqueline R. Smith, *Nuclear Ambitions* (Boulder, CO.: Westview Press, 1990), pp. 73–75; "Delhi Signs Accord on Supply of Heavy Water," Delhi, *All India Radio Network*, April 8, 1994, in *FBIS-EAS-94-069*, April 11, 1994, p. 46; "Romania to Import 350 Tonnes of Indian Heavy Water," *Reuters*, September 23, 1994.

Additional References

1991: "World Survey: Waiting for a New Dawn," *Nuclear Engineering International*, June 1991, p. 22. **1992:** "Hope for Foreign Reactors Ends in Both India and Pakistan," *Nucleonics Week*, January 23, 1992, p. 3; Shahid-ur-Rehman Khan, "India and Pakistan Exchange Lists of Nuclear Facilities," *Nucleonics Week*, January 9, 1992, p. 10; Mark Hibbs, "Second Indian Enrichment Facility Using Centrifuges Is Operational," *Nucleonics Week*, March 26, 1992, pp. 9–10; Mark Hibbs, "India and Pakistan Fail to Include New SWU Plants on Exchanged Lists," *Nuclear Fuel*, March 30, 1992, p. 6; "Kakrapur Startup," *Nuclear Engineering International*, November 1992, p. 12; "AEC Denies Reports on Making Atomic Bombs," *Patriot*, October 23, 1992, in *JPRS-TND-92-046*, December 11, 1992, p. 11. **1993:** Interview with Indian official, February 1993; "World Nuclear Industry Handbook," *Nuclear Industry International*, 1993; Neel Patri, "Indian Budget Gives No Increase in Nuclear Plant Building Money," *Nucleonics Week*, March 11, 1993, p. 11; Neel Patri, "India Scaling Down Kundankulam as Russian Reactor Plan Fades," *Nucleonics Week*, April 15, 1993, p. 13; Neel Patri, "Thorium-Burning Kakrapar-1 Declared Commercial by NPC," *Nucleonics Week*, May 13, 1993, p. 4; "India: FBTR Raising Power," *Nucleonics Week*, December 16, 1993, p. 15. **1994:** Neel Patri, "Narora-1 Turbine Fire Spoils Indian Nuclear Production, Profits," *Nucleonics Week*, April 7, 1994, p. 3; Neel Patri, "Indian Lawmakers Criticize Cost, Delays in Nuclear Power Program," *Nucleonics Week*, April 28, 1994, p. 2. **1995**: Neel Patri, "Narora-1 Returns to Service, After Fire Prevention Backfits," *Nucleonics Week*, January 5, 1995, p. 3.

Pakistan

Pakistan, which is not a party to the Nuclear Non-Proliferation Treaty (NPT), secretly launched its nuclear program in 1972, in the aftermath of its defeat in the 1971 Indo-Pakistani War. The program, which accelerated dramatically after India's nuclear test in May 1974, made substantial progress by the early 1980s. A 1983 U.S. State Department analysis of the Pakistani nuclear-weapons effort declared that there was "unambiguous evidence that Pakistan is actively pursuing a nuclear-weapons development program." The report highlighted Pakistan's progress in key areas of weapons manufacture, its critical dependence on clandestine efforts to procure nuclear equipment from private Western firms, and its receipt of nuclear assistance from China, including assistance "in the area of fissile material production and possibly also nuclear device design."[1] The centerpiece of the program is Pakistan's Kahuta enrichment plant, which is not subject to International Atomic Energy Agency (IAEA) safeguards.

In October 1990, the Bush Administration terminated all economic and military aid to Pakistan after being unable to certify to Congress that Pakistan did not "possess a nuclear explosive device," as required by the U.S. law known as the Pressler Amendment.[2]

In April 1994, the U.S. State Department submitted a report to Congress projecting that Pakistan "could assemble a limited number of nuclear weapons in a relatively short timeframe."[3] A portion of Pakistan's potential arsenal apparently consists of a number of complete, but unassembled, nuclear weapons, which could be readied for use in hours. The remainder consists of weapons-grade nuclear material in bulk form and the key non-nuclear components that together could be fashioned into weapons in weeks or possibly days. In all, Pakistan might be able to deploy between fifteen and twenty-five nuclear weapons. Pakistan's nuclear weapons are thought to have yields comparable to the device used on Nagasaki.[4]

In August 1994, former Pakistani Prime Minister Nawaz Sharif declared that Pakistan possessed nuclear weapons, but the official position of the Pakistani government is that, though able to manufacture such weapons, Pakistan has not done so.[5] According to Pakistani declarations that have been confirmed privately by U.S. officials, in July 1991 Pakistan froze the further production of weapons-grade nuclear material at the Kahuta uranium enrichment plant and the manufacture of key nuclear weapons components.[6]

However, Pakistan's ability to produce weapons-usable nuclear materials will be further enhanced upon completion of a plutonium-production reactor now under construction at Khusab. The reactor, which is being built with Chinese assistance according to U.S. officials, is not subject to IAEA inspection and, when completed, will provide Pakistan with its first source of unsafeguarded plutonium-bearing spent fuel. If plutonium from that fuel is extracted at the near-by Chasma reprocessing plant or at the pilot-scale plant at Rawalpindi—both of which are thought to be ready to operate, but neither of which is currently subject to IAEA inspection—Pakistan could obtain plutonium that it would be legally free to use for nuclear arms.[7] (China is also supplying Pakistan a nuclear power plant, which is under construction at Chasma; it will be placed under IAEA inspection.)

Delivery Capabilities. Pakistan possesses a variety of nuclear-capable fighter-bomber aircraft, including the U.S.-supplied F-16s, that could be modified to deliver nuclear weapons in a crisis. There is also growing evidence that Pakistan has received nuclear-capable, 280-km range M-11 missiles from China, or key components for the system. It had not deployed this system as of early 1995, but apparently could take this step relatively quickly.[8]

In August 1993, the United States imposed sanctions on Pakistan's space agency and on China's Ministry of Aerospace Industries because of the sale of M-11 components. The sanctions against the latter were lifted in October 1994 after China agreed to a ban on the sale of missiles inherently capable of carrying a 500-kg payload to a distance of 300 km, or more, a ban which China agreed prohibited further exports of the M-11.[9] In the mid-1980s, also with Chinese assistance, Pakistan launched a program to develop two short-range nuclear-capable ballistic missiles, the Hatf-I and Hatf-II, with ranges of 80 km and 300 km, respectively. U.S. intelligence sources believe that the Hatf-I has probably already been deployed but that the Hatf-II will not be available for a number of years.[10]

Confidence Building and Arms Control. Pakistan, whose security concerns are dominated by the threat from its western neighbor, has stated that it is prepared to join the NPT or accept other non-proliferation measures if India does so, but India has rejected these proposals on the grounds that they do not address the nuclear threat it faces from China.[11] In June 1991, Pakistani Prime Minister Nawaz Sharif attempted to meet these concerns, in part, by proposing that the United States, the Soviet Union, and China mediate nuclear arms control negotiations between Pakistan and India. Although the United States, Russia (as the nuclear-weapon-state successor to the Soviet Union), and China have stated they would participate in such talks, India has rejected this proposal.

Bilateral nuclear arms control agreements remain elusive, but Pakistan and India have implemented a number of bilateral confidence-building measures, including a military-to-military hot-line and an agreement, which entered into force in January 1991, prohibiting the two states from attacking each other's nuclear installations. Lists of facilities covered by this agreement were exchanged in January 1992 and January 1993, although the first such data exchange was marred by accusations that both sides had failed to list at least one important nuclear plant.[12] In August 1992, the two states brought into force agreements on mutual advance notification of military exercises and on the avoidance of over-flights of military aircraft. They also signed a bilateral accord banning the possession, manufacture, and use of chemical weapons. The last, however, did not contain any verification measures. Both states also became original signatories to the Chemical Weapons Convention in mid-January 1993, but neither has ratified the pact.[13] According to U.S. officials, both have chemical weapons programs.

Over the last two years, in addition to enforcing the Pressler Amendment, U.S. diplomacy in South Asia has supported Indo-Pakistani confidence-building measures and has encouraged negotiations between the two states on nuclear issues, within the context of the five-power talks proposed by Pakistan.

In late 1992, the U.S. Congress added new provisions to the Foreign Assistance Act, encouraging the president to pursue regional nuclear non-proliferation initiatives in South Asia and requiring him to submit twice-yearly reports, beginning in April 1993, on the nuclear weapon and ballistic missile programs in China, India, and Pakistan. Among other issues, the president is to determine whether any of these states possesses a nuclear explosive device. While not imposing sanctions, the legislation for the first time specifically treated India on a par with Pakistan as a proliferation concern.

In March 1994, in the context of its global initiative aimed at a verifiable ban on the production of fissile material for nuclear explosives, the Clinton Administration presented proposals to both Pakistan and India intended to advance that goal in a South Asia-specific context. Its proposal to the government of Pakistan would "verifiably cap Pakistan's nuclear weapons material production in return for which Pakistan would be provided some relief from existing legislative sanctions [namely, those imposed under the Pressler Amendment]."[14] One element of the relief would be the release of up to thirty-six F-16 fighter aircraft previously purchased by Pakistan. With respect to India, the administration sought a "commitment similar to, but separate from, that sought from Pakistan," using, *inter alia*, the prospect of increased scientific and technological cooperation as an incentive.[15]

However, both Pakistan and India rejected the regional "Fissile Material Cut-off" proposal, the former on the grounds that it called for a unilateral capping of the Pakistani nuclear program without explicitly calling for similar restraints from India. Pakistani Prime Minister Benazir Bhutto stated that "[if Pakistan was] unilaterally pressed for the capping, it [would] be discriminatory, and Pakistan [would] not agree to it." She added that Pakistan might soften its position if India did the same.[16] India oppposed this regional arms control framework because it would place constraints only on itself and Pakistan, leaving China free to maintain its current nuclear status. From India's perspective, any regional approach would have to include all "geopolitically relevant" states, i.e. China, among others. As an alternative, India called for a global denuclearization accord that would eliminate all nuclear weapons by the year 2010, including those of the superpowers.[17]

Accordingly, India—together with the United States and others—is co-sponsoring a multilateral treaty at the Conference on Disarmament in Geneva that would impose a prospective global ban on the production of fissile materials for nuclear weapons or not under IAEA safeguards. Pakistan, however, is blocking its implementation by demanding that it extend to existing stocks of fissile material.

In early 1995, the Clinton Administration was recasting its South Asia-specific proposal as a long-term goal and was seeking to improve relations with both countries through the signing of military cooperation agreements.[18]

NOTES

[1]See U.S. Department of State, "The Pakistani Nuclear Program," June 23, 1983, SECRET/NOFORN/ORCON released under the Freedom of Information Act to the National Security Archive, January 17, 1991. (The National Security Archive is a private research organization based in Washington, DC.)

[2]The Pressler Amendment was adopted in 1985. (See Foreign Assistance Act of 1961, section 620(e).) Until 1990, U.S. presidents had certified that Pakistan did not possess a nuclear explosive device. During the spring of 1990, however, it is believed that the threat of war with India led Pakistan to fabricate cores for several nuclear weapons from pre-existing stocks of weapons-grade uranium; this led to the U.S. aid cut-off later in the year.

[3]See U.S. State Department, "Report to Congress: Update on Progress Toward Regional Nonproliferation in South Asia," April 1994.

[4]See "Pakistan Has Seven Nuclear Weapons," *Reuters*, December 1, 1992 (reporting on an NBC News report stating that Pakistan possessed "at least seven" nuclear devices); "Pakistan's Atomic Bomb," *Foreign Report*, January 12, 1989, p. 1; Hedrick Smith, "A Bomb Ticks in Pakistan," *New York Times Magazine*, March 6, 1988, p. 38; interview with senior U.S. official, fall 1992; David Albright and Mark Hibbs, "Pakistan's Bomb: Out of the Closet," *Bulletin of the Atomic Scientists*, July/August 1992, p. 38; U.S. Department of State, "Memorandum for Dr. Kissinger; Subject: Official Visit of Pakistan Prime Minister Mohammad Khan Junejo: Background and Talking Points," July 18, 1986, SECRET/SENSITIVE, released under the Freedom of Information Act to the National Security Archive.

[5]See Alistair Lyon, "Pakistani Leaders Deny Nuclear Bomb Claim," *Reuters*, August 24, 1994; Steve Pagani, "IAEA Says Unable to Verify Pakistan Atom Bomb Report," *Reuters*, August 24, 1994; Alistair Lyon, "Pakistani Ex-Premier Stands By Nuclear Revelation," *Reuters*, August 25, 1994.

[6]See U.S. State Department, "Report to Congress," *op. cit.*; R. Jeffrey Smith, "Pakistan Can Build One Nuclear Device, Foreign Official Says," *Washington Post*, February 7, 1992; "Khan Notes Freeze on Program," Karachi, *AMN*, February 9, 1992, in *JPRS-TND*, April 3, 1992, p. 6; Gene Kramer, "U.S.-Pakistan," *Associated Press*, February 10, 1992; Rauf Siddiqi, Ann MacLachlan, "No 'Direct Progress' in Talks, But Pakistan, U.S. Continue Effort," *Nucleonics Week*, February 20, 1992, p. 15; Ali Sarwar Naqvi, "Don't Blame Pakistan," *Washington Post*, July 16, 1992.

[7]See Mark Hibbs, "Bhutto May Finish Plutonium Reactor Without Agreement on Fissile Stocks," *Nucleonics Week*, October 6, 1994, p. 10; interview with U.S. official, July 1994.

China is a nuclear-weapon state party to the NPT. If Chinese assistance for the Khusab reactor includes equipment that is especially designed or prepared for use in a nuclear reactor, the transfer would violate China's obligations under Article III.2 of the Treaty, which prohibits such transfers unless placed under IAEA safeguards in the recipient state. In addition, any Chinese assistance to the Pakistani nuclear weapons program would violate China's obligation under Article I of the Treaty. Pakistan is not a party to the NPT, however, and has not accepted any international obligation that would prohibit its operation of the Khusab reactor without IAEA monitoring or prohibit its manufacture of nuclear arms. See also note 1 to Pakistan chart, p. 102.

[8]See William C. Potter and Harlan W. Jencks, *The International Missile Bazaar* (Boulder, CO: Westview Press, 1994), p. 81; "U.S. Warns China, Pakistan Against Missile Sale," *Reuters*, September 7, 1994; R. Jeffrey Smith and Thomas W. Lippman, "Pakistan M-11 Funding Is Reported," *Washington Post*, September 8, 1994; Sid Balsam, "China-U.S.: China Rebuts U.S. Missile Claim," *United Press International*, October 3, 1994; interviews with U.S. officials, fall 1994.

[9]See Elaine Sciolino, "U.S. and Chinese Reach Agreement on Missile Export," *New York Times*, October 5, 1994; Daniel Williams, "U.S. Deal With China Allows High-Tech Sales in Exchange for Pledge," *Washington Post*, October 5, 1994.

[10]Interviews with U.S. officials, fall 1994; William C. Potter and Harlan W. Jencks, *The International Missile Bazaar, op. cit.*, p. 84.

[11]Various Pakistani nuclear arms control and non-proliferation initiatives are listed in " 'Text' of Sharif Speech on Nuclear Issue," *Nation*, June 7, 1991, in *FBIS-NES*, June 10, 1991, p. 68.

[12]Pakistan protested the absence of a gas centrifuge uranium enrichment facility in Karnataka state (presumably the Rattehalli plant) from the Indian list, while India objected to Pakistan's failure to list the Golra enrichment facility near Islamabad. Mark Hibbs, "Second Indian Enrichment Facility Using Centrifuges Is Operational," *Nucleonics Week*, March 26, 1992; "India and Pakistan Fail to Include New SWU Plants on Exchanged Lists," *Nuclear Fuel*, March 30, 1992.

[13]There is some question as to whether the two will ratify the convention, because of its intrusive inspection provisions. In theory, under the accord, either state could demand a challenge inspection of the other's sensitive nuclear sites, subject to certain restrictions, if it had a reasonable basis for believing that chemical weapons were present. India has charged that Pakistan is making chemical arms at the Kahuta enrichment plant complex. See Mark Hibbs, "Regional Nuclear Gambit Checked, U.S. Has Few Cards to Move India," *Nucleonics Week*, April 2, 1992.

[14]See U.S. State Department, "Report to Congress," *op. cit.*

[15]*Ibid.*

[16]John Ward Anderson, "Pakistan Rebuffs U.S. on A-Bomb," *Washington Post*, April 8, 1994.

[17]India also opposed the envisioned release of the nuclear-capable F-16s to Pakistan because they would increase the threat to its security. See John F. Burns, "India Rejects U.S. Bid for Nuclear Pact With Pakistan," *New York Times*, March 26, 1994; John-Thor Dahlburg, "Plan to Ship F-16s to Pakistan Raises India's Ire," *Los Angeles Times*, March 17, 1994; John F. Burns, "India Resists Plan to Curb Nuclear Arms," *New York Times*, May 15, 1994; Thomas W. Lippman, "U.S. Effort to Curb Nuclear Weapons in Peril as India Insists on Limits for China," *Washington Post*, July 7, 1994.

[18]Dana Priest, "U.S., Pakistan to Renew Talks," *Washington Post*, January 11, 1995; John F. Burns, "U.S.-India Pact on Military Cooperation," *New York Times*, January 13, 1995; Dana Priest, "U.S. Hopes India Accord Will Reduce Nuclear Threat in South Asia," *Washington Post*, January 14, 1995.

Large-scale uranium enrichment plant designed to produce enough weapons-grade uranium for a number of nuclear devices per year: not subject to IAEA inspection.

Uranium enrichment R&D facility/pilot plant(?): not subject to IAEA inspection.

Pakistan Institute of Nuclear Science and Technology (PINSTECH). *Laboratory and pilot-scale plant for plutonium extraction (the second not yet operating): neither subject to IAEA inspection. U.S.-supplied PARR-1 research reactor: subject to IAEA safeguards; may have been used clandestinely to produce tritium for advanced nuclear weapons; power increased to 10 megawatts in 1992.*

50-70 Mwt research/ plutonium production reactor under construction with Chinese assistance: not under IAEA inspection. If completed, in conjunction with the nearby large plutonium extraction plant at Chasma and the pilot-scale plant at Rawalpindi, the reactor could be the source of a significant inventory of unsafeguarded weapons-usable plutonium.

Possible nuclear test site.

Large plutonium extraction plant presumed near completion: not subject to IAEA inspection. Chinese-supplied 300 MWe nuclear power reactor in early stages of construction: to be subject to IAEA inspection.

Canadian-supplied KANUPP nuclear power reactor: subject to IAEA inspection.

Arabian Sea

0   250
MILES

Italicized names represent nuclear-related sites. See chart.

Carnegie Endowment for International Peace, *Tracking Nuclear Proliferation*, 1995.

UZBEKISTAN
TAJIK.
TURKMENISTAN
CHINA
Kashmir (disputed)
AFGHANISTAN
Golra
Islamabad ★ *Kahuta*
Rawalpindi *Sihala*
Chasma *Khusab*
Lahore
Multan
Dera Ghazi Khan
PAKISTAN
Chagai Hills
IRAN
INDIA
Karachi
INDIA

PAKISTAN: Nuclear Infrastructure

NAME/LOCATION OF FACILITY	TYPE/STATUS	IAEA SAFEGUARDS
POWER REACTORS		
KANUPP Karachi	Heavy-water, natural U, 125 MWe; operating.	Yes
Chasma	Light-water, LEU, 300 MWe; under construction.	Planned
RESEARCH REACTORS		
Pakistan Atomic Research Reactor (PARR), Rawalpindi	Light-water, originally HEU, modified to use LEU fuel, 10 MWt; operating.	Yes
PARR 2, Rawalpindi	Pool-type, light-water, enriched uranium, 27 KWt; operating.	Yes
Research/Plutonium Production Reactor, Khusab	HEU, 50 MWt; under construction.	No
URANIUM ENRICHMENT		
Kahuta	Large-scale ultracentrifuge facility; operating (no current production of weapons-grade uranium).	No
Sihala	Experimental-scale ultracentrifuge facility; operating.	No
Golra	Ultracentrifuge plant reportedly to be used as testing facility; under construction? operating?	No
REPROCESSING (PLUTONIUM EXTRACTION)		
Chashma	Terminated by France (1978); construction may be nearly complete using indigenous resources.	No[1]
New Labs Rawalpindi	Cold tests conducted; not known to be operating.	No
PINSTECH, Rawalpindi	Experimental-scale plant	No
URANIUM PROCESSING		
Dera Ghazi Khan	Uranium mining and milling; operating.	N/A (Not applicable)
Lahore	Milling; operating.	N/A
Dera Ghazi Khan	Uranium conversion (UF_6); operating.	No
Chashma/Kundian	Fuel fabrication; operating.	No
HEAVY WATER PRODUCTION		
Multan	Operating	No
Karachi	Operating	No
TRITIUM PURIFICATION		
150 km south of Rawalpindi	Tested in 1987	No

Abbreviations:

HEU	=	highly enriched uranium
LEU	=	low-enriched uranium
nat. U	=	natural uranium
MWe	=	millions of watts of electrical output
MWt	=	millions of watts of thermal output
KWt	=	thousands of watts of thermal output

NOTES (Pakistan Chart)

1. Safeguards may be required because of the use of French technology supplied in the 1970s, under the Franco-Pakistani bilateral supply agreement for the plant, which requires such monitoring. Because France refused to complete the facility, however, Pakistan has never acknowledged that it is obligated to place the facility under IAEA inspection, despite its incorporation of the French technology.

Additional References

1990: Leonard S. Spector with Jacqueline R. Smith, *Nuclear Ambitions* (Boulder, CO: Westview Press, 1990). **1991:** ''U.S.-Supplied Nuclear Research Reactor Modified,'' *Agence France Presse*, March 17, 1991, in *FBIS-NES*. **1992:** ''France and Pakistan in Accord on Compensation,'' *Nuclear Engineering International*, March 1992, p. 7; ''Work on Plant Begins,'' *Frontier Post*, July 31, 1992, in *JPRS-TND-92-027*, August 5, 1992, p. 12; Shahid-ur-Rehman, ''Chinese Official Says Chasma Design is Near Completion,'' *Nucleonics Week*, December 17, 1992, pp. 8–9. **1993:** Shahid-ur-Rehman Khan, ''Construction Officially Underway by CNNC for Pakistan's Chashnupp,'' *Nucleonics Week*, August 5, 1993, p. 5.

North Korea

North Korea, a state party to the Nuclear Non-Proliferation Treaty (NPT) since 1985, is believed to have pursued an active nuclear weapons program, in violation of the Treaty, centered around a number of facilities at the Yongbyon Nuclear Research Center. In October 1994, as part of a complicated understanding with the United States, North Korea froze operations at most of these facilities, effectively halting the production of new weapons-usable nuclear materials. It may be continuing work, however, on other aspects of its nuclear weapons program, such as designing a nuclear weapon or fabricating such weapons from materials it already possesses.

The key facilities at Yongbyon include an operational 5 MWe experimental nuclear power reactor, a partially completed large-scale reprocessing plant for plutonium extraction, a number of radiochemistry laboratories (or ''hot cells'') that can be used for plutonium extraction, a high-explosive testing facility, a fuel fabrication plant, and a partially completed 50 MWe power reactor. It was also building a 200 MWe reactor at Teachon until agreeing to freeze construction of the facility under its October 1994 understanding with the United States.[1]

Although North Korea signed the NPT in 1985, it did not permit the International Atomic Energy Agency (IAEA) to conduct inspections, as required by the Treaty, until May 1992. In the interim, U.S. intelligence agencies believe that North Korea has extracted plutonium at the Yongbyon reprocessing plant—and possibly at a number of hot cells—using irradiated fuel rods from the 5 MWe reactor, which is thought to have been partially or fully refueled in 1989. They estimate that North Korea may have obtained as much as 12 kg of plutonium and that there is a ''better than even chance'' it has manufactured one or two nuclear weapons.[2]

The 5 MWe reactor's inventory of spent fuel was again unloaded in May 1994. If reprocessed, this material could provide enough plutonium for four or five nuclear weapons. In addition, if completed, the 50 MWe reactor would have the potential to produce enough material for ten to twelve nuclear bombs a year.[3]

Under the terms of the U.S.-North Korean ''Agreed Framework'' concluded on October 21, 1994, however, North Korea has pledged:(1) to freeze operations at, or construction of, all of these reactors and at the Yongbyon reprocessing plant, with the freeze to be verified by the IAEA; (2) not to separate plutonium from the spent fuel removed from the 5 MWe reactor in May 1994 (the status of the fuel to be monitored by the IAEA); (3) to ship, at some point, the spent fuel out of North Korea, and (4) to dismantle thereafter all facilities of proliferation concern. In exchange, North Korea will receive two, less proliferation-prone, light-water reactors (LWRs) and a number of other energy-related inducements as well as security assurances.[4]

The Inspection Controversy. The U.S.-North Korean Agreed Framework culminated a decade of ups and downs in the relationship between North Korea and the international non-proliferation regime. As noted above, North Korea became a party to the NPT in 1985 but did not ratify a safeguards agreement with the IAEA, as required by the Treaty, until April 9, 1992. Under the agreement, North Korea is required to place all of its nuclear materials and related facilities under IAEA monitoring. In May 1992, the IAEA initiated a series of inspections and ''visits'' to verify North Korea's initial inventory of nuclear facilities and materials.[5] During this process, in the summer and fall of 1992, the IAEA found discrepancies in North Korea's declaration of levels of past plutonium production.

Specifically, the IAEA's chemical analysis of samples of plutonium provided by Pyongyang contradicted the latter's claim that it had previously separated only grams of plutonium in a one-time "experiment." Instead, the IAEA results indicated that the North had separated plutonium in four campaigns over three years, starting in 1989.[6]

The findings raised further concern because they also appeared to contradict North Korea's claim that it had not replaced the core of the 5 MWe reactor since the unit began operating in 1986 but had separated plutonium only from a handful of defective fuel rods that it had removed from the facility. U.S. intelligence analysts believed, however, that the reactor's core had been replaced during a 100-day period when the unit was shut down in 1989, providing the North with a stockpile of plutonium-bearing spent fuel from which it had subsequently extracted a significant amount of plutonium at the Yongbyon reprocessing plant—possibly enough for one or two nuclear devices.[7] The IAEA finding that the North had engaged in multiple plutonium separation campaigns thus lent credence to the U.S. view that North Korea might have a substantial plutonium stockpile.

In an effort to resolve the discrepancies that the IAEA found in North Korea's declaration regarding plutonium production, the IAEA called, in early 1993, for a "special inspection" of two undeclared sites near the Yongbyon nuclear complex that were thought to contain wastes from the plutonium separation process. North Korea refused to accept the inspection and announced it was withdrawing from the NPT, which permits such action on 90 days notice if a party's "supreme national interests" are jeopardized. After a round of negotiations with the United States in June 1993, North Korea agreed to suspend its withdrawal. However, North Korea asserted that since it was no longer a full party to the NPT, the IAEA no longer had the right to conduct even normal "ad hoc and routine" inspections. Over the ensuing nine months, Pyongyang severely constrained IAEA inspection activities needed to preserve the "continuity safeguards," leading IAEA Director General Hans Blix to declare, in December 1993, that agency safeguards in North Korea could no longer provide "any meaningful assurances" that nuclear materials were not being diverted to weapons uses.[8]

In March 1994, under the threat of UN economic sanctions, North Korea once again agreed to an IAEA inspection of its declared facilities but at the last moment blocked the agency from taking key radioactive samples at the plutonium extraction plant at Yongbyon.[9] The crisis escalated further in mid-May 1994, when North Korea started to defuel the 5 MWe reactor, while refusing to implement procedures demanded by the IAEA to segregate 300 care-fully selected fuel rods from the 8,000-rod core.[10] Analysis of the radioactive signature of the segregated rods would have indicated how long they had been in the reactor, permitting the IAEA to determine whether it had been refueled in 1989—and, thus, whether North Korea might have been able to obtain plutonium for one or two nuclear devices.

As Pyongyang accelerated and completed the defueling, Hans Blix declared in a letter to the UN Security Council, on June 2, 1994, that the "agency's ability to ascertain, with sufficient confidence, whether nuclear material from the reactor has been diverted in the past, has been . . . lost."[11] A special inspection of the two undeclared waste sites thus apparently remained the IAEA's principal option for determining past levels of plutonium production. However, North Korea continued to insist that it would never allow inspections at the two sites, which it claimed were military facilities and therefore off-limits to the agency. To penalize North Korea for refusing to comply with IAEA inspection requirements during the defueling of the Yongbyon reactor, in early June, the agency suspended all technical assistance to the North. This led Pyongyang to announce on June 13, 1994, that it was withdrawing from the IAEA (a step that did not, however, amount to a renunciation of its safeguards obligations under the NPT).[12]

These developments prompted the United States to circulate a two-phase proposal to the Security Council on June 15, 1994, for sanctions against North Korea. The first phase of the sanctions, which were to be activated after a grace period, was a worldwide ban on arms imports from, and arms exports to, North Korea, along with a downgrading of diplomatic ties. In the second phase, to be triggered if the North continued to reject the IAEA's demands, a worldwide ban on financial dealings with Pyongyang would be implemented.[13]

The crisis eased after former President Jimmy Carter met with North Korean President Kim Il Sung on June 16–17, 1994. The North Korean leader agreed to freeze his country's nuclear program if the United States resumed high-level talks. These negotiations, which did not take place until early August because of the sudden death of Kim Il Sung on July 9, proved successful in hammering out an "Agreed Statement" on August 12, 1994, under which, in broad terms, North Korea agreed to dismantle the elements of its nuclear program that appeared to be linked to the production of nuclear arms in return for the supply of two, less proliferation-prone, light-water reactors and a number of other energy and security-related inducements.[14]

The "Agreed Framework." The two sides proceeded with a series of expert-level discussions and another round of high-level talks to work out the modalities of the agreement. After a period of stalemate, they managed to conclude an "Agreed Framework," which was signed on October 21, 1994.[15] The accord provides, *inter alia,* for the establishment of an international consortium, represented by the United States, that will finance and supply to North Korea two LWRs by the target date 2003. In return, North Korea agreed immediately to freeze its nuclear program, an undertaking that included pledges not to refuel the 5 MWe Yongbyon reactor, to halt construction of the 50 MWe reactor at that site and of the 200 MWe reactor at Taechon, to seal the Yongbyon plutonium separation plant and the fuel fabrication plant at the site, and to provide for the storage, without plutonium separation, of the spent fuel discharged from the 5 MWe reactor in June 1994. Pyongyang also agreed that the spent fuel would be removed from North Korea as nuclear components for the first LWR are supplied and that all of the facilities where activities were frozen would be dismantled by the time that the second LWR began operating.

To offset the supposed energy deficit that will result by the "freezing" of North Korea's graphite-moderated reactors and related facilities, the United States was to arrange, within one month of the agreement, for the delivery to North Korea (within three months) of heavy oil for heating and electricity production "that will reach a rate of 500,000 tons annually."

Under the agreement, North Korea will remain a party to the NPT. However, it will not be required to come into full compliance with its safeguards agreement with the IAEA until a "significant portion of the LWR project is completed, but before delivery of key nuclear components." This delay, of from four to six years, will result in postponment of IAEA verification of the accuracy and completeness of North Korea's initial report on the nuclear materials in its possession. More specifically, it will postpone IAEA special inspections of the two waste sites noted above and thus a determination of whether the North possesses sufficient plutonium for a nuclear weapon.

The pact also provided for steps toward normalization of relations between North Korea and the United States, U.S. assurances against the threat or use of nuclear weapons against the North, and a North Korean commitment to implement the 1992 North-South Joint Declaration on the Denuclearization of the Korean Peninsula.[16]

Proponents of the agreement have pointed to the security benefits inherent in the accord. They stress that it freezes, and then dismantles, a nuclear program that would have eventually given North Korea the capability to produce dozens of nuclear weapons per year, a portion of which might have been exported. Another advantage cited is that North Korea has effectively agreed, for the first time, to IAEA inspection of the two undeclared waste sites, which will help reveal the history of past plutonium production. Moreover, proponents note that the agreement places restrictions on North Korea beyond those imposed by the NPT by banning reprocessing of existing spent fuel and requiring the dismantling of North Korea's most sensitive nuclear facilities.[17]

On the other hand, critics maintain that the agreement may be giving away too much. First, by postponing IAEA inspection of the two undeclared sites for an extended period (four to six years), the agreement delays attaining full compliance with IAEA safeguards and creates an unprecedented "special" safeguards status for North Korea. These steps, it is argued, compromise the integrity of IAEA safeguards, especially as they relate to the conduct of the agency's newly inaugurated "special inspections." The accord also will not attempt to rule out, for four to six years, the possibility that North Korea possesses a pre-existing stock of plutonium or possibly one or two nuclear weapons. Moreover, the critics stress, the agreement preserves North Korea's ability, for a somewhat longer period, to acquire additional nuclear weapons rapidly, since, if implementation of the pact breaks down, Pyongyang would have immediate access to the stored spent fuel from the 5 MWe reactor, as well as to the Yongbyon reprocessing plant. Finally, the agreement sets a precedent for others to "toy" with the NPT. Iran, for example, has already hinted it might withdraw from the Treaty because it is the object of a U.S.-led nuclear embargo.[18]

Ballistic Missile Program. North Korea has an expanding ballistic missile program, which was based at first on the reverse engineering of Soviet Scud-B missiles reportedly supplied by Egypt. The progress of North Korea's missile program has subsequently relied heavily on Iranian financing. In return, Iran has received the nuclear-capable Scud Mod. B (320- to 340-km range and 1,000-kg payload) and the nuclear-capable Scud Mod. C (500-km range and 700-to 800-kg payload), as well as the infrastructure to assemble and, apparently, to produce the missiles.[19]

In May 1993, North Korea reportedly flight-tested the Nodong 1, a medium-range ballistic missile (1,000-km range) capable of carrying nuclear, chemical, or biological payloads. When deployed,

Nodong 1 will give North Korea the capability to hit targets throughout South Korea; Niigata and Osaka in Japan; Khabarovsk in Russia; and Beijing and Shanghai in China. According to some sources, North Korea is also developing more advanced missiles including the Nodong 2 (1,500- to 2,000-km range) and the Taepo Dong (TD) series of two-stage missiles, with ranges from 2,000 km to 3,500 km. Particularly worrisome is the fact that North Korea is trying to sell the Nodong 1 to a number of anti-Western countries, including Iran and Libya. If deployed in Iran, the missile could reach Israel, and if deployed in Libya, it could reach U.S. bases and allied capitals in the Mediterranean region.[20]

NOTES

[1]See "IAEA Director General Completes Official Visit to the Democratic People's Republic of Korea," IAEA Press Release (PR 92/25), May 15, 1992; "Democratic People's Republic of Korea (DPRK) Submits Initial Report to IAEA Under Comprehensive Safeguards Agreement in Connection With the Non-Proliferation Treaty," IAEA Press Release (PR 92/24), May 5, 1992; Mark Hibbs, "North Korea Said to Have Converted Separated Plutonium into Metal," *Nucleonics Week*, July 8, 1993, p. 2; Lally Weymouth, "Peninsula of Fear: Will North Korea Start an Asian Nuke Race?" *Washington Post*, October 24, 1993; Mark Hibbs, "No U.S. Agency Consensus on DPRK Nuclear Progress," *Nucleonics Week*, January 6, 1994, p. 9; Mark Hibbs, "North Korea Obtained Reprocessing Technology Aired by Eurochemic," *Nuclear Fuel*, February 28, 1994, p. 6; "Remarks by Secretary of Defense William Perry: U.S. Security Policy in Korea," National Press Club, Washington, DC, May 3, 1994.

[2]See Stephen Engelberg, "Intelligence Study Says North Korea Has Nuclear Bomb," *New York Times*, December 26, 1993; Mark Hibbs, "No U.S. Agency Consensus on DPRK Nuclear Progress," *op. cit.*

[3]"Remarks by Secretary of Defense William Perry: U.S. Security Policy in Korea," *op. cit.*

[4]"Testimony of Leonard S. Spector, Director of the Nuclear Non-Proliferation Project, Carnegie Endowment for International Peace," before the Senate Foreign Relations Committee, January 25, 1995; "Agreed Framework Between the United States of America and the Democratic People's Republic of Korea," October 21, 1994.

[5]See IAEA Director General Hans Blix, "Travel Report: Visit to the Democratic People's Republic of Korea, 11–16 May 1992 (Vienna: IAEA, June 11, 1992); "IAEA Director General Completes Official Visit to the Democratic People's Republic of Korea," IAEA Press Release (PR 92/25), May 15, 1992; "Democratic People's Republic of Korea (DPRK) Submits Initial Report to IAEA Under Comprehensive Safeguards Agreement in Connection With the Non-Proliferation Treaty," IAEA Press Release (PR 92/24), May 5, 1992; Ann MacLachlan, "North Korea Files Initial Report With IAEA, Declares Reprocessing Facility," *Nucleonics Week*, May 5, 1992.

[6]Mark Hibbs, "IAEA Special Inspection Effort Meeting Diplomatic Resistance," *Nucleonics Week*, February 18, 1993, p. 16; R. Jeffrey Smith, "N. Korea and the Bomb: High-Tech Hide-and-Seek," *Washington Post*, April 27, 1993; Mark Hibbs, "U.S. Might Help North Korea Refuel Reactor," *Nuclear Fuel*, November 8, 1993, p. 1; R. Jeffrey Smith, "West Watching Reactor for Sign of North Korea's Nuclear Intentions," *Washington Post*, December 12, 1993.

[7]*Ibid.*

[8]See David Sanger, "U.N. Agency Finds No Assurance North Korea Bans Nuclear Arms," *New York Times*, December 3, 1993.

[9]R. Jeffrey Smith, "N. Korean Conduct in Inspection Draws Criticism of U.S. Officials," *Washington Post*, March 10, 1994; R. Jeffrey Smith, "Inspection of North Korea's Nuclear Facilities Is Halted," *Washington Post*, March 16, 1994; David E. Sanger, "North Korea Said to Block Taking Of Radioactive Samples From Site," *New York Times*, March 16, 1994; Michael R. Gordon, "U.S. Goes to U.N. to Increase the Pressure on North Korea," *New York Times*, March 22, 1994.

[10]Mark Hibbs, "Fuel Readiness Means North Korea Can Start Reactors Up on Schedule," *Nucleonics Week*, April 7, 1994, p. 14; R. Jeffrey Smith, "N. Korea Refuses Demand to Inspect Reactor Fuel," *Washington Post*, April 28, 1994; "Remarks by Secretary of Defense William Perry: U.S. Security Policy in Korea," *op. cit.*; Mark Hibbs, "U.S. Warns North Koreans to Accept IAEA Presence at Reactor Refueling," *Nuclear Fuel*, May 9, 1994, p. 10; David E. Sanger, "Nuclear Agency to Send a New Inspection Team to North Korea," *New York Times*, May 13, 1994; R. Jeffrey Smith, "Inspectors Returning to North Korea," *Washington Post*, May 14, 1994; "IAEA Safeguards in the DPRK," IAEA Press Release, May 19, 1994; Mark Hibbs, "North Korea Needs 6–9 Months to Reprocess Discharged Core," *Nucleonics Week*, May 26, 1994, p. 17; Mark Hibbs, "North Korea Has Machines to Refuel Faster Than West's Experts Thought," *Nucleonics Week*, June 2, 1994, p. 1; Mark Hibbs and Kathleen Hart, "IAEA, U.S. Agencies Underestimated North Korea's Refueling Capability," *Nuclear Fuel*, June 6, 1994, p. 5.

[11]See "Letter From the Director General of the IAEA Addressed to the Secretary-General [of the United Nations] Relating to North Korea," June 2, 1994.

[12]R. Jeffrey Smith and T.R. Reid, "North Korea Quits U.N. Nuclear Body," *Washington Post*, June 14, 1994.

[13]Ann Devroy, "U.S. to Seek Sanctions on N. Korea," *Washington Post*, June 3, 1994; Michael Gordon, "White House Asks Global Sanctions on North Koreans," *New York Times*, June 3, 1994; David B. Ottaway, "N. Korea Forbids Inspections," *Washington Post*, June 8, 1994; Julia Preston, "U.S. Unveils Proposal for Sanctions," *Washington Post*, June 16, 1994;

[14]T. R. Reid, "Leaders of 2 Koreas Seek First Summit," *Washington Post*, June 19, 1994; Michael R. Gordon, "Back from Korea, Carter Declares the Crisis is Over," *New York Times*, June 20, 1994; T. R. Reid, "North Korean President Kim Il Sung Dies at 82," *Washington Post*, July 9, 1994; "Agreed Statement Between the United States of America and the Democratic People's Republic of Korea, Geneva, August 12, 1994," IAEA Media Talking Points, August 16, 1994;

"Seoul Says North Must Accept South's Model Reactor," *Reuters*, August 18, 1994.

[15]See Mark Hibbs, "U.S., DPRK to Meet in Berlin on LWR Transfer, Spent Fuel Details," *Nucleonics Week*, September 8, 1994, p. 17; "North Korea Rejects Special Nuclear Inspections," *Reuters*, September 16, 1994; Jan Kremar, "IAEA Wants Action on N. Korea, Nuclear Smuggling," *Reuters*, September 23, 1994; "N. Korea to Allow Inspections Once Pact Agreed," *Reuters*, September 24, 1994; "Pyongyang Rejects IAEA Call to Open Atomic Plants," *Reuters*, September 25, 1994; R. Jeffrey Smith, "Stalemate in North Korea Talks May Strain Relations, Officials Say," *Washington Post*, October 2, 1994; "Agreed Framework Between the United States of America and the Democratic People's Republic of Korea," October 21, 1994.

[16]Under this accord, which was signed by the two Koreas on December 31, 1991, and came into force on February 19, 1993, both states pledged not to "test, manufacture, produce, receive, store, deploy, or use nuclear weapons." Two provisions of the agreement were particularly noteworthy—one mandating bilateral nuclear inspections (separate from the IAEA inspections required in both states under the NPT) and a second prohibiting both states from building or operating plutonium reprocessing or enrichment plants, which could provide access to weapons-usable nuclear materials. (See Joint [North/South Korea] Declaration on the Denuclearization of the Korean Peninsula, February 19, 1992, Articles III and IV.) Bilateral talks on implementing the agreement foundered over the issue of mutual inspections, and it has not been implemented. In addition, North Korea has claimed that the Yongbyon reprocessing plant is merely a radiochemistry laboratory and therefore is not covered by the accord. Thus, it was not until the signing of the October 21, 1994, Agreed Framework with the United States that the North implemented a freeze on all activities at the facility.

[17]"Testimony of Leonard S. Spector, Director of the Nuclear Non-Proliferation Project, Carnegie Endowment for International Peace," *op. cit.*; Douglas Hamilton, "IAEA Concerned by Terms of U.S.-N.Korea Pact," *Reuters*, October 20, 1994; R. Jeffrey Smith, "N. Korea Accord: A Troubling Precedent?" *Washington Post*, October 20, 1994; "IAEA Comments on Agreed Framework Between United States and Democratic People's Republic of Korea," IAEA Press Release, October 20, 1994.

[18]See references in note 17.

[19]See "Statement by Joseph S. Bermudez Jr.," before the House Commitee on Foreign Affairs, Subcommittee on International Security, International Organizations and Human Rights, September 14, 1993; William C. Potter and Harlan W. Jencks, eds., *The International Missile Bazaar* (Boulder, CO: Westview Press, 1994), p. 65.

[20]See David E. Sanger, "Missile Is Tested by North Koreans," *New York Times*, June 13, 1993; "Testimony by Director of Central Intelligence R. James Woolsey," before the House Foreign Affairs Committee, Subcommittee on International Security, International Organizations, and Human Rights, July 28, 1993; "Statement by Joseph S. Bermudez Jr.," September 14, 1994, *op. cit.*; Barbara Starr, "N. Korea Casts a Longer Shadow With TD-2," *Jane's Defence Weekly*, March 12, 1994, p. 1; "North Korea Grasps at the Stage Beyond Nodong 1," *Jane's Defence Weekly*, March 19, 1994, p. 18.

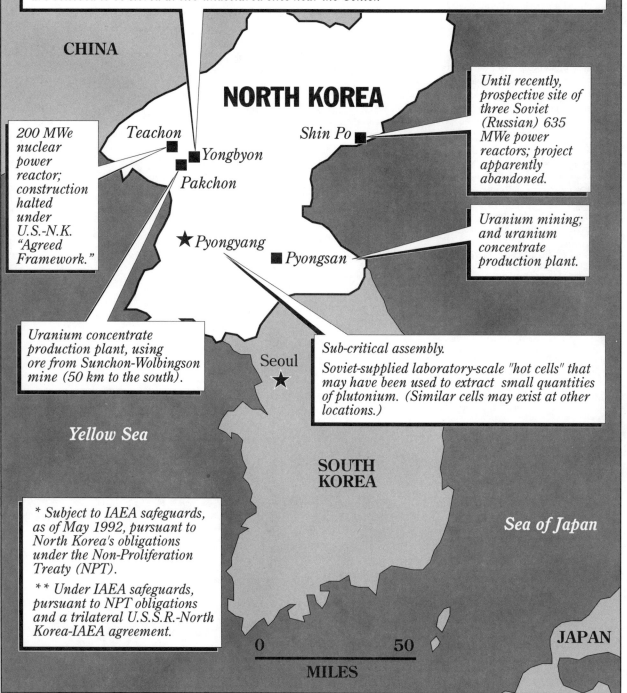

Yongbyon Nuclear Research Center.
Site of a 5 MWe experimental nuclear power reactor;* a partially completed plutonium extraction facility;* a fuel fabrication plant;* fuel storage facilities;* and a Soviet-supplied IRT research reactor** and critical assembly.** 50 MWe power reactor also under construction.

Under the Oct. 21, 1994, U.S.-North Korean "Agreed Framework," activities at the 5 MWe gas-graphite reactor, the fuel fabrication facility, and the reprocessing plant have been frozen; construction also has been halted on the 50 MWe gas-graphite reactor.

U.S. intelligence agencies believe that North Korea has used the 5 MWe reactor and extraction plant to produce plutonium (possibly enough for 1 or 2 nuclear weapons). Wastes from the extraction process are believed to be stored at two undeclared sites near the Center.

CHINA

NORTH KOREA

Teachon

Shin Po

200 MWe nuclear power reactor; construction halted under U.S.-N.K. "Agreed Framework."

Yongbyon

Pakchon

Until recently, prospective site of three Soviet (Russian) 635 MWe power reactors; project apparently abandoned.

★ *Pyongyang*

■ *Pyongsan*

Uranium mining; and uranium concentrate production plant.

Uranium concentrate production plant, using ore from Sunchon-Wolbingson mine (50 km to the south).

Seoul
★

Sub-critical assembly.

Soviet-supplied laboratory-scale "hot cells" that may have been used to extract small quantities of plutonium. (Similar cells may exist at other locations.)

Yellow Sea

SOUTH KOREA

Sea of Japan

* Subject to IAEA safeguards, as of May 1992, pursuant to North Korea's obligations under the Non-Proliferation Treaty (NPT).

** Under IAEA safeguards, pursuant to NPT obligations and a trilateral U.S.S.R.-North Korea-IAEA agreement.

JAPAN

0   50

MILES

Carnegie Endowment for International Peace, *Tracking Nuclear Proliferation*, 1995.

NORTH KOREA: Nuclear Infrastructure

NAME/LOCATION OF FACILITY	TYPE/STATUS	IAEA SAFEGUARDS
P O W E R R E A C T O R S		
Yongbyon	Gas-graphite, natural U, 5 MWe; operations frozen.	Yes
Yongbyon	Gas-graphite, natural U, 50 MWe; construction halted.	IAEA verifying construction freeze.
Taechon	Gas-graphite, natural U, 200 MWe; construction halted.	IAEA verifying construction freeze.
R E S E A R C H R E A C T O R S		
IRT, Yongbyon	Pool-type, HEU, 4 MWt; operating.	Yes[1]
Yongbyon	Critical assembly	Yes[2]
Pyongyang	Sub-critical assembly	Yes
R E P R O C E S S I N G (P L U T O N I U M E X T R A C T I O N) [3]		
Yongbyon	Partially completed; operations frozen.	Yes[4]
Pyongyang	Soviet-supplied laboratory-scale ''hot cells''	No
U R A N I U M P R O C E S S I N G		
Pyongsan	Uranium mining; operating?	N/A (Not applicable)
Pakchon (Sanchon-Wolbingson mine)	Uranium mining; operating?	N/A
Pyongsan	Uranium milling; operating?	N/A
Pakchon	Uranium milling; operating?	N/A
Yongbyon	Uranium purification (UO_2) facility; operating?	Yes
Yongbyon	Fuel fabrication facility; operations frozen.[5]	Yes

Abbreviations:

HEU	=	highly enriched uranium
LEU	=	low-enriched uranium
nat. U	=	natural uranium
MWe	=	millions of watts of electrical output
MWt	=	millions of watts of thermal output
KWt	=	thousands of watts of thermal output

NOTES (North Korea Chart)

1. This facility is covered by the 1992 IAEA safeguards agreement and an earlier trilateral U.S.S.R.-North Korea-IAEA agreement.

2. This facility is covered by the 1992 IAEA safeguards agreement and the earlier trilateral U.S.S.R.-North Korea-IAEA agreement.

3. There have been allegations that North Korea is constructing a uranium enrichment facility, but U.S. officials discount these reports.

4. North Korea has consistently maintained that the 600-foot-long, plutonium separation facility at Yongbyon, should be characterized as a ''radiochemical laboratory'' because it had not been fully tested and because, when first observed by the IAEA in mid-1992, only 80 percent of its civil engineering had been completed and only 40 percent of its equipment, installed. U.S. officials believe, however, that the facility was designed to handle all the spent fuel from the 5 MWe reactor and the 50 MWe reactor at Yongbyon. They theorize that, even in its incomplete state, the plant had the capacity to process all the spent fuel produced by the smaller reactor and thus could have separated one to two bombs' worth of plutonium prior to 1992 from the spent fuel thought to have been discharged from the 5 MWe unit in 1989.

During their March 1994 inspection of this facility, IAEA inspectors made certain observations that led them to believe that, since their previous inspection a year earlier, North Korea had built and possibly operated a second, unsafeguarded plutonium separation line. (See Mark Hibbs and Naoaki Usui, ''Second, Hidden Reprocessing Line Feared Opened at Yongbyon Plant,'' *Nucleonics Week*, March 24, 1994, p. 1; Mark Hibbs, ''North Korea Needs 6–9 Months to Reprocess Discharged Core,'' *Nucleonics Week*, May 26, 1994, p. 17.) All operations at the facility are currently frozen, pursuant to the U.S.-North Korean Agreed Framework, and the IAEA has verified this status.

5. Associated with this plant are fuel storage facilities, which are covered by North Korea's 1992 safeguards agreement with the IAEA.

Additional References

1990: Leonard S. Spector with Jacqueline R. Smith, *Nuclear Ambitions* (Boulder, Colo.: Westview Press), 1990. **1992:** Gary Milhollin, ''North Korea's Bomb,'' *New York Times*, June 4, 1992; Gerald F. Seib, ''U.S. Analysts Worry North Korea May Be Hiding Nuclear Potential,'' *Wall Street Journal*, June 11, 1992; ''North Korea's Nuclear Power Programme Revealed,'' *Nuclear Engineering International*, July 1992, pp. 2; David Albright and Mark Hibbs, ''North Korea's Plutonium Puzzle,'' *Bulletin of the Atomic Scientists*, November 1992, p. 39.

8

NORTH AFRICA AND THE MIDDLE EAST

Algeria

In early 1991, U.S. intelligence agencies discovered that Algeria was secretly building a sizable research reactor at the Ain Oussera nuclear complex. Because the facility was unusually large in view of Algeria's rudimentary nuclear research program, was being built in secret, and was not subject to International Atomic energy Agency (IAEA) inspection, Washington feared the facility might be used to produce plutonium for a nuclear weapons program.[1]

Algeria soon acknowledged it was building the reactor, which it stated was being supplied by China. It also stated that the unit had a power rating of 10-15 MWt and would use low-enriched uranium as fuel and heavy water as its moderator. Noting the facility's unusually large cooling towers, however, U.S. and other foreign sources worried that the reactor might have a capacity as high as 60 MWt. Other factors also suggested a possible military use of the reactor: its long distance from major population centers, the initial absence of electrical generation facilities and transmission lines, and the location of SA-5 surface-to-air missile defense batteries near the facility. In addition, several unconfirmed reports indicated that Algeria had also begun to construct a nuclear fuel reprocessing plant next to the reactor, a facility that presumably could have been used to separate weapons-usable plutonium from the reactor's spent fuel. These developments aroused suspicions that Algeria was embarking on a nuclear weapons program.[2]

In May 1991, following the exposure of the nuclear reactor construction program, Algiers agreed to place the reactor at Ain Oussera (denominated the Es Salam reactor) under International Atomic Energy Agency (IAEA) safeguards.[3] This step significantly reduced the immediate threat of nuclear weapons development in Algeria. In addition, during the December 21, 1993, inauguration of the Es Salam reactor, Algerian Foreign Minister Salah Dembri pledged that Algeria "resolved to adhere to the Non-Proliferation Treaty [NPT]." He added that Algeria was "absolutely dedicated to the peaceful use of the atom" and "confidently and unequivocally affirms its commitment to the non-proliferation regime."[4] Algiers completed the constitutional process needed for adhering to the pact in late 1994, and, on January 12, 1995, formally acceded to the Treaty.[5]

While the apparent commitment to nuclear restraint on the part of Algeria's current military-dominated government is a positive development, some observers remain concerned that it continues to harbor an intention to develop nuclear arms, especially considering the suspicious circumstances surrounding the initial construction of the Es Salam reactor.

Moreover, Algeria's political future remains uncertain. The Algerian government is under increasing pressure from Islamic fundamentalist rebels operating under the banner of the Islamic Salvation Front (FIS). Should these fundamentalists come to power, development of nuclear weapons could be a tempting prize for a newly formed militant Islamic state searching for legitimacy, prestige, and military power in a hostile international environment. The risk of proliferation could be significantly increased if such a new Islamic fundamentalist government were to work with Iran in a common effort to acquire nuclear arms.

NOTES

[1]Elaine Sciolino and Eric Schmitt, "Algerian Reactor: A Chinese Export," *New York Times*, November 15, 1991, p A12; "China Helps Algeria Build First Arab Atom Bomb, " *Sunday Times*, April 28, 1991; Bill Gertz, "China Helps Algeria Develop Nulcear Weapons," *Washington Times*, April 11, 1991.

[2]See Ann MacLachlan and Mark Hibbs, "Algeria Confirms Secret Reactor; Questions About Purpose Remain," *Nucleonics Week*, May 2, 1991, p. 3; Barbara Gregory, *Algeria: Contemplating A Nulcear Weapons Option?*, (McLean, VA: Science Applications International Corporation), March 25, 1995; interviews with former U.S. officials.

[3]"Algeria: IAEA, Algeria Sign Safeguards Agreement," *Nuclear Fuel*, March 16, 1992, p. 15; "Atomic Energy Inspectors Tour Nuclear Reactor," *Algiers Radio*, January 19, 1992, in *FBIS-NES-92-014*, January 22, 1992, p. 15; Gamini Senevirante, "IAEA Governors Defer Decision on Expanding Safeguards Powers," *Nucleonics Week*, December 12, 1991, p. 10.

[4]"Algeria Pledges Peaceful Use of PRC-Built Nuclear Reactor," Beijing, *Xinhua Domestic Service*, December 24, 1993, in *JPRS-TND-93-003*, January 31, 1994, p. 45; "Decision to Join Nuclear Non-Proliferation Treaty Announced," *Radio Algiers Network*, December 21, 1993, in *JPRS-TND-94-002*, January 18, 1994, p. 12; "Reactions to Dedication of Nuclear Reactor," Algiers, *El Moudjahid*, December 22, 1993, in *JPRS-TND-94-005*, February 25, 1994, p. 10.

[5]"Algeria Accedes to the Treaty on the Non-Proliferation of Nuclear Weapons," IAEA Press Release PR 95/2, (Vienna: IAEA), January 13, 1995. Algeria deposited its instruments of accession to the NPT in Washington, Moscow, and London.

Algeria:
Map and Chart

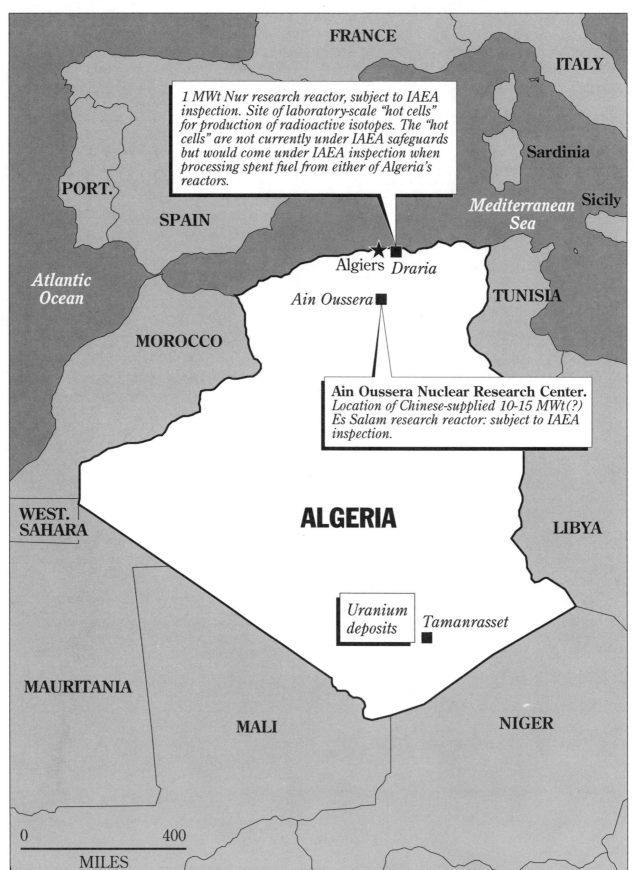

1 MWt Nur research reactor, subject to IAEA inspection. Site of laboratory-scale "hot cells" for production of radioactive isotopes. The "hot cells" are not currently under IAEA safeguards but would come under IAEA inspection when processing spent fuel from either of Algeria's reactors.

Ain Oussera Nuclear Research Center. *Location of Chinese-supplied 10-15 MWt(?) Es Salam research reactor: subject to IAEA inspection.*

FRANCE

ITALY

Sardinia

PORT.

SPAIN

Mediterranean Sea Sicily

★ Algiers *Draria*

Atlantic Ocean

Ain Oussera ■

TUNISIA

MOROCCO

ALGERIA

LIBYA

WEST. SAHARA

Uranium deposits ■ *Tamanrasset*

MAURITANIA

MALI

NIGER

0   400

MILES

Carnegie Endowment for International Peace, *Tracking Nuclear Proliferation*, 1995.

ALGERIA: Nuclear Infrastructure

NAME/LOCATION OF FACILITY	TYPE/STATUS	IAEA SAFEGUARDS
RESEARCH REACTORS		
Nur, Draria (Algiers)	Small pool-type, LEU, 1 MWt; operating.	Yes
Es Salam, Ain Oussera	Heavy water, LEU, 10-15(?) MWt; operating.	Yes[1]
REPROCESSING (PLUTONIUM EXTRACTION)		
Draria	Hot cells for use in the production of radioactive isotopes	No[2]
URANIUM PROCESSING		
West of Tamanrasset, southern Algeria	Uranium deposits; status unknown.	(Not applicable)

Abbreviations:

HEU	=	highly enriched uranium
LEU	=	low-enriched uranium
nat. U	=	natural uranium
MWe	=	millions of watts of electrical output
MWt	=	millions of watts of thermal output
KWt	=	thousands of watts of thermal output

NOTES (Algeria Chart)

1. On February 27, 1992, Algeria and the IAEA signed a facility-specific safeguards agreement. The agreement provides for the inspection of the reactor, its nuclear fuel, and its heavy water, but apparently does not guarantee access to other facilities in the Ain Oussera nuclear research complex. Since Algeria recently acceded to the NPT, it is now required to sign a comprehensive inspection agreement with the IAEA that will place all nuclear activities in the country under IAEA monitoring.

2. Will be subject to IAEA inspection when processing material from either of Algeria's reactors.

Additional References

1992: Vipin Gupta, "Algeria's Nuclear Ambitions," *International Defense Review*, April 1992, p. 329; "Reports of the Global Activities of the International Atomic Energy Agency," *IAEA Newsbriefs*, February/March 1994, p. 3–4; Interviews with former U.S. officials.

Iran

Iran, which is a party to the Nuclear Non-Proliferation Treaty (NPT), is believed by U.S. authorities to be pursuing a secret nuclear weapons program. According to CIA estimates, Iran's nuclear weapons program is still at a relatively rudimentary stage and is at least eight to ten years away from producing nuclear arms, although this period could be shortened depending on the sophistication and magnitude of foreign assistance. China has been the primary supplier of nuclear-related technology to Iran and is believed by some U.S. officials to be assisting Iran's nuclear weapons program. In addition, according to former CIA Director R. James Woolsey, Iran's Muslim fundamentalist regime appears to be accelerating the pace of the program since it has been recently seeking to purchase nuclear materials and technology illicitly from Russian sources and to acquire complete Russian nuclear devices.[1]

Western intelligence sources believe that Iran has established a procurement network to support experimental programs in fissile material production at Sharif University, in Tehran, and possibly at other locations. These programs reportedly include research and development in both centrifuge uranium enrichment and plutonium separation (reprocessing). According to these reports, the Iranians have approached West European companies seeking to acquire nuclear-related dual-use technologies or have purchased small companies—particularly in Germany—which could serve as export platforms for sensitive equipment to Iran.[2]

The most specific statement on Iran's ''crash'' nuclear weapons program was given by former CIA Director R. James Woolsey in September 1994. He stated:

> We pay particular attention to Iran's efforts to acquire nuclear and missile technology from the West in order to enable it to build its own nuclear weapons, despite being a signatory to the NPT. We believe that Iran is 8–10 years away from building such weapons, and that help from the outside will be critical in reaching this timetable. Iran has been particularly active in trying to purchase nuclear materials or technology clandestinely from Russian sources. Iran is also looking to purchase fully-fabricated nuclear weapons in order to accelerate sharply its timetable.[3]

In an effort to dispel suspicions about its nuclear program, in addition to accepting International Atomic Energy Agency (IAEA) inspections on all nuclear activities as required by the NPT, Iran has agreed to permit the IAEA to visit any location within the country to check for undeclared nuclear activities. The agency has made two such special ''visits.'' A February 1992 visit observed several locations not on Iran's list of declared nuclear sites but found no violations of the NPT. In a follow-on visit in November 1993, IAEA officials viewed facilities in Esfahan, Karaj, and Tehran, but again found no violations of the pact.[4]

Because of its belief that Iran is developing nuclear weapons, the United States has attempted to gain approval for an international embargo on the transfer of nuclear goods to Iran. Western governments have imposed such an embargo, but China and Russia have rejected it, and each has signed agreements to sell Iran nuclear power plants.

China will supply two 300 MWe units based on its Qinshan-1 design, to be located at Esteghlal, a site adjacent to Bushehr on Iran's Persian Gulf coast. The Chinese reportedly have conducted a full seismic study at that location and have received a down payment for the construction of the reactors.[5]

Iran and Russia signed a $1 billion agreement on January 8, 1995, in which Russia will help to complete one and possibly two partially constructed nuclear power reactors at Bushehr. These reactors were originally being built by Siemens of Germany starting in 1976, but completion was halted after the 1979 Iranian Revolution. At that point approximately 85 percent of the civil work on Bushehr I was complete: the inner steel containment vessel had been completed and tested; the outer concrete dome was incomplete. Work on Bushehr II was also partially finished when construction stopped in 1979.[6] In the intervening years, both reactors were damaged during bombing raids in the Iran-Iraq war, and Iran was subsequently unsuccessful at convincing Siemens to complete construction, largely due to pressure from the United States.

The Russian-Iranian nuclear agreement envisions the installation of a VVER-1000 power reactor at Bushehr I. Although the original facility was a Siemens-designed 1,300 MWe pressurized water reactor, the Russians plan to retrofit as much of their VVER-1000 technology into the original structure as possible.[7] Russia's Minister of Atomic Energy, Viktor Mikhailov, also stated in February 1995 that an additional contract for completion of Bushehr II was ready to be signed.[8]

Russia plans to ship over 7,000 tons of equipment to the Bushehr site as work begins in mid-1995. Several Russian nuclear specialists have been active in Iran since April 1994 performing preliminary studies of the coastal site, and some 150 Russian technicians are currently at the site. The nuclear deal also includes the training of approximately 500 Iranian technicians in Russia and the supply of fuel for the facilities. As of March 1995, Russia did not plan to take back the plutonium-bearing spent fuel from the reactors, a practice which had been a standard feature of Soviet nuclear export agreements. The planned start-up date for the facility is within four years.[9]

In addition to Iran's plans to complete the reactors at the Bushehr site, Tehran has expressed strong interest in the possible purchase of two V-213 VVER-440 power reactors and a research reactor from Russia.

The Russia-Iran reactor deal caused considerable concern in Washington. The Clinton Administration, while acknowledging that the deal is legal under international non-proliferation law, strongly protested it as a boost to Iran's efforts to gain expertise and material that could be used to further its ''crash'' nuclear weapons program. In addition, several Republican congressman have even gone as far as to suggest that the United States substantially curtail its aid to Russia unless it cancels the deal.[10]

At the third Preparatory Committee (PrepCom) session for the Review and Extension Conference of the NPT in September 1994, Iran threatened to withdraw from the NPT on the grounds that the Western embargo violates Article IV of the Treaty, guaranteeing ''the inalienable right of all Parties to the Treaty to develop research, production and use of nuclear energy for peaceful purposes'' as well as full access to ''equipment, materials and scientific and technological information'' for such uses. Subsequently Iranian officials toned down the threat of withdrawal, and did not renew it at the fourth PrepCom in January 1995. On October 3, 1994, IAEA Director General Hans Blix said that his agency would continue to provide technical assistance to Iran until conclusive evidence was presented that Iran is violating its NPT obligations.[11]

Iran reportedly has been seeking to acquire ballistic missile capabilities that could be used for delivering nuclear weapons, turning to North Korea and China for missile systems and related technologies. Iran possesses two versions of the nuclear-capable, North Korea-supplied, Scud ballistic missile, the Mod. B (320- to 340-km range and 1,000-kg payload) and the Mod. C (500-km range and 700- to 800-kg payload). According to some sources, it can also manufacture these systems, but U.S. analysts with access to classified information discount these reports.[12]

It has been reported that North Korea has agreed to sell Iran the Mod. D (Nodong 1), with a range of 1,000-km and, according to some reports, Iran may already have flight-tested the missile. Other sources have reported that North Korea has postponed the Nodong 1 sale indefinitely, possibly at the request of Israel, which would be within the range of the system. Iran has reportedly acquired much of its current ballistic missile capabilities in exchange for providing long-term financing for North Korea's missile program.[13] China reportedly agreed in 1988 to provide Iran with ''M-class'' missile technology that would enable the production of missiles with ranges of 600 km to 1,000 km. Whether any technology has been transfered under the contract is unclear.[14]

NOTES

[1] See "Testimony by Director of Central Intelligence R. James Woolsey," before the House Foreign Affairs Committee, Subcommittee on International Security, International Organizations, and Human Rights, July 28, 1993; Patrick Worsnip, "CIA Chief Attacks Iran, Iraq Weapons Programs," *Reuters*, September 26, 1994.

[2] See Mark Hibbs, "U.S. Officials Say Iran Is Pursuing Fissile Material Production Research," *Nuclear Fuel*, December 7, 1992, p. 5; "Iran and the Bomb," *Frontline*, PBS Network, April 13, 1993; Mark Hibbs, "German-U.S. Nerves Frayed Over Nuclear Ties to Iran," *Nuclear Fuel*, March 14, 1994, p. 9; Mark Hibbs, "Sharif University Activity Continues Despite IAEA Visit, Bonn Agency Says," *Nuclear Fuel*, March 28, 1994, p. 10.

[3] "Challenges to the Peace in the Middle East," Address of R. James Woolsey, Director, Central Intelligence Agency, to the Washington Institute for Near East Policy, Wye Plantation, MD, September 23, 1994 (revised version).

[4] Mark Hibbs, "IAEA Explores Iran's Intentions, Minus Evidence of Weapons Drive," *Nucleonics Week*, February 13, 1992, p. 12; "Atomic Team Reports on Iran Probe," *Washington Post*, February 14, 1992; "Iran: IAEA Inspection Team Finds Nothing Suspicious," *Nuclear Engineering International*, April 1992, p. 67; Steve Coll, "Nuclear Inspectors Check Sites in Iran," *Washington Post*, November 20, 1993; Mark Hibbs, "IAEA Says It Found No Non-Peaceful Activity During Recent Iran Visit," *Nucleonics Week*, December 16, 1993, p. 11.

[5] See "World Survey: Iran," *Nuclear Engineering International*, June 1993, p. 21; "China in Pact to Help Iran Build A-Plant," *New York Times*, July 7, 1993; "Nuclear Energy Chief on Iran's Program, Israel," Tehran, *Tehran Times*, August 18, 1993, in *FBIS-NES-93-166*, August 30, 1993, p. 75; Mark Hibbs, "Russian, Chinese Reactors Might Be Sited at Bushehr," *Nucleonics Week*, October 14, 1993, p. 9; "Beijing Exports Nuclear Power Plants to Pakistan, Iran," Beijing, *Xinhua Domestic Service*, in *JPRS-TND-93-038*, December 29, 1993, p. 1; "China Goes Ahead With Nuclear Plants in Iran," *United Press International*, November 21, 1994.

[6] "Russian German Hybrid for Bushehr?," *Nuclear Engineering International*, November 1994, p. 10.

[7] One source noted that the primary circuit for the VVER-1000 reactor, which utilizes horizontal steam generators, occupies a much larger space that the original German construction and, thus, the current structure will have to be enlarged. See "Russian-German Hybrid for Bushehr?" *Nuclear Engineering International*, November 1994, p.10.

[8] C.J. Hanley, "Russian's Don't Blink at Gingrich," *Washington Times*, February 26, 1995.

[9] "Agreement Signed for Bushehr," *Nuclear Engineering International*, November 1994, p. 4.
For general background on the deal see "Russia to Help Set Up Nuclear Plant in Bushehr," Cairo, *Mena*, April 13, 1994, in *FBIS-NES-94-072*, April 14, 1994; "Russia Helps Build Bushehr Nuclear Power Plant," Tehran, *Jomhuri-Yeeslami*, April 13, 1994, in *FBIS-NES-94-079*, April 25, 1994, p. 82; "IAEO Officials on Nonproliferation, Bushehr," Tehran, *First Program Network*, April 21, 1994, in *JPRS-TND-94-011*, May 16, 1994; Mark Hibbs, "Minatom Says It Can Complete One Siemens PWR in Iran in Five Years," *Nucleonics Week*, September 29, 1994; "IAEA Delegate Protests German, U.S. Actions," *Nuclear News*, November 1994, p. 36; "Iran Says Russians Begin Work on Nuclear Plant," *Reuters*, November 20, 1994..

[10] Thomas W. Lippman, "Russia-Iran Atomic Deal Irks U.S.," *Washington Post*, February 12, 1995; Elaine Sciolino, "Congress Presses Russia, and Clinton, Over Iran Deal," *New York Times*, February 23, 1995.

[11] See Mark Hibbs, "Iran May Withdraw From NPT Over Western Trade Barriers," *Nucleonics Week*, September 22, 1994, p. 1; Mark Hibbs, "Western Group Battles Iran at Third Prep Com Session," *Nucleonics Week*, September 22, 1994, p. 9; Mark Hibbs, "It's 'Too Early' for Tehran to Leave NPT, Delegates Say," *Nuclear Fuel*, September 26, 1994, p. 9; Mark Hibbs, "IAEA Sees No Current Grounds to Deny Iran Technical Assistance," *Nucleonics Week*, October 6, 1994, p. 11.

[12] See "Statement by Joseph S. Bermudez Jr.," before the House Committee on Foreign Affairs, Subcommittee on International Security, International Organizations and Human Rights, September 14, 1993; William C. Potter and Harlan W. Jencks, eds., *The International Missile Bazaar* (Boulder, CO: Westview Press, 1994), p. 65.

[13] See "Testimony by Director of Central Intelligence R. James Woolsey," *op. cit.*; "Statement by Joseph S. Bermudez Jr.," *op. cit.*; Ron Kampeas, "Israel-Missiles," *Associated Press*, January 4, 1994; "Allegations of 'Secret' Contacts With DPRK on Missiles to Iran," Tel Aviv, *IDF Radio*, March 22, 1994, in *JPRS-TND-94-008*, April 1, 1994, p. 34; "Foreign Ministry Denies Contacts," Tel Aviv, *IDF Radio*, March 22, 1994, in *JPRS-TND-94-008*, April 1, 1994, p. 34; "Iran's Testing of DPRK Missile Denied," Tokyo, *Kyodo*, June 13, 1994, in *FBIS-EAS-94-113*, June 13, 1994, p. 13.

[14] "Statement by Joseph S. Bermudez Jr.," *op. cit.*

University of Tehran. *U.S.-supplied, Argentine-fueled 5 MWt research reactor, subject to IAEA inspection.*
Sharif University of Technology. *Alleged experimental centrifuge program for uranium enrichment, and possible research on plutonium separation.*

Esfahan Nuclear Research Center. *Chinese-supplied mini research reactors and sub-critical assemblies: subject to IAEA inspection. Possible location of nuclear-weapons design research.*

Yazd Province. Location of uranium deposits.

Partially completed Bushehr I and II power reactors (1300 MWe each). Damaged during the Iran-Iraq War; construction restarted with Russian assistance. Site of nuclear power reactors to be purchased from China.

0   400
MILES

Carnegie Endowment for International Peace, *Tracking Nuclear Proliferation*, 1995.

IRAN: Nuclear Infrastructure

NAME/LOCATION OF FACILITY	TYPE/STATUS	IAEA SAFEGUARDS
P O W E R R E A C T O R S		
Bushehr I	Light-water, LEU, 1300 MWe; under construction; damaged by Iraqi air strikes (1987, 1988).	Planned[1]
Bushehr II	Light-water, LEU, 1300 MWe; under construction; damaged by Iraqi air strikes (1987, 1988).	Planned[2]
R E S E A R C H R E A C T O R S		
Tehran	Light-water, HEU, 5 MWt; operating.	Yes
Esfahan	Miniature Neutron Source Reactor (MNSR), 900 grams of HEU, 27 kw; operating.[3]	Yes
U R A N I U M E N R I C H M E N T		
Tehran	Alleged centrifuge research program, Sharif University of Technology[4,5]	
U R A N I U M P R O C E S S I N G		
Yazd Province	Discovery of uranium deposits announced in 1990[6]	N/A (Not applicable)
Tehran	Uranium-ore concentration facility; incapacitated.[7]	N/A

Abbreviations:

HEU	=	highly enriched uranium
LEU	=	low-enriched uranium
MWe	=	millions of watts of electrical output
MWt	=	millions of watts of thermal output
KWt	=	thousands of watts of thermal output

NOTES (Iran Chart)

1. This facility is not under IAEA safeguards (as there is no nuclear material present at the site); the Bushehr complex, however, reportedly was among the locations "visited" by the IAEA in February 1992.

U.S. government sources have indicated that, during the Iran-Iraq War, Iran was planning to move 22.4 kg of uranium hexafluoride (UF$_6$) to the Bushehr site to trigger limited IAEA monitoring, which Iran apparently believed might deter recurrent Iraqi air strikes on the Bushehr plants. However, the plan apparently was not implemented. Interviews with U.S. officials, December 1993.

2. See note 1.

3. Another Chinese-supplied miniature research reactor at the Esfahan Nuclear Research Center is the heavy-water zero-power reactor (HWZPR). In addition, there are two Chinese-supplied sub-critical assemblies, the light-water sub-critical "reactor" (LWSCR) and the graphite sub-critical "reactor" (GSCR). These units, in themselves, do not pose a proliferation threat since their operation does not yield significant amounts of sensitive nuclear materials. (Interview with U.S. State Department official, December 1993.) Nevertheless, they provide for the development of nuclear technical expertise.

4. Sharif University was one of the sites "visited" by the IAEA in November 1993, but reportedly no suspicious activity was discovered there.

5. During their February 1992 "visit," IAEA officials reportedly observed a small Chinese-supplied calutron at Karaj and concurred with Iran's assertion that it was being used only for stable isotope production and not for uranium enrichment purposes. After the IAEA discovery in 1991 that Iraq was using large-size calutrons in the electromagnetic isotope separation (EMIS) process to enrich uranium, concerns increased that Iran might be pursuing a similar path.

6. During its February 1992 "visit," the IAEA went to the desert town of Saghand in Yazd Province to check on

reports that Iran was constructing a uranium-ore processing plant there, but only uranium-ore drilling rigs were found.

7. Located at the University of Tehran, the facility was viewed by IAEA officials during their February 1992 "visit."

Additional References

1990: Leonard S. Spector with Jacqueline R. Smith, *Nuclear Ambitions* (Boulder, CO: Westview Press), 1990; "Esfahan Reactors Become Operational," *Tehran Domestic Service*, March 14, 1990, in *FBIS-NES*, March 14, 1990, p. 36; "World Survey," *Nuclear Engineering International*, June 1990, p. 24. **1992:** "Nuclear Threat," *Associated Press*, February 3, 1992; Mark Hibbs, "Iran Sought Sensitive Nuclear Supplies From Argentina, China," *Nucleonics Week*, September 24, 1992, p. 2; Mark Hibbs, "Sensitive Iran Reactor Deal May Hinge on MFN for China," *Nucleonics Week*, October 1, 1992, p. 5; Mark Hibbs, "U.S. Warned Not to Try Using IAEA to Isolate or Destabilize Iran," *Nucleonics Week*, October 8, 1992, p. 9; "U.S. Halted Nuclear Bid by Iran," *Washington Post*, November 17, 1992. **1993:** IAEA, *The Annual Report for 1992* (Vienna: IAEA, July 1993), pp. 157, 163.

Iraq

As of early 1995, Iraq's potential to develop nuclear weapons in the near term had been substantially curtailed as a result of the implementation of United Nations (UN) Security Council Resolution 687. The resolution, adopted by the Security Council in April 1991 following Iraq's defeat in the 1991 Gulf War, established procedures for the destruction of Iraq's unconventional weapons and ballistic missile capabilities and for a subsequent monitoring program to prevent their reconstruction.

While conducting inspections under the auspices of the United Nations Special Commission on Iraq (UNSCOM), the International Atomic Energy Agency (IAEA) discovered that, since the early 1980s, Iraq had repeatedly violated its obligations under the Nuclear Non-Proliferation Treaty (NPT),[1] by pursuing a multi-billion-dollar covert nuclear weapons program, code named "Petrochemical 3." Specifically, Iraq had simultaneously pursued multiple strategies for enriching uranium to weapons-grade, including the electromagnetic isotope separation (EMIS) process, the use of gas centrifuges, lasers, and chemical enrichment. Iraqi scientists had also engaged in laboratory-scale activities to separate plutonium.[2]

The UN-IAEA inspections also revealed details of Baghdad's efforts to design an implosion-type nuclear explosive device and to test its non-nuclear components, including its plans to produce large quantities of lithium-6, a material used exclusively for the production of "boosted" atomic bombs and hydrogen bombs. In addition, the inspectors found that Iraq was pursuing a parallel program to develop a missile-delivery system for its nuclear arms. IAEA officials estimated that Iraq might have been able to manufacture its first atomic weapons, using indigenously produced weapons-grade uranium, as early as the fall of 1993.

On July 18 and August 9, 1991, the IAEA formally declared Iraq to be in non-compliance with its safeguards agreement with the Agency (INFCIRC/172). Specific violations included: Iraq's possession of significant amounts of unsafeguarded nuclear materials related to uranium enrichment, including uranium dioxide (UO_2), uranium tetrachloride (UCl_4), and uranium hexafluoride (UF_6); its undeclared construction of a large-scale facility at Al Tarmiya for the production of enriched uranium through the EMIS method, which had produced approximately a half kilogram of 4 percent enriched (non-weapons-usable) uranium; and the undeclared separation of minute quantities of plutonium from irradiated fuel in safeguarded facilities at Al Tuwaitha.[3]

Iraq had also engaged in nuclear weapons research and development activities in violation of Article II of the NPT, prohibiting the "manufacture" of such weapons.[4] These activities did not constitute a violation of Iraq's IAEA safeguards agreement, however, since IAEA safeguards are intended only to verify that nuclear materials (and the facilities that produce and use them) are not employed for nuclear weapons. Activities, such as the development of nuclear weapons designs, that do not involve nuclear materials are not subject to IAEA monitoring or any other verification mechanism under the NPT. Nevertheless, the far more comprehensive inspections mandated by Security Council Resolution 687 enabled the United States to determine that Iraq's nuclear activities were indeed in violation of its obligations under NPT Article II. (The United States also declared that "Iraq's noncompliance with its Safeguards Agreement constitutes a violation of Article III of the NPT.")[5]

The 1991 Gulf War and its aftermath set back Iraq's nuclear-weapons program many years. Most of the installations involved in the effort were destroyed by U.S. bombing raids during the conflict. Other facilities—many of which had been unknown to the United States and its coalition partners—were leveled by Iraq itself after the war in an effort to deceive the UN-IAEA inspectors about the nature of the facilities. French- and Soviet-origin weapons-usable uranium that Iraq had obtained for running research reactors supplied by these countries was placed in IAEA custody and was eventually removed from Iraq. During the seventh UN-IAEA inspection, in October 1991, the inspectors started to destroy the enrichment-related equipment, as well as equipment related to the separation of plutonium from spent reactor fuel (known as ''reprocessing''), which they had discovered in earlier inspections. In April 1992, during the eleventh inspection, inspectors destroyed buildings and equipment at the Al Atheer/Al Hateen site, which was found to be Iraq's key complex for designing nuclear weapons, conducting high-explosive experiments relating to their detonation, producing nuclear weapons components, and assembling them. On September 19, 1994, following an additional fifteen inspections, IAEA Director General Hans Blix stated that his agency had completed the destruction, removal, or rendering harmless of all known nuclear weapons-usable material, facilities, and equipment in Iraq that might have the potential to contribute to the development of nuclear weapons.[6]

On November 26, 1993, Iraq formally agreed to accept long-term monitoring of its industries to insure that it would not revive its programs to manufacture weapons of mass destruction. In order to implement fully this long-term plan for monitoring and verification, the IAEA established a continuous presence in Iraq in August 1994.[7] In early October 1994, Ambassador Rolf Ekeus, head of UNSCOM, reported to the Security Council that the ''commission's ongoing monitoring and verification system [in Iraq] is provisionally operational,'' and that a period of testing of the system had begun.[8]

While Ekeus had earlier indicated that a six-month period of testing would have been sufficient for determining the effectiveness of the system, his report did not set a time limit. This was a result of successful U.S. efforts at the United Nations to

delay, for an unspecified period, the lifting of UN economic sanctions against Iraq imposed at the end of the 1991 Gulf War.[9] For the Iraqis, the lack of a specific testing period for the monitoring system implied an indefinite extension of the sanctions. The impending release of the Ekeus report apparently contributed to the eruption of a week-long crisis highlighted by the massing of Iraqi troops on the Kuwaiti border and the redeployment of U.S. forces to the region.[10]

*

Prior to the 1991 Gulf War, Iraq had extensive ballistic missile capabilities, including a stockpile of Soviet-supplied Scud-Bs (300-km range and 1,000-kg payload) and two indigenously-produced variants of the Scud-B, the *Al-Husayn* (600-km range and 150- to 500-kg payload) and the *Al-Hijarah/Abbas* (750-km range and 100- to 300-kg payload).[11] UNSCOM officials believe that Iraq's ballistic missile infrastructure was fairly sophisticated and had gradually enabled Iraq to modify Scud-Bs to produce the *Al-Husayn* without the need to cannibalize parts from other Scuds in the Iraqi stockpile.

Under the terms of Security Council Resolution 687, UNSCOM has destroyed Iraq's known ballistic missiles with a range of greater than 150 km and has dismantled the related infrastracture. A dispute is continuing, however, between UNSCOM and the United States over whether all of Iraq's missiles in this category have been accounted for. The U.S. intelligence community believes that Iraq may have hidden up to a hundred such missiles.[12]

As part of the long-term plan for on-going monitoring and verification, UNSCOM is regularly inspecting facilities involved in research and production of missiles with a range of less than 150 km, which are permitted under the terms of the Gulf War ceasefire agreement. There are, however, no UN restrictions on Iraq's development of cruise missiles.

NOTES

[1]Iraq ratified the Non-Proliferation Treaty on October 29, 1969, pledging not to manufacture nuclear weapons and agreeing to place all its nuclear materials and facilities under IAEA safeguards.

[2]This review of both the Iraqi nuclear weapons program and related UN-IAEA activities is based on the following sources: IAEA, ''IAEA Reports on On-Site Inspections in Iraq Under Security Council Resolution 687 (1-14),'' 1991/1992; David Albright and Mark Hibbs, ''Iraq's Bomb: Blueprints and Artifacts,'' *Bulletin of the Atomic Scientists,* January/February 1992, pp. 30-40; Gary Milhollin, ''Building Saddam Hussein's Bomb,'' *New York Times Magazine,* March 8, 1992, pp. 30-36; IAEA, ''IAEA Inspections and Iraq's Nuclear Capabilities,''

IAEA/PI/A35E, April 1992; David Albright and Mark Hibbs, ''Iraq's Shop-Till-You Drop Nuclear Program,'' *Bulletin of the Atomic Scientists,* April 1992, pp. 27–37; Jay C. Davis and David A. Kay, ''*Iraq's Secret Nuclear Weapons Program,*'' *Physics Today,* July 1992, p. 21; Paul Lewis, ''U.N. Experts Now Say Baghdad Was Far From Making an A-Bomb Before Gulf War,'' *New York Times,* May 20, 1992; Maurizio Zifferero, ''The IAEA: Neutralizing Iraq's Nuclear Weapons Potential,'' *Arms Control Today,* April 1993, p. 7.

[3]See IAEA, ''Iraq's Non-Compliance With Its Safeguards Obligations,'' IAEA Document GC(XXXV)/978, Attachments 1 and 3, September 16, 1991.

[4]Saudi Arabia is reported by one source to have provided financial and technological support to the Iraqi nuclear weapons program during the 1980s in exchange for access to nuclear weapons technology. This allegation was made by Mohammed Khilewi, a Saudi diplomat assigned to the Saudi mission to the United Nations in New York, who defected in May 1994. Specifically, Mr. Khilewi maintained that, as part of a secret 20-year campaign to acquire nuclear weapons, Saudi Arabia gave Saddam Hussein as much as $5 billion of assistance for his nuclear-weapons program as well as specialized equipment needed to advance the centrifuge enrichment component of the program. In return, the Iraqis were to share nuclear technology with Saudi Arabia and also provide training for Saudi nuclear scientists. The funding was suspended following the outbreak of the 1991 Gulf War. Mr. Khilewi also asserted that Saudi Arabia's nuclear weapons-related effort included attempts in 1989 to buy nuclear research reactors from China and an American company. (See "Britain's Gulf War Ally Helped Saddam Build a Nuclear Bomb," *Sunday Times* (London), July 24, 1994; *New York Times*, August 7, 1994.)

In 1988, Saudi Arabia acquired from China the nuclear-capable, intermediate-range CSS-2 (DF-3) missile (2,650-km range and 2,150-kg payload). The missiles carry conventional warheads, and Saudi Arabia and China insisted that the missiles were acquired for this purpose. Since, at the time, there had been no evidence of Saudi interest in nuclear weapons, this claim was generally accepted. If the allegations are true that Saudi Arabia was actively seeking nuclear weapons at the very time it was acquiring the missiles, it is reasonable to speculate that the missiles were intended for use with such weapons to create a Saudi nuclear deterrent. See David Ottoway, "U.S. Asks Soviets, Chinese to Cease Ballistic Missile Sales in the Middle East," *Washington Post*, May 26, 1988; Doug Rabnif, "Fallout from Saudi Missiles," *Christian Science Monitor*, March 30, 1988; "Testimony of Richard Murphy, Assistant Secretary of State for Near Eastern and South Asian Affairs," before the Subcommittee on Arms Control, International Security, and Science, and the Subcommittee on Europe and the Middle East of the House Commitee on Foreign Affairs, May 10, 1988 (processed); Yitzhak Shichor, *East Wind Over Arabia: Origins and Implications of the Sino-Saudi Missile Deal* (Berkley, CA.: Institute of East Asian Studies, University of California, Berkley, 1989).

Saudi Arabia signed the NPT in 1988 to help allay concerns over its acquisition of the missile. Since then, it has made repeated statements forswearing nuclear weapons, but as of early 1995, it had not concluded the NPT-mandated full-scope safeguards agreement with the IAEA. There are no known nuclear facilities in Saudi Arabia. See *20/20*, ABC Network, June 24, 1994; Steve Coll and John Mintz, "Saudi Aid to Iraqi A-Bomb Alleged; Asylum-Seeking Diplomat," *Washington Post*, July 25, 1994; communication with IAEA official, January 1995.

[5]See U.S. Arms Control and Disarmament Agency, "Adherence to and Compliance with Arms Control Agreements and the President's Report to Congress on Soviet Non-Compliance with Arms Control Agreements," January 14, 1993, p. 17.

[6]IAEA, "Highlights of IAEA Director General's Statement to the 38th Regular Session of the IAEA General Conference," 94 PR/33, September 19, 1994.

[7]Evelyn Leopold, "IAEA Says Iraqi Nuclear Capacity 'Neutralized,'" *Reuters*, November 1, 1993; Paul Lewis, "Bowing to U.N., Iraq Will Permit Arms Monitors," *New York Times*, November 27, 1993; "U.N. Gives Iraq Thick Document on Monitoring," *Reuters*, June 23, 1994; Evelyn Leopold, "U.N. to Finish First Phase on Iraqi Arms in September," *Reuters*, June 29, 1994; Jack Redden, "Long-Term U.N. Arms Monitoring Readied for Iraq," *Reuters*, August 18, 1994; Mark Hibbs, "Permanent IAEA Monitors Now on the Job in Iraq," *Nucleonics Week*, September 1, 1994, p. 16.

[8]Louis Meixler, "U.N.-Iraqi Monitoring," *Associated Press*, October 6, 1994; Leon Barkho, "U.N. Says Iraq's Arms Monitoring Operational," *Reuters*, October 6, 1994; Evelyn Leopold, "Ekeus Report Starts Testing for Iraqi Monitoring," *Reuters*, October 10, 1994; Barbara Crossette, "Head of U.N. Inspection Team Says Baghdad Threatens Weapons-Monitoring Effort," *New York Times*, October 12, 1994.

As one component of a long-term monitoring plan called for by the United Nations to prevent a resurgence of the Iraqi nuclear weapons effort, the IAEA, in September 1992, initiated a program providing for the periodic testing, at selected locations, of the principal bodies of water and waterways in Iraq, to help detect any sizeable nuclear activity. This was later accompanied by the use of helicopters equipped with radiation sensors. Two other elements of the plan are the on-going monitoring of selected "dual-use" facilities and equipment that could be utilized in reconstructing the Iraqi nuclear weapons program and the continued use of short-notice inspections. See IAEA, "Report on the Fourteenth IAEA On-Site Inspection in Iraq Under Security Council Resolution 687 (1991)," S/24593, September 28, 1992; Maurizio Zifferero, "The IAEA: Neutralizing Iraq's Nuclear Weapons Potential," *Arms Control Today*, *op. cit.*, p. 9; Paul Lewis, "U.N. Sends Atom-Detecting Copters to Iraq," *New York Times*, September 19, 1993.

[9]On September 23, 1994, for example, then-CIA Director R. James Woolsey stated that Iraq was violating U.N. resolutions by "still hiding Scud missiles, chemical munitions, and its entire biological-weapons warfare program." He added that "Iraq has the largest pool of scientific and technical expertise in the Arab world—over 7,000 nuclear scientists and engineers alone." (See Sid Balman, Jr., "CIA: Saddam Building and Hiding Weapons," *United Press International*, September 26, 1994; Patric Worsnip, "CIA Chief Attacks Iran, Iraq Weapons Programs," *Reuters*, September 26, 1994.) A statement in the speech that "Iraq [was] accelerating construction of deep underground shelters and tunnels to produce and store weapons of mass destruction" was subsequently retracted by the CIA. See Al Kamen, "Tunnel Vision," *Washington Post*, November 4, 1994.

[10]See "U.S. Sends Force as Iraqi Soldiers Threaten Kuwait; Iraqi Denounces Sanctions," *New York Times*, October 8, 1994; "October 2-8: Threat to Kuwait; Iraq Moves Its Troops Toward the Brink Again; Clinton Responds Quickly," *New York Times*, October 9, 1994; "Threats in the Gulf: The Military Buildup; At Least 36,000 U.S. Troops Going to Gulf in Response to Continued Iraqi Buildup," *New York Times*, October 10, 1994; "Iraq Pledges Pullback; Clinton Orders 350 Aircraft to Gulf," *Los Angeles Times*, October 11, 1994; "U.S. Says Iraqis Start Pullback But Crisis is not Over," *Los Angeles Times*, October 12, 1994; "U.S. Puts Limit on its Military Buildup in Gulf," *New York Times*, October 21, 1994.

[11]See U.S. Congress, Office of Technology Assessment, *Technologies Underlying Weapons of Mass Destruction*, OTA-BP-ISC-115 (Washington, DC: U.S. Government Printing Office, December 1993), pp. 209, 220-21.

[12]Rolf Ekeus, head of UNSCOM, has stated his belief that his commission has accounted for all the missiles. On the other hand, in his September 1994 speech (noted above), then CIA Director Woolsey said that Iraq is still hiding Scud missiles. See David C. Isby, "Iraq's Residual Scud Force," *Jane's Intelligence Review*, March 1995; Sid Balman, Jr., "CIA: Saddam Building and Hiding Weapons," *United Press International*, *op. cit.*; Patric Worsnip, "CIA Chief Attacks Iran, Iraq Weapons Programs," *Reuters*, *op. cit.*

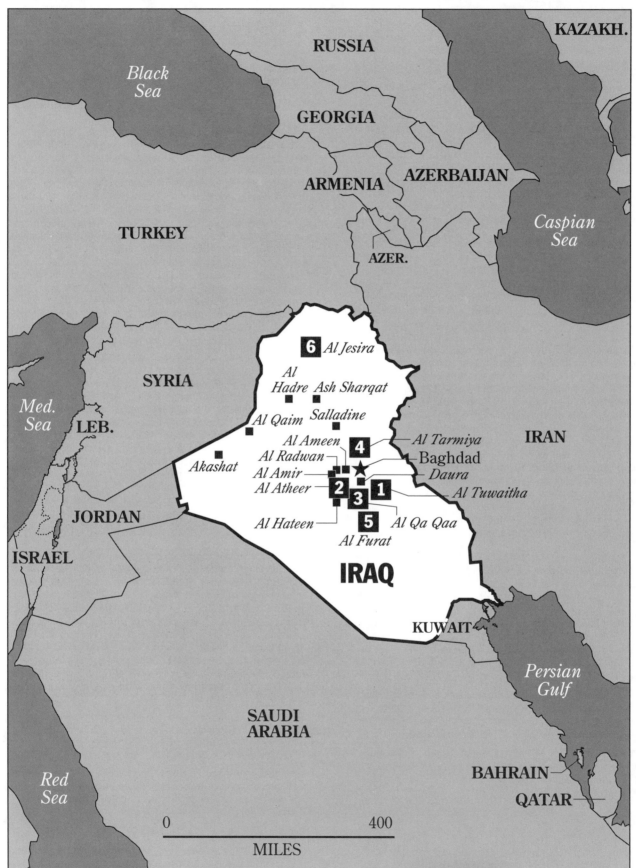

Carnegie Endowment for International Peace, *Tracking Nuclear Proliferation*, 1995.

KEY TO IRAQ MAP

1 **Al Tuwaitha Nuclear Research Center.** *Tammuz I (Osirak), Tammuz II (ISIS), and IRT-5000 research reactors (the first destroyed by Israel in 1981); subject to IAEA inspection prior to Gulf War.*

Site of research and development (R&D) programs in uranium enrichment, including gas centrifuges, Electromagnetic Isotope Separation (EMIS), chemical separation, and gaseous diffusion. *

Location of "hot cells" used for separation of grams of plutonium. * Experimental program for the production of lithium-6 which, if irradiated in a reactor, yields tritium for use in advanced nuclear weapons.

Weapons-related R&D activities in nuclear physics, uranium metallurgy and triggering system capacitors. * *

2 **Al Atheer.** *Prime development and testing site for nuclear weaponization program, including facilities and equipment for large-scale uranium metallurgy and production of weapons components; computer simulations of nuclear weapon detonations; and experiments for the development of an implosion-type explosive structure in nearby "bunker" at Al-Hateen. Possible testing of explosive structures at Al Hadre. * **

3 **Al Qa Qaa High Explosives and Propellant Facility.** *Military and nuclear weapons R&D facility: development of exploding bridge wire detonators (EBW) used in the firing system of nuclear weapons; storage of large quantities of HMX high explosive used in nuclear weapons.*

4 **Al Tarmiya.** *Industrial-scale complex for EMIS designed for the installation of 70 1,200-millimetre separators plus 20 600-millimetre separators. Eight units were operational prior to Desert Storm bombings; if all separators had been installed, plant could have yielded 15 kg of HEU annually, possibly enough for one nuclear weapon. Replica facilities were under construction at Ash-Sharqat. **

5 **Al Furat Project.** *Large-scale manufacturing and testing facility, designed for the production of up to 2,000 maraging steel centrifuges for uranium enrichment, according to IAEA estimates. Site of a planned 100-centrifuge experimental cascade, with an initial operational capability by mid-1993. A 500-centrifuge cascade was to be built at an unknown location. **

6 **Al Jesira.** *Large-scale facility for the production of uranium dioxide (UO_2) and uranium tetrachloride (UCl_4), feed materials for EMIS. Intended site for the production of uranium hexafluoride (UF_6) to feed the centrifuge enrichment program. **

---

* Activities found by IAEA to be in violation of Iraq's safeguards agreement with the IAEA.
* * Activities found by the United States to be in violation of Iraq's obligations under Article II of the Non-Proliferation Treaty (NPT) prohibiting the "manufacture" of nuclear weapons.

Italicized names on map represent nuclear-related sites either declared by Iraq or discovered by IAEA inspectors during implementation of Security Council Resolution 687 adopted at the end of the 1991 Gulf War. The facilities and equipment at these sites that escaped damage during the war were subsequently dismantled or destroyed by the IAEA or came under IAEA monitoring; sensitive nuclear materials have been removed. See chart.

IRAQ: Nuclear Infrastructure

NAME/LOCATION OF FACILITY	TYPE/STATUS	IAEA SAFEGUARDS[1]
FORMER NUCLEAR-WEAPONS (R&D) COMPLEX[2]		
Al Atheer	Prime development and testing facility for nuclear weaponization program; large-scale uranium metallurgy that could produce reflectors, tampers, and other weapons components; location of two isostatic presses (hot and cold) suitable for making shaped charges, plus other remote-controlled machining equipment suitable for production of explosive structures. Operational until damaged by Coalition air attacks (1991); subsequently destroyed by IAEA inspectors.	NPT-violation
Al Tuwaitha	Nuclear physics and uranium metallurgy laboratories; research and development (R&D) in triggering system capacitors; possible site for experimental work on neutronic initiators. Operational until damaged by Coalition air attacks (1991); under IAEA monitoring.	NPT-violation
Al Qa Qaa	Military R&D facility; development of exploding bridge wire detonators; storage of large quantities of HMX high explosive; under IAEA monitoring.	NPT-violation
Al Musaiyib (Al Hateen Establishment)	High-explosive testing site; facility for hydrodynamic studies; facilities and equipment destroyed by the IAEA.	NPT-violation
Al Hadre	Open firing range for air-fuel bombs and fragmentation testing, suitable for experimentation with entire non-nuclear explosive structure of an implosion-type nuclear device; under IAEA monitoring.	NPT-violation
RESEARCH REACTORS[3]		
Osiraq/Tammuz I	Light-water, HEU, 40 MWt; destroyed by Israeli air attack (1981).	NPT-violation
Isis/Tammuz II	Light-water, HEU, 800 KWt; operational until destroyed by Coalition air attack (1991).	Yes
IRT-5000	Light-water, HEU, 5 MWt; operational until destroyed by Coalition air attack (1991).	Yes
URANIUM ENRICHMENT		
Al Tuwaitha	Prototype-scale, electromagnetic isotope separation (EMIS) method[4]; operational until damaged by Coalition air attack (1991).	IAEA-violation
Al Tuwaitha	Prototype-scale, gas centrifuge method[5, 6]; operations terminated as a result of Gulf War (1991).	IAEA-violation
Al Tuwaitha	Laboratory-scale, chemical exchange isotope separation method; operational until damaged by Coalition air attack (1991).	IAEA-violation
Al Tarmiya	Industrial-scale, EMIS method[7]; partially operational until damaged by Coalition air attack (1991).	IAEA-violation
Ash Sharqat	Industrial-scale, EMIS method; under construction until damaged by Coalition air attack (1991).	IAEA-violation
Al Furat	Large manufacturing and testing facility for centrifuge production[8]; under construction until it came under IAEA monitoring after the Gulf War.	IAEA-violation

IRAQ (cont'd.)

NAME/LOCATION OF FACILITY	TYPE/STATUS	IAEA SAFEGUARDS[1]
R E P R O C E S S I N G (P L U T O N I U M E X T R A C T I O N)		
Al Tuwaitha	Laboratory-scale; three hot cells used for separating plutonium from irradiated uranium; operations terminated as a result of Gulf War (1991); equipment largely escaped damage; destroyed or rendered inoperable subsequently by IAEA inspectors.	IAEA-violation[9]
U R A N I U M P R O C E S S I N G		
Akashat	Uranium mine; operational until damaged by Coalition air attack (1991).	N/A (Not applicable)
Al Qaim	Phosphate plant that produced uranium concentrate (U_3O_8); operational until damaged by Coalition air attack (1991); recovered material under IAEA monitoring.	N/A
Al Tuwaitha	Laboratory-scale uranium purification facility (UO_2); operational until heavily damaged by Coalition air attack (1991); recovered equipment under IAEA monitoring.	IAEA-violation
Al Tuwaitha	Laboratory-scale, uranium tetrachloride facility (UCl_4); operational until heavily damaged by Coalition air attack (1991); recovered equipment under IAEA monitoring.	IAEA-violation
Al Tuwaitha	Laboratory-scale production of uranium hexafluoride (UF_6); operational until damaged by Coalition air attack (1991).	IAEA-violation
Al Tuwaitha	Fuel fabrication laboratory; operational until destroyed by Coalition air attack (1991); recovered nuclear material under IAEA monitoring.	IAEA-violation
Mosul (Al Jesira)	Industrial-scale, uranium tetrachloride facility (UCl_4); operational until damaged by Coalition air attack (1991).	IAEA-violation
Mosul (Al Jesira)	Production-scale uranium purification facility (UO_2); operational until heavily damaged by Coalition air attack (1991); production area sustained greatest damage by subsequent Iraqi deception activities.	IAEA-violation

Abbreviations:

HEU	=	highly enriched uranium
LEU	=	low-enriched uranium
nat. U	=	natural uranium
MWe	=	millions of watts of electrical output
MWt	=	millions of watts of thermal output
KWt	=	thousands of watts of thermal output

NOTES (Iraq Chart)

1. For the purposes of this chart, the designations "Yes" and "N/A" ("Not applicable") are used to describe the safeguards in place prior to the 1991 Gulf War at facilities processing or using nuclear materials that were declared by Iraq to the IAEA under Iraq's safeguards agreement with the IAEA (INFCIRC/172). "IAEA-violation" denotes clandestine facilities involved in processing or using nuclear materials that were discovered in the course of the postwar UN-IAEA inspections and found by the IAEA to be violations of the IAEA-Iraq safeguards agreement. "NPT-violation" denotes clandestine facilities that were discovered in the course of the post-war UN-IAEA inspections and were involved in nuclear weapons-related *activities* inconsistent with Iraq's NPT pledge not to manufacture nuclear arms.

2. The Iraqi nuclear weapons program was massive in scope, employing several thousand individuals and spread out over many facilities. The Al Atheer complex was found by UN-IAEA inspectors to be the prime "weaponization" site, with the Al Qa Qaa site and the Al Hatteen High Explosive Site also playing a role in this facet of the program.

Estimates of the time it would have taken Iraq to build a nuclear weapon if its program had continued uninterrupted depend on assessments regarding (1) how long it would have taken Iraq to build up its uranium enrichment infrastructure and produce enough fissionable material for a nuclear device and (2) how long it would have taken Iraq to design and fabricate the non-nuclear components of the devices. David Kay, who led three UN-IAEA teams in Iraq, and Jay C. Davis, who served on two UN-IAEA inspections as an expert on accelerators and construction techniques, have estimated that Iraq was about 18-30 months away from producing enough fissile material for one nuclear weapon when the Gulf War began.

However, a panel of experts convened by the IAEA in April 1992 to review the findings of the inspections up to that point concluded that Iraqi President Saddam Hussein was from three to five years away from acquiring a crude nuclear device. This panel noted that the Iraqis were experiencing delays in manufacturing the approximately 80 EMIS units needed for efficient uranium enrichment (see note 6) and were also encountering problems in designing a practical implosion-type explosive assembly, in which shaped charges made of conventional high explosives would detonate, imploding and compressing the highly enriched uranium core into a supercritical mass. The Iraqis also had difficulties understanding how materials would react if subjected to extreme pressures. See Jay C. Davis and David A. Kay, "Iraq's Secret Nuclear Weapons Program," *Physics Today*, July 1992, p. 21; Paul Lewis, "U.N. Experts Now Say Baghdad Was Far From Making an A-Bomb Before Gulf War," *New York Times,* May 20, 1992; Maurizio Zifferero, "The IAEA: Neutralizing Iraq's Nuclear Weapons Potential," *Arms Control Today*, April 1993, p. 7; David Albright and Mark Hibbs, "Iraq's Bomb: Blueprints and Artifacts," *Bulletin of the Atomic Scientists*, January/February 1992, p. 31.

3. When the UN-IAEA inspections began, the first priority was to locate and remove from Iraq an inventory of weapons-grade uranium that had been provided by France and the Soviet Union for use as reactor fuel and had been subject to regular IAEA inspection prior to the Gulf War. This inventory included stocks of fresh unirradiated fuel from the IRT-5000 research reactor (10.97 kg of 80 percent enriched uranium) plus two other small additional quantities of fresh fuel (1.27 kg of 36 percent-enriched uranium and 372 g of 93 percent enriched uranium). It also included 35.6 kg of irradiated fuel (93 percent enriched uranium). The fresh fuel was of particular concern to the UN-IAEA inspectors and, consequently, it was the first to be airlifted to Russia in mid-November 1991 for isotopic dilution and subsequent placement under IAEA custody. The irradiated fuel was sent to Russia in two shipments, one in December 1993 and another in February 1994. See IAEA, "IAEA Inspections and Iraq's Nuclear Capabilities," IAEA/PI/A35E, April 1992; "IAEA To Transfer Batch of Enriched Uranium to Russia," *AFP*, January 9, 1994, reported in *JPRS-TND-93-003*, January 31, 1994; "Last of HEU in Iraq Shipped to Russia," *Arms Control Today*, March 1994, p. 40.

4. As a result of their inspections through the early fall of 1991, the UN-IAEA inspectors concluded of Iraq's various efforts to produce fissile material for nuclear weapons, its pursuit of electro-magnetic isotope separation (EMIS) technology for enriching uranium had progressed the farthest. Nonetheless, the inspectors found that Iraq had built and operated only a small number of EMIS units at an experimental facility at the Al Tuwaitha Nuclear Research Center near Baghdad and at a partially completed industrial-scale facility in Al Tarmiyah. The ultimate plan of the Iraqi Atomic Energy Commission (IAEC) was to install a total of 90 separators at the Al Tarmiyah plant and to build a replica facility at Ash Sharqat. At the time of the Coalition bombings, eight separators were operational and 17 were in the process of installation at Al Tarmiyah; if all separators had been installed, the plant could have yielded 15 kg of HEU annually, possibly enough for one nuclear weapon. The Ash Sharqat facility was about 85 percent completed, with no separators installed. The attacks, along with the Iraqis' subsequent dismantlement and deception activities, extensively damaged both installations.

All equipment at the Al Tuwaitha and Al Tarmiya sites that might have revealed the existence of the EMIS program was removed and transported by the Iraqi Army to six locations where Iraqi personnel attempted to destroy the telltale signs of the EMIS effort. After UN-IAEA inspection teams obtained access to those locations, the inspectors concentrated their efforts on identifying key EMIS components that were still recognizable to verify Iraqi statements regarding their program. This equipment was then destroyed under the supervision of the UN-IAEA inspectors.

5. Iraq's gas centrifuge program for uranium enrichment was started much later than the EMIS program but, judging by its scope, the Iraqis appeared to be attaching an equal

degree of importance to it. The program relied heavily on foreign sources willing, for example, to provide classified design information of early Western-type centrifuges and to circumvent export controls by providing large quantities of high-tensile "maraging" steel necessary for the manufacture of high-speed enrichment centrifuges. Iraq also obtained approximately 20 carbon-fiber rotors for its centrifuge research and development program from RO-SCH Verbundwerkstoff GmbH of Kaufbeuren, Germany, whose directors were subsequently convicted of violating German export control laws. See David Albright and Mark Hibbs, "Iraq: Supplier-Spotting," *Bulletin of the Atomic Scientists,* January/February 1993, p. 8; Mark Hibbs, "German Couple Convicted for Centrifuge Exports to Iraq," *Nucleonics Week,* November 11, 1993, p. 8.

Early development and testing work was carried out at Al Tuwaitha. The program intensified in mid-1987 and, within a year, work centered on two prototype centrifuges, one using a carbon fiber cylinder, the other using a maraging steel cylinder. Iraq apparently decided to concentrate its centrifuge development and production efforts on the maraging steel option and, based on significant assistance from foreign concerns, Iraq moved rapidly toward the construction of an industrial-scale plant to manufacture centrifuge components, code-named the Al Furat Project and located south of Baghdad near the Badr Engineering Complex. This manufacturing and testing facility, which was slated for completion by mid-1991, was designed to make all the components for the maraging steel centrifuges. The program called for the construction of a prototype 100-centrifuge cascade at Al Furat by the end of 1992 and commencement of cascade operations by mid-1993. In addition, a 500-machine cascade was to be built and operated by early 1986 at an unknown location.

6. All known centrifuge components and manufacturing equipment have been destroyed or rendered inoperable by IAEA inspection teams.

7. Component manufacturing facilities for the Iraqi EMIS program were located at: Al Ameen (prototype components); Al Radwan and Al Amir (magnet cores, return irons, ion sources, collector parts); Sehee at Daura (vacuum chamber parts); Salladine (electrical control panel assembly); and Tuwaitha (coil manufacturing). In January 1993, a U.S. cruise missile attack destroyed Al Rabee, an EMIS-related industrial complex near Zaafarniyah (about 20 km from Baghdad) in retaliation of Iraqi violations of Security Council resolutions establishing no-fly zones in Iraq. Al Rabee and Al Dijjla—another site at Zaafarniyah that was not hit in the attack—were manufacturing plants whose activities were useful in producing EMIS components. Their capabilities included coil winding, chassis assembly, computer-aided design, printed circuit-board fabrication, and control system design and assembly. Reportedly the two plants had manufactured some EMIS equipment installed at the Al Tarmiya facility. See Mark Hibbs, "IAEA in 'Difficult Position' After U.S. Attack on Iraq Site," *Nucleonics Week,* January 21, 1993.

8. These facilities, which escaped damage during the Gulf War, were far from completion when work stopped in August 1990.

9. One of the fuel elements processed was from the IRT-5000 reactor and was exempt from safeguards under Article 37 of INFCIRC/172, Iraq's safeguards agreement with the IAEA. The other three were fabricated indigenously from undeclared nuclear material, in violation of the safeguards agreement. A total of 6 grams of plutonium was recovered.

Additional References

1990: Leonard S. Spector with Jacqueline R. Smith, *Nuclear Ambitions* (Boulder, Colo.: Westview Press, 1990). **1991/1992:** IAEA, "IAEA Reports on On-Site Inspections in Iraq Under Security Council Resolution 687 (1–14)," 1991/1992. **1992:** David Albright and Mark Hibbs, "Iraq's Bomb: Blueprints and Artifacts," *Bulletin of the Atomic Scientists,* January/February 1992, pp. 30–40; Gary Milhollin, "Building Saddam Hussein's Bomb," *New York Times Magazine,* March 8, 1992, pp. 30–36; IAEA, "IAEA Inspections and Iraq's Nuclear Capabilities," IAEA/PI/A35E, April 1992;

David Albright and Mark Hibbs, "Iraq's Shop-Till-You Drop Nuclear Program," *Bulletin of the Atomic Scientists,* April 1992, pp. 27–37; Jay C. Davis and David A. Kay, "Iraq's Secret Nuclear Weapons Program," *Physics Today,* July 1992, p. 21; Paul Lewis, "U.N. Experts Now Say Baghdad Was Far From Making an A-Bomb Before Gulf War," *New York Times,* May 20, 1992. **1993:** Maurizio Zifferero, "The IAEA: Neutralizing Iraq's Nuclear Weapons Potential," *Arms Control Today,* April 1993, p. 7.

Israel

Israel, which is not a party to the Nuclear Non-Proliferation Treaty (NPT), is considered a de-facto nuclear-weapon state. In recent years, unclassified estimates of Israel's nuclear capabilities have been based in large part on analyses of the revelations made by former Israeli nuclear technician Mordechai Vanunu to the *Sunday Times* of London in October 1986.[1] Based on the data he supplied concerning Israeli plutonium production, the *Sunday Times* projected that Israel might have as many as 200 nuclear devices.[2] U.S. officials who attempted at the time to harmonize Vanunu's testimony with other relevant information concluded, however, that, given the relatively small size of Israel's only plutonium-producing reactor, located at the Dimona research complex, Israel's nuclear armory probably contained fewer than 100 weapons, and perhaps no more than 50 or 60. Extrapolating from these lower figures to the present, the Israeli nuclear arsenal might be in the range of 70–80 weapons today. Vanunu also provided detailed information indicating that Israel had produced tritium and lithium deuteride, suggesting that the Israeli arsenal consists, at least in part, of "boosted" nuclear weapons, weapons that use nuclear fusion to increase their efficiency. Since Israel is not known to have conducted any nuclear tests (see below), it is assumed that it could not have advanced to the point of producing thermonuclear weapons ("hydrogen bombs").

A 1991 book by Seymour Hersh, a prominent American investigative journalist, stated that Israel's arsenal was considerably larger and more advanced than the earlier estimates suggested. Relying largely on interviews with U.S. intelligence analysts and Israeli figures knowledgeable about the country's nuclear program, Hersh claimed that Israel possessed "hundreds" of low-yield, neutron-bomb type warheads, many in the form of artillery shells and land mines, as well as full-fledged thermonuclear weapons.[3]

A recent press report has provided new details about Israel's nuclear weapons infrastructure. The report alleges that Nahal Soreq is the installation where Israel conducts research on nuclear weapons design. It goes on to state that Israel's nuclear weapons are assembled at a facility in Yodefat and that Israel's nuclear missile base and bunker for storing nuclear gravity bombs is in Kfar Zekharya. Tactical nuclear weapons, it continues, are stored at Eilabun.[4]

The Israeli nuclear weapons program was launched in the fall of 1956, in the wake of the Suez crisis. At the time, France's Socialist government, led by Guy Mollet, was deeply committed to Israel's survival, and the two states confronted threats stemming from Arab nationalism—Israel because of its isolated position in the Middle East and France because of growing unrest in French Algeria. France secretly pledged to assist Israel in developing nuclear arms and agreed to supply it with a sizable plutonium-bearing reactor to be built at Dimona, in the Negev, some 40 miles from Beersheba.[5]

In mid-1957, with French Atomic Energy Commission approval, Israel signed an agreement with the French firm of St. Gobain Techniques Nouvelles for the construction of several additional facilities at the Dimona site, including the key installation—where Vanunu would subsequently work—for extracting plutonium from the Dimona reactor's spent fuel. Soon thereafter, France also gave Israel important information on the design and manufacture of nuclear weapons themselves.

Francis Perrin, the scientific head of the French Atomic Energy Commission from 1951 to 1970, was intimately involved with the French-Israeli nuclear program. In an on-the-record 1986 interview with the London *Sunday Times*, Perrin acknowledged that France supplied the Dimona reactor and the plutonium extraction plant and that, for at least two years during the late 1950s, France and Israel collaborated on the design and development of nuclear weapons.[6]

There has been no conclusive proof that Israel has ever conducted a full-scale nuclear test. Its nuclear arsenal is thought to have been developed, in part, through the testing of non-nuclear components and computer simulations—and through the acquisition of weapons design and test information from abroad. Israel is thought, for example, to have obtained data from France's first nuclear test, in 1960.[7] It may also have obtained data from U.S. nuclear tests at approximately that time. According to a May 1989 U.S. television documentary, Israel was able to gain access to information concerning U.S. tests from the 1950s and early 1960s. The test data could have included the results of U.S. boosted and thermonuclear weapons that were being developed at the time.[8]

In addition, there has been speculation that a signal detected on September 22, 1979, by a U.S. VELA monitoring satellite over the South Atlantic, was, in fact, the flash from a low-yield Israeli nuclear test—possibly of a tactical nuclear weapon or of the fission trigger of a thermonuclear device.

Seymour Hersh reports that "according to Israeli officials whose information about other aspects of Dimona's activities has been corroborated," the September 1979 event was indeed an Israeli test—and was actually the third of a series of tests conducted at that time.[9] The first two tests, Hersh's sources stated, were obscured by storm clouds. The claim that clouds would prevent detection of an atmospheric nuclear detonation by a VELA satellite has been challenged, however, since the satellite is said to rely in part on infra-red sensors that can penetrate cloud cover. Thus this critical matter remains unresolved.

Israel currently deploys two nuclear-capable ballistic missile systems: the Jericho I and Jericho II. Up to fifty Jericho I solid fuel, two-stage missiles with an approximate range of 660 km are deployed in shelters on mobile launchers possibly at a facility located midway between Jerusalem and the Mediterranean. The Jericho II solid fuel, two-stage missile can travel an estimated 1,500 km; commercial satellite photos indicate that the missile base between Jerusalem and the Mediterranean was enlarged between 1989 and 1993 to allow for Jericho II deployment. Furthermore a U.S. government study indicates that Israel's Shavit space launch vehicle could be modified to carry 500 kg over 7,800 km, in effect making it an intercontinental ballistic missile (ICBM).[10]

Senior Israeli officials reportedly are divided over how to respond to the Clinton Administration's proposal for a global treaty prohibiting the further production of plutonium and weapons-grade uranium for nuclear weapons or not under IAEA safeguards, a proposal familiarly known as the "Fissile Material Cut-off." The proposal would permit the five nuclear-weapon states and the three de facto nuclear powers (India, Israel, and Pakistan) to retain existing stocks of unsafeguarded fissile material, in effect permitting the retention of undeclared nuclear weapons capabilities in the latter states. Some Israeli officials argue that Israel should not limit its nuclear options, while others believe Israel's inventory of fissionable materials could be capped without injuring the country's strategic capabilities. As of early 1995, the government of Prime Minister Yitzhak Rabin appeared unlikely to embrace the freeze proposal. During 1995, Rabin may make concessions regarding the status of the strategically important Golan Heights as part of peace treaty negotiations with Syria, concessions that are likely to be bitterly attacked by the right-wing, opposition Likud party. Most observers believe that, in this situation, it will be politically impossible for Rabin simultaneously to accept restraints on Israel's nuclear program.[11]

NOTES

[1]"Revealed: The Secrets of Israel's Nuclear Arsenal," *Sunday Times* (London), October 5, 1986.

[2]Given what is known about Israel's nuclear infrastructure, it has long been assumed that its weapons use plutonium rather than highly enriched uranium for their cores.

[3]Seymour M. Hersh, *The Samson Option* (New York: Random House, 1991), pp. 291, 312, 319.

[4]See Harold Hough, "Israel's Nuclear Infrastructure," *Jane's Intelligence Review*, November 1994, p. 508.

[5]See Leonard S. Spector, *The Undeclared Bomb* (Cambridge, MA: Ballinger Publishing Company, 1988), pp. 165– 87; Pierre Péan, *Les Deux Bombes* (Paris: Fayard, 1981) Chapters V, VII, VIII.

[6]"France Admits It Gave Israel A-Bomb," *Sunday Times* (London), October 12, 1986.

[7]*Ibid.;* Steven Weissman and Herbert Krosney, *The Islamic Bomb* (New York: Times Books, 1981), p. 114.

[8]See "Israel: The Covert Connection," *Frontline*, PBS Network, May 16, 1989.

[9]See Seymour M. Hersh, *The Samson Option, op. cit.*, p. 271.

[10]See David A Fulghum and Jeffery M. Lenorovitz, "Israeli Missile Base Hidden in Hill," *Aviation Week and Space Technology*, November 8, 1993, p. 29; Steven E. Gray, "Israeli Missile Capabilities: A Few Numbers to Think About" (Livermore, CA.: Lawrence Livermore National Laboratories, Z Division, October 7, 1988).

[11]See "Commentator Attacks Egyptian Position on NPT," *Ha'aretz*, Tel Aviv, September 29, 1994, in *FBIS-NES-94-190*, September 30, 1994, p. 35.

Israel:
Map and Chart

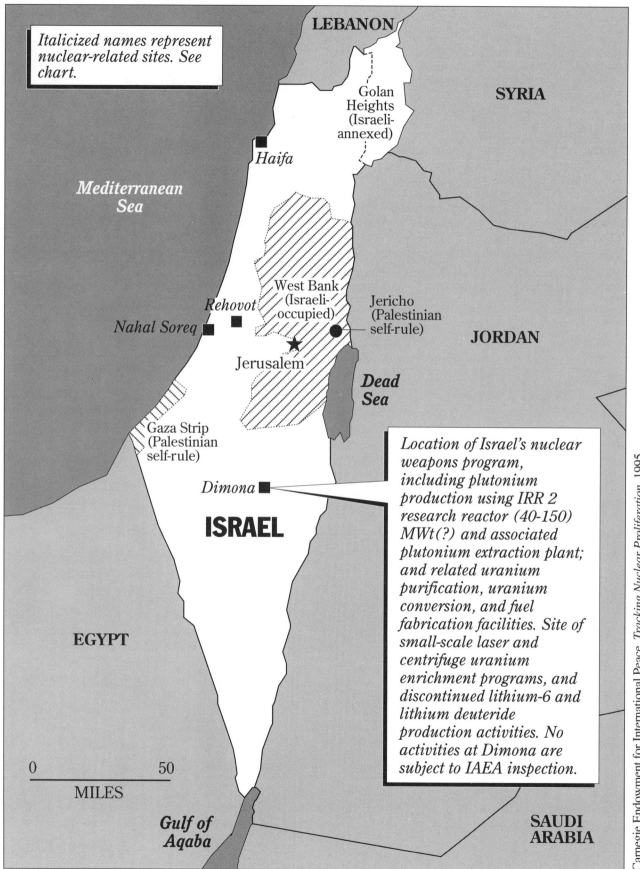

Italicized names represent nuclear-related sites. See chart.

LEBANON

SYRIA

Golan Heights (Israeli-annexed)

Haifa

Mediterranean Sea

West Bank (Israeli-occupied)

Rehovot

Nahal Soreq

Jericho (Palestinian self-rule)

JORDAN

Jerusalem

Dead Sea

Gaza Strip (Palestinian self-rule)

Dimona

ISRAEL

EGYPT

Location of Israel's nuclear weapons program, including plutonium production using IRR 2 research reactor (40-150) MWt(?) and associated plutonium extraction plant; and related uranium purification, uranium conversion, and fuel fabrication facilities. Site of small-scale laser and centrifuge uranium enrichment programs, and discontinued lithium-6 and lithium deuteride production activities. No activities at Dimona are subject to IAEA inspection.

0 ————— 50

MILES

Gulf of Aqaba

SAUDI ARABIA

Carnegie Endowment for International Peace, *Tracking Nuclear Proliferation*, 1995.

ISRAEL: Nuclear Infrastructure

NAME/LOCATION OF FACILITY[1]	TYPE/STATUS	IAEA SAFEGUARDS[2]
RESEARCH REACTORS		
IRR I, Nahal Soreq	Light water, HEU, 5 MWt; operating.	Yes
IRR 2, Dimona	Heavy water, natural U; 40(?), 70(?), 150(?) MWt; operating.[3]	No
URANIUM ENRICHMENT		
Dimona	Experimental/pilot-scale laser and centrifuge-enrichment programs; operating.	No
REPROCESSING (PLUTONIUM EXTRACTION)		
Dimona	Operating	No
Nahal Soreq	Pilot-scale; operating.	No
URANIUM PROCESSING		
Negev area, near Beersheeba	Uranium phosphate mining; operating.	N/A (Not applicable)
Haifa	Yellowcake produced in two phosphate plants; operating.	N/A
Southern Israel	Yellowcake produced in phosphate plant; operating.	N/A
Dimona	Uranium purification (UO_2); operating.	No
Dimona	Uranium conversion (UF_6); operating.	No
Dimona	Fuel fabrication facility; operating.	No
HEAVY WATER PRODUCTION		
Rehovot	Pilot-scale plant; operating.	No
TRITIUM, LITHIUM DEUTERIDE		
Dimona	Lithium-6 production, allowing the production of both tritium and lithium deuteride; decommissioned.	No

Abbreviations:

HEU	=	highly enriched uranium
LEU	=	low-enriched uranium
nat. U	=	natural uranium
MWe	=	millions of watts of electrical output
MWt	=	millions of watts of thermal output
KWt	=	thousands of watts of thermal output

NOTES (Israel Chart)

1. The Israel Electric Corporation (IEC) has expressed a strong interest in importing foreign reactor technology to construct a nuclear power plant, possibly at Shivta in the Negev desert. However, Israel's inquiries in this regard have not been answered because of its unwillingness to sign the NPT or otherwise place its entire nuclear program under international safeguards.

2. On September 30, 1994, the International Atomic Energy Agency (IAEA) announced that it had "decided to restore technical assistance to Israel and expressed its wish for closer cooperation between the IAEA and Israel in Agency activities in accordance with the Agency's statute and objectives." The IAEA had suspended such assistance following Israel's 1981 attack on Iraq's Osiraq research reactor. See "IAEA Restores Technical Assistance to Israel," *Reuters*, September 30, 1994.

3. Estimates of the reactor's capacity have varied widely. See Leonard S. Spector, *The Undeclared Bomb* (Cambridge, MA: Ballinger Publishing Company, 1988), pp. 165-87.

Additional References

1990: Leonard S. Spector with Jacqueline R. Smith, *Nuclear Ambitions* (Boulder, CO: Westview Press, 1990). **1994:** "Israel: Production Halt Idea Debated," *Nucleonics Week*, January 6, 1994, p. 18; "Israel Wants Nuclear Plant Once Nonproliferation Issue Cleared," *Nucleonics Week*, February 24, 1994, p. 15.

Libya

For nearly twenty-five years, Libya's mercurial leader, Colonel Muammer Khadafi, has sought to obtain nuclear arms and other weapons of mass destruction to advance the cause of radical Arab nationalism. Libya made its first attempt at nuclear arming in 1970, when it attempted to purchase nuclear weapons from China but was rebuffed. In the intervening years, Libyan officials have repeatedly expressed interest in acquiring nuclear weapons, although Libya has made little progress in that regard.

Libya ratified the Nuclear Non-Proliferation Treaty (NPT) in 1975, but it did not enter into a formal safeguards agreement with the International Atomic Energy Agency (IAEA) until 1980. Libya currently operates a Soviet-supplied 10 MWt research reactor at Tajoura and apparently is no longer pursuing plans to build a 440 MWe power reactor near the Gulf of Sidra, originally promised by the Soviet Union in 1977. The Tajoura reactor is subject to IAEA inspection.

Currently, Libya's nuclear program has not advanced beyond a rudimentary level, and thus does not pose a short- or medium-term proliferation threat. Still, since the early 1990s, unconfirmed reports about Libyan attempts to purchase nuclear technology suggest that Libya's nuclear ambitions continue. Tripoli could be awaiting an opportunity to purchase weapons-grade material on the black market in order to restart or accelerate a nuclear-weapons program.[1]

Although Libya has been unsuccessful in its attempts to develop a nuclear weapons capability, it is nonetheless perceived as a growing threat to its neighbors, and to southern Europe, because of its programs to pursue other weapons of mass destruction and ballistic missiles. Its bid to acquire chemical weapons in the late 1980s has been well documented, and it is now believed to have a substantial chemical weapon stockpile.[2]

Throughout the late 1980s and early 1990s Libya made several apparently unsuccessful attempts to purchase missiles from abroad, such as the SS-23 and SS-21 from the Soviet Union and the DF-3A, M-9, and M-11 from China. Libya's missile arsenal remains relatively limited. It currently deploys a number of basic 300 km–range Scud-B missiles that it obtained from the Soviet Union. Tripoli, however, continues to develop its indigenous missile, the al-Fateh, with a reported range of 950 km. This missile is not yet operational. In addition, Tripoli may be continuing to cooperate with North Korea on the future purchase of the Nodong-1 (and/or related technologies) which is also still under development. Libya is not known to have purchased either the Scud Mod. B or Mod. C missiles from North Korea.[3]

NOTES

[1]Mark Hibbs, *Nucleonics Week*, August 22, 1991, p. 7, noted in *Eye On Supply* (Monterey, CA.: Monterey Institute for International Studies, Spring 1992), p. 40; Bill Gertz, *Washington Times*, February 24, 1992, p. A1, noted in *Eye On Supply* (Monterey, CA.: Monterey Institute for International Studies, Fall 1992), p. 25; R. Jeffery Smith, *Washington Post*, April 28, 1992, p. A2, noted in *Eye On Supply* (Monterey, CA.: Monterey Institute for International Studies, Winter 1993), p. 37.

[2]Stephen Engelberg with Michael Gordon, ''Germans Accused of Helping Libya Build Nerve Gas Plant,'' *New York Times*, January 1, 1989.

For Libya's recent efforts to develop a chemical weapon capability including the construction of underground facilities see ''Challenges to Peace in the Middle East,'' Address of R. James Woolsey, DCI, to the Washington Institute for Near East Policy, Wye Plantation, MD, September 23, 1994 (revised version).

[3]''Testimony of Joseph S. Bermudez Jr.,'' before the House Committee on Foreign Affairs, Subcommittee on International Security, International Organizations, and Human Rights, February 14, 1993.

Most recently, in June 1993, Libya tried to obtain chemicals for solid rocket fuel from Russia via Ukraine—a move confirming Libya's continued interest in ballistic missile development. See ''Libya: Rocket Racket,'' *Africa Confidential*, July 16, 1993.

Sardinia

ITALY

ALB.

Tyrrhenian Sea

GREECE

Aegean Sea

TURKEY

Sicily

Ionian Sea

⌐ MALTA

Sea of Crete

Crete

Mediterranean Sea

TUNISIA

★
Tripoli ■

Tajoura

Gulf of Sidra

Soviet-supplied 10 MWt research reactor: subject to IAEA inspection.

LIBYA

EGYPT

ALGERIA

NIGER

CHAD

SUDAN

0   400

MILES

Carnegie Endowment for International Peace, *Tracking Nuclear Proliferation*, 1995.

LIBYA: Nuclear Infrastructure[1]

NAME/LOCATION OF FACILITY	TYPE/STATUS	IAEA SAFEGUARDS
RESEARCH REACTORS		
Tajoura	Light water, HEU, 10 MWt; operating.	Yes
POWER REACTORS		
Gulf of Sidra	Light water, LEU, 440 MWe; planned but apparently abandoned.	Not applicable

Abbreviations:

HEU = highly enriched uranium
LEU = low-enriched uranium
MWe = millions of watts of electrical output
MWt = millions of watts of thermal output

References

1990: Leonard S. Spector with Jacqueline R. Smith, *Nuclear Ambitions* (Boulder, CO: Westview Press, 1990); *Nuclear Developments*, November 15, 1990, p. 9, noted in *Eye On Supply* (Monterey, CA: Monterey Institute for International Studies, Spring 1991), p. 40. **1992:** IAEA, *The Annual Report for 1992* (Vienna: IAEA, July 1993); "Libya Ready to Invite Inspection of Any Site," *Disarmament Newsletter*, April 1992.

9
LATIN AMERICA

Argentina

Argentina became a party to the Nuclear Non-Proliferation Treaty (NPT) on February 10, 1995.[1] The event was the culmination of a twelve-year process through which Argentina gradually ruled out the development of nuclear weapons by accepting increasingly stringent non-proliferation controls.

Until this process began, Argentina had steadfastly refused to accept such restrictions, and, in late 1983, just prior to the inauguration of its first elected government in more than two decades, evidence emerged that the country had taken the first steps toward developing nuclear arms. At that time, Argentina's departing military junta revealed that since 1978, the country had been secretly constructing a uranium enrichment plant at Pilcaniyeu that was not subject to International Atomic Energy Agency (IAEA) inspections. Although the junta claimed that the facility was intended for peaceful purposes, the secrecy surrounding the plant and the fact that Argentina's nuclear power reactors did not require enriched uranium fuel gave rise to suspicions that it was to be part of a clandestine nuclear weapons development program.[2]

The inauguration of Argentine President Raul Alfonsín in December 1983 led to a major shift in Argentine nuclear policy. Military involvement in the country's nuclear affairs was ended, and nuclear confidence-building measures with neighboring Brazil initiated earlier were accelerated. These included reciprocal visits to all nuclear installations in both countries (including those not subject to IAEA inspection) beginning in 1987 and a series of bilateral nuclear agreements (see below).

No weapons-grade highly enriched uranium is believed to have been produced at the Pilcaniyeu facility, and Argentina has pledged not to produce any in the future. Since Argentina does not possess a plutonium separation (''reprocessing'') plant, it currently has no source of weapons-grade nuclear materials.

On July 18, 1991, Brazilian President Fernando Collor de Mello and Argentine President Carlos Saúl Menem signed a formal bilateral agreement to allow mutual inspections of nuclear installations in their respective countries and to establish the Argentine-Brazilian Accounting and Control Commission (ABACC) to implement the bilateral inspection accord. A quadripartite agreement to integrate the bilateral inspection system with that of the IAEA was signed by the two nations, the IAEA, and ABACC on December 13, 1991, in Vienna. Exchanges of nuclear materials inventories and mutual inspections under the July 1991 bilateral accord began in the fall of 1992 following the inauguration of ABACC. However, inspections under the Quadripartite Safeguards Agreement were delayed until after the Brazilian Congress approved it on February 25, 1994, and it entered into force on March 4, 1994. The Argentine Congress had approved the agreement on August 5, 1992.[3]

In January 1994, Argentina brought into force the Treaty for the Prohibition of Nuclear Weapons in Latin America (Treaty of Tlatelolco), thus making the commitment not to acquire, manufacture, test, use, or permit the stationing of a nuclear explosive device on its territory and accepting IAEA inspection of all peaceful nuclear activities in Argentina.[4] Under the Quadripartite Agreement, ABACC and the IAEA must now establish an initial inventory of all nuclear materials in Argentina as a basis for future inspections. This task will be complicated by the years of unsafeguarded activities at Pilcaniyeu.

Missile Restraints. On November 29, 1994, Argentine Foreign Ministry officials announced that Argentina had become a member of the Missile Technology Control Regime (MTCR). The announcement followed President Menem's earlier decision, under U.S. pressure, to scrap Argentina's program to develop the nuclear-capable, 1,000-km, two-stage Condor II missile. The Condor program had been a joint Argentine-Egyptian-Iraqi endeavor.[5] Argentina is no longer conducting research and development on ballistic missiles or on an indigenous space-launch vehicle.

NOTES

[1]Embassy of Argentina, "Argentina Accesses the Non-Proliferation Nuclear-Weapons Treaty," Press Release, February 10, 1995.

[2]For an extensive review of the Argentine nuclear program during the 1980s see Leonard S. Spector with Jacqueline R. Smith, *Nuclear Ambitions* (Boulder, CO: Westview Press, 1991), pp. 223-41.

[3]See "Brazil and Argentina Move Towards Safeguards," *Nuclear Engineering International*, September 1991, p. 4; "Brazil's Military May Block Safeguards with Argentina," *Nucleonics Week*, November 28, 1991, p. 8; James Brooke, "Brazil and Argentina Join Up to Open Their Nuclear Sites," *New York Times*, December 13, 1991; Statement by Michael McCurry, "Argentina and Brazil: Ratification of the Quadripartite Safeguards Agreement," U.S. Department of State, March 4, 1994; John R. Redick, Julio C. Carasales, and Paulo S.

Wrobel, "Nuclear Rapprochement: Argentina, Brazil, and the Nonproliferation Regime," *Washington Quarterly,* vol. 18, no. 1, Winter 1995, pp. 107-22; John R. Redick, "Nuclear Weapon-Free Zones in a Changing Global Environment," in J.B. Poole and R. Guthrie, eds., *Verification 1994,* VERTIC, United Kingdom, 1994.

[4]See "Brazil, Argentina and Chile Bring Into Force the Treaty for the Prohibition of Nuclear Weapons in Latin America (The Treaty of Tlatelolco)," Arms Control and Disarmament Agency Press Release, June 3, 1994.

[5]See "Nation Joins Missile Technology Control Regime," Buenos Aires, *Buenos Aires Herald*, November 30, 1994, in *JPRS-TND-93-001*, January 6, 1994, p. 11; U.S. Congress, Office of Technology Assessment, *Technologies Underlying Weapons of Mass Destruction*, OTA-BP-ISC-115 (Washington, DC: U.S. Government Printing Office, December 1993), p. 224.

Argentina:
Map and Chart

BOLIVIA

PARAGUAY

BRAZIL

ARGENTINA

URUGUAY

Los Gigantes

Cordoba

*Rio Tercero
(Embalse)*

Rosario

La Estella

Atucha

*Pacific
Ocean*

San Rafael

Sierra Pintada

Marlague

*Buenos
Aires
(Constituyentes)
(Ezeiza)*

CHILE

Arroyito

Pilcaniyeu

*San Carlos
de Bariloche*

*Previously unsafeguarded
uranium enrichment plant.
No known production of
weapons-grade uranium.
Argentina has declared it will
enrich uranium to no more
than 20 percent, precluding
its use for nuclear weapons.
Under inspection by the
Argentine-Brazilian
Accounting and Control
Commission (ABACC),
pursuant to bilateral
agreement of July 18, 1991;
and under initial "ad hoc"
inspection by the
International Atomic Energy
Agency (IAEA), pursuant to
quadripartite safeguards
agreement between Argentina,
Brazil, ABACC, and the
IAEA that entered into force
on March 4, 1994.*

*Atlantic
Ocean*

*Falkland
Islands
(Br.)*

0   500

MILES

Carnegie Endowment for International Peace, *Tracking Nuclear Proliferation*, 1995.

ARGENTINA: Nuclear Infrastructure

NAME/LOCATION OF FACILITY	TYPE/STATUS	SAFEGUARDS[1]
P O W E R R E A C T O R S		
Atucha I	Heavy-water, natural U, 320 MWe; operating.	IAEA/ABACC
Embalse	Heavy-water, natural U, 600 MWe; operating.	IAEA/ABACC
Atucha II	Heavy-water, natural U, 745 MWe; under construction.	Planned
R E S E A R C H R E A C T O R S		
RA-0, Cordoba	Light-water, medium-enriched uranium, 1 Wt; operating.	IAEA/ABACC
RA-1, Constituyentes	Light-water, medium-enrched uranium, less than 100 KWt; operating.	IAEA/ABACC
RA-2, Constituyentes	Light-water, HEU, less than 1 MWt; operating.	IAEA/ABACC
RA-3, Ezeiza	Light-water, LEU, 5 MWt; operating.	IAEA/ABACC
RA-4, Rosario	Light-water, medium-enriched uranium, less than 1 MWt; operating.	IAEA/ABACC
RA-6, San Carlos de Bariloche	Light-water, HEU, 500 KWt; operating.	IAEA/ABACC
RA-10, Cordoba	20% enriched uranium, graphite reflector; not operating.	IAEA/ABACC[2]
U R A N I U M E N R I C H M E N T		
Pilcaniyeu	Gaseous diffusion method; partially operating; full operations planned for 1995.[3]	IAEA/ABACC
R E P R O C E S S I N G (P L U T O N I U M E X T R A C T I O N)		
Ezeiza	Construction suspended, 1990	N/A (Not applicable)
U R A N I U M P R O C E S S I N G		
Los Gigantes	Uranium mining; operating.	N/A
La Estella	Uranium mining; operating.	N/A
Sierra Pintada	Uranium mining; operations deferred for financial reasons.	N/A
La Estella	Uranium milling; operating.	N/A
San Rafael	Uranium milling; operating.	N/A
Marlague	Uranium milling; shut-down(?); stand-by(?).	N/A
Cordoba	Uranium purification (UO_2) plant; operating.	IAEA/ABACC
Cordoba	Uranium purification (UO_2) plant; operating(?).	IAEA/ABACC
Cordoba	Uranium purification (UO_2) plant; shut-down.	IAEA/ABACC
Constituyentes	Uranium conversion plant; operating.	IAEA/ABACC
Pilcaniyeu	Uranium conversion (UF_6) facility; operating.	IAEA/ABACC
Ezeiza	Fuel fabrication facility (Atucha); operating.	IAEA/ABACC
Ezeiza	Fuel fabrication facility (CANDU); operating.	IAEA/ABACC
Constituyentes	Pilot-scale plant to fabricate HEU; operating.	IAEA/ABACC
Constituyentes	Research reactor fuel fabrication plant; operating.	IAEA/ABACC

ARGENTINA (cont'd.)

NAME/LOCATION OF FACILITY	TYPE/STATUS	SAFEGUARDS[1]
H E A V Y W A T E R P R O D U C T I O N		
Arroyito	Production-scale; operating.	IAEA/ABACC
Atucha	Pilot-scale; under construction.	IAEA/ABACC

Abbreviations:

HEU	=	highly enriched uranium
LEU	=	low-enriched uranium
nat. U	=	natural uranium
MWe	=	millions of watts of electrical output
MWt	=	millions of watts of thermal output
KWt	=	thousands of watts of thermal output

NOTES (Argentina Chart)

1. IAEA and ABACC are conducting parallel inspections at the indicated facilities. At the Pilcaniyeu enrichment plant, the IAEA has only recently been permitted to conduct inspections, following the ratification of the Quadripartite Safeguards Agreement. These inspections are still in the initial or ''ad hoc'' phase, pending completion of formal IAEA ''facility attachments'' for this facility. See Mark Hibbs, ''Tough Safeguards Negotiations Ahead for Argentine-Brazilian Agreement,'' *Nuclear Fuel*, September 26, 1994, p. 3.

2. This facility is not listed as under safeguards in the *IAEA Annual Report for 1993*. However, an official of the Argentine Embassy stated in March 1993 that by that time the reactor had come under IAEA safeguards (Document INFCIRC/62).

3. Mark Hibbs, ''Brazil Mulling New Centrifuge Plant to Serve Two Reactors at Angra Site,'' *Nuclear Fuel*, September 26, 1994, p. 3. Argentina has not produced weapons-grade uranium at the facility and has pledged not to do so in the future.

Additional References

1990: Ismael Bermudez, ''Report on Nuclear Projects, Privatization Plan,'' *Clarin*, August 5, 1990, in *FBIS-LAT*, August 9, 1990, p. 22. **1991:** ''World Survey: Still Waiting for a New Dawn,'' *Nuclear Engineering International*, June 1991, p. 20. **1992:** *World Nuclear Industry Handbook*, 1992 (Sutton, Surrey, U.K.: Nuclear Engineering International, 1992); ''Nuclear Reactor Reactivated After 17 Years,'' *Telam*, July 7, 1992, in *JPRS-TND-92-023*, July 16, 1992, p. 4; ''Heavy Water Plant To Open in Late 1992,'' *Efe*, April 29, 1992, in *FBIS-LAT-92-087*, May 5, 1992, p. 24; ''Arroyito Startup,'' *Nuclear Engineering International*, July 1992, p. 4. **1993:** IAEA, *The Annual Report for 1992* (Vienna: IAEA, July 1993), pp. 152-64; interview with Argentine official, March 1993. **1994:** Maria O'Donnell, ''Menem Announces Support for Nonproliferation Treaty,'' Buenos Aires, *Pagina/12*, June 22, 1994, in *JPRS-TND-94-014*, July 13, 1994, p. 26.

Brazil

In the fall of 1990, Brazil's President, Fernando Collor de Mello, declared that he was terminating a secret nuclear weapons program that Brazil had been pursuing over the previous decade. Begun when the country was under military control and code-named the Solimoes Project, the secret effort included research on nuclear weapons design, the excavation of a 100-meter-deep shaft for underground nuclear tests at a military base near Cachimbo in the Amazon jungle, and the development of two uranium enrichment facilities not subject to International Atomic Energy Agency (IAEA) safeguards. These installations—a laboratory-scale plant at the Institute for Energy and Nuclear Research (IPEN), in São Paulo, and the initial module of an industrial-scale plant at the Brazilian Navy's Aramar Research Center, in Ipéro—are potentially capable of producing uranium enriched to the level needed for nuclear weapons. Neither plant is known to have produced such material, however, and Brazil has declared that, at the facilities, it intends to produce only low-enriched uranium, which cannot be used for nuclear arms.

Underscoring his decision to end Brazil's nuclear weapons program, President Collor closed the Cachimbo test site in a public ceremony, on September 17, 1990, by symbolically throwing a shovelful of cement into the test shaft. A week later he announced at the United Nations that Brazil was rejecting "the idea of any test that implies nuclear explosions, even for peaceful ends."[1]

On July 18, 1991, President Collor and Argentine President Carlos Saúl Menem signed a bilateral agreement to allow mutual inspections of nuclear installations in their respective countries and to establish the Argentine-Brazilian Accounting and Control Commission (ABACC) to implement the bilateral inspection accord. The accord was the culmination of a bilateral program of confidence-building in the nuclear sphere begun in 1987. A quadripartite agreement to integrate ABACC's bilateral inspection system with that of the IAEA was signed by the two nations, the IAEA, and ABACC on December 13, 1991, in Vienna. Exchanges of nuclear materials inventories and mutual inspections under the July 1991 bilateral accord began in the fall of 1992 following the inauguration of ABACC. However, inspections under the Quadripartite Safeguards Agreement were delayed until the Brazilian Congress approved it on February 25, 1994, and it entered into force on March 4, 1994. The Argentine Congress had approved the agreement on August 5, 1992.[2]

On May 30, 1994, Brazil brought into force the Treaty for the Prohibition of Nuclear Weapons in Latin America (Treaty of Tlatelolco) thus making the commitment not to acquire, manufacture, test, use, or permit the stationing of a nuclear explosive device on its territory and accepting IAEA inspection of all peaceful nuclear activities in Brazil.[3] Brazil has also indicated that it may soon join the Nuclear Non-Proliferation Treaty (NPT).

Under the Quadripartite Agreement, ABACC and the IAEA must establish an initial inventory of all nuclear materials in Brazil, as a basis for future inspections. This task will be complicated by the years of unsafeguarded activities at IPEN and Ipéro, and at other sites, some of which may still remain undisclosed, that contributed to the Brazilian nuclear weapons program.

Missile Program. During the 1970s and early 1980s, Brazil developed a series of sounding rockets, some of them modified into short-range surface-to-surface missiles for export to Libya and Iraq, among others. During the late 1980s and early 1990s, however, Brazil terminated programs to develop more capable missiles, such as the Avibras SS-300 and the Orbita–MB/EE-600 and 1000—whose ranges in excess of 300 kilometers would have placed them in the class of systems that the Missile Technology Control Regime (MTCR) sought to restrict. This led the Brazilian government to announce its decision on February 11, 1994, to comply with the criteria and standards of the MTCR, agreeing to restrict the export of missiles (and key components of missiles) able to carry weapons of mass destruction to distances above the 300-km threshold.[4] Nevertheless, Brazil is continuing research and development on certain space-launch systems with potential military applications, such as the Sonda IV rocket, which has a 600- to 1,000-km range and can carry a 500-kg maximum payload. Because of these continuing efforts, Brazil has not been invited to become a member of the MTCR, in contrast to Argentina, which has cancelled its sensitive space-launch and missile development programs.[5]

NOTES

[1]See James Brooke, "Brazil Uncovers Plan by Military to Build Atom Bomb and Stops It," *New York Times*, October 9, 1990; David Albright, "Brazil Comes in From the Cold," *Arms Control Today*, December 1990, p. 13.

[2]"Brazil and Argentina Move Towards Safeguards," *Nuclear Engineering International*, September 1991, p. 4; Mark Hibbs, "Brazil's Military May Block Safeguards with Argentina," *Nucleonics Week*, November 28, 1991, p. 8; James Brooke, "Brazil and Argentina Join Up to Open Their Nuclear Sites," *New York Times*, December 13, 1991; Statement by Michael McCurry, "Argentina and Brazil: Ratification of the Quadripartite Safeguards Agreement," U.S. Department of State, March 4, 1994; John R. Redick, Julio C. Carasales, and Paulo S. Wrobel, "Nuclear Rapprochement: Argentina, Brazil, and the Nonproliferation Regime," *Washington Quarterly,* vol. 18, no. 1, Winter 1995, pp. 107-22; John R. Redick, "Nuclear Weapon-Free Zones in a Changing Global Environment," in J.B. Poole and R. Guthrie, eds., *Verification 1994,* VERTIC, United Kingdom, 1994.

[3]See "Brazil, Argentina and Chile Bring Into Force the Treaty for the Prohibition of Nuclear Weapons in Latin America (The Treaty of Tlatelolco)," ACDA Press Release, June 3, 1994.

[4]Raquel Stenzel, "Government Agrees to Comply With Missile Control Pact," *Gazeta Mercantil* (São Paulo) February 12, 1994, in *JPRS-TND-94-006,* March 16, 1994, p. 16.

[5]See William C. Potter and Harlan W. Jencks, eds., *The International Missile Bazaar: The New Suppliers' Network* (Boulder, CO: Westview Press, 1994), pp. 99, 101, 102, 104, 115; U.S. Congress, Office of Technology Assessment, *Technologies Underlying Weapons of Mass Destruction,* OTA-BP-ISC-115 (Washington, DC: U.S. Government Printing Office, December 1993), p. 209.

Brazil:
Map and Chart

VENEZUELA

COLOMBIA

GUYANA

SURINAME

FR. GUIANA

*Nuclear test site (dismantled). Part of
nuclear weapons program pursued by Brazil
in 1980s until terminated in 1990 by
President Fernando Collor de Mello.*

Itataia

■ *Cachimbo*

BRAZIL

PERU

★ Brasilia

BOLIVIA

*Belo
Horizonte*

*Pocos de
Caldas*

*São Paulo
(IPEN)*

Resende

*Atlantic
Ocean*

*Pacific
Ocean*

Ipero

Rio de Janeiro

PARAGUAY

Angra dos Reis
Sao Jose dos Campos

ARGENTINA

Aramar Research Center. *First module of
industrial-scale centrifuge uranium enrichment
plant. No known production of weapons-grade
uranium. Facility was apparently key component
of now-terminated Brazilian nuclear-weapons
program of 1980s. Brazil has declared it will
enrich uranium to no more than 20 percent,
precluding its use for nuclear weapons.*

URUGUAY

*Under inspection by Argentine-Brazilian
Accounting and Control Commission (ABACC),
pursuant to bilateral agreement of July 18, 1991;
and under initial "ad hoc" inspection by the
IAEA, pursuant to quadripartite safeguards
agreement between Argentina, Brazil, ABACC,
and the IAEA that entered into force on March
4, 1994.*

0   500
MILES

Carnegie Endowment for International Peace, *Tracking Nuclear Proliferation*, 1995.

BRAZIL: Nuclear Infrastructure

NAME/LOCATION OF FACILITY	TYPE/STATUS	SAFEGUARDS[1]
P O W E R R E A C T O R S		
Angra I	Light-water, LEU, 626 MWe; operating.	IAEA/ABACC
Angra II	Light-water, LEU, 1,300 MWe; under construction.	IAEA/ABACC (planned)
Angra III	Light-water, LEU, 1,300 MWe; under construction (indefinitely deferred).	N/A (Not applicable)
R E S E A R C H R E A C T O R S		
IEAR-1, São Paulo	Pool, HEU, 5 MWt; operating.	IAEA/ABACC
RIEN-1, Rio de Janeiro	Medium-enriched uranium, 10 KWt; operating.	IAEA/ABACC
Triga-UMG, Belo Horizonte	Medium-enriched uranium, 100 KWt; operating.	IAEA/ABACC
IPEN-Zero Power, São Paulo	Light-water, LEU, 100W; operating.	IAEA/ABACC
Renap-11, Aramar Research Center, Ipéro	Pressurized-water; under development.	IAEA/ABACC
U R A N I U M E N R I C H M E N T		
Resende[2]	Pilot-scale, jet-nozzle method; completed; program cancelled.[3]	IAEA/ABACC
Belo Horizonte	Laboratory-scale, jet nozzle method; shut-down(?).	IAEA/ABACC
Aramar Research Center, Ipéro	First-stage, industrial-scale plant, ultracentrifuge method; operating.	IAEA/ABACC
IPEN, São Paulo	Laboratory-scale ultracentrifuge method; operating.	IAEA/ABACC
R E P R O C E S S I N G (P L U T O N I U M E X T R A C T I O N)		
Resende	Indefinitely postponed	IAEA/ABACC
IPEN, São Paulo	Laboratory-scale; completed; not known to have operated.	IAEA/ABACC
U R A N I U M P R O C E S S I N G		
Pocos de Caldas	Uranium mining site; operating.	N/A
Pocos de Caldas	Uranium milling site; operating.	N/A
Itataia	Uranium milling site; not operating.	N/A
IPEN, São Paulo	Uranium purification (UO_2) site	IAEA/ABAAC
Aramar Research Center, Ipéro	Laboratory-scale uranium purification (UO_2) facility; operating.	IAEA/ABACC[4]
Resende	Uranium conversion facility (UF_6); indefinitely postponed.	IAEA/ABACC
IPEN, São Paulo	Pilot-scale uranium conversion facility (UF_6); operating.	IAEA/ABACC
IPEN, São Paulo	Laboratory-scale uranium conversion facility (UF_6); operating.	IAEA/ABACC
Aramar Research Center, Ipéro	Uranium conversion plant (UF_4); construction postponed.	IAEA/ABACC[5]
Resende	Fuel fabrication plant; operating.	IAEA/ABACC

Abbreviations:

HEU	=	highly enriched uranium
LEU	=	low-enriched uranium
nat. U	=	natural uranium
MWe	=	millions of watts of electrical output
MWt	=	millions of watts of thermal output
KWt	=	thousands of watts of thermal output

NOTES (Brazil Chart)

1. IAEA and ABACC are conducting parallel inspections at the indicated facilities. At the IPEN and Aramar Center enrichment plants, the IAEA has only recently been permitted to conduct inspections, following the ratification of the Quadripartite Safeguards Agreement. These inspections are still in the initial or "ad hoc" phase, pending completion of formal IAEA "facility attachments" for these facilities. See José Maria Tomazela, "IAEA Team Inspects Navy Nuclear Center," *Agencia Estado*, São Paulo, July 7, 1994, in *FBIS-LAT-94-131*, July 8, 1994, p. 40; Mark Hibbs, "Tough Safeguards Negotiations Ahead for Argentine-Brazilian Agreement," *Nuclear Fuel*, September 26, 1994, p. 3.

2. The Brazilian nuclear industry is exploring the possibility of building a centrifuge uranium enrichment plant at Resende, utilizing a type of centrifuge manufactured in Brazil and now operating at the Aramar Center (see entry below). The projected capacity would be sufficient to supply fuel for the Angra I and II power reactors. The fuel for the reactors is low-enriched uranium, which is not usable for nuclear weapons. See Mark Hibbs, "Brazil Mulling New Centrifuge Plant to Serve Two Reactors at Angra Site," *Nuclear Fuel*, September 26, 1994, p. 3.

3. In March 1994, Brazil dropped its project to enrich uranium using the German jet nozzle process. It is not clear from the press reports whether this decision affects only the facilities at Resende or also involves the laboratory-scale plant at Belo Horizonte, listed below. George Vidor, "Jet Nozzle Uranium Enrichment Project Cancelled,"*O Globo*, Rio de Janeiro, March 19, 1994, in *FBIS-LAT-94-056*, March 23, 1994, p. 48; Mark Hibbs, "Brazil Mulling New Centrifuge Plant to Serve Two Reactors at Angra Site," *op. cit.*

4. This facility, commissioned in early July 1994, was inspected by ABACC and IAEA officials on July 29, 1994. José Maria Tomazela, "IAEA Team Inspects Ipéro Uranium Hexafluoride Plant,"*Agencia Estado*, São Paulo, July 29, 1994, in *JPRS-TND-94-016*, August 19, 1994, p. 19.

5. José Maria Tomazela, "IAEA Team Inspects Ipéro Uranium Hexafluoride Plant," *op. cit.*; Tania Malheiros, "Navy Confirms Project for Hexafluoride Conversion," *Agencia Estado*, São Paulo, August 4, 1994, in *JPRS-TND-94-016*, August 19, 1994, p. 19.

Additional References

1990: Leonard S. Spector with Jacqueline R. Smith, *Nuclear Ambitions* (Boulder, CO: Westview Press, 1990). **1992:** "Construction of Angra-2 Nuclear Plant to Resume," *O Estado de São Paulo*, January 31, 1992, in *FBIS-LAT-92-022*, February 3, 1992, p. 37; *World Nuclear Industry Handbook 1992* (Sutton, Surrey, U.K.: Nuclear Engineering International, 1992); Mark Hibbs, "Furnas Gets German Bank Credits for Completion of Angra-2," *Nucleonics Week*, July 23, 1992, p.4; "New Financing Agreement Aims to Kick Start Construction at Angra-2," *Nuclear Engineering International*, September 1992, p. 2; "Indigenous Mastery of Nuclear Fuel Cycle Seen," *Manchete*, June 27, 1992, in *FBIS-LAT-92-161*, August 19, 1992, p. 27. **1993:** Mark Hibbs, "Brazil Gives Quiet Go-Ahead to Resuming Work on Angra-2," *Nucleonics Week*, April 1, 1993, p. 3; IAEA, *The Annual Report for 1992* (Vienna: IAEA, July 1993), pp. 152-164. **1994:** Armin Schmid, "Angra-1 Now Set to Return to Service in Early March," *Nucleonics Week*, January 20, 1994, p. 15; Armin Schmid, "Brazilian Senate Approves Nuclear Safeguards Agreement," *Nucleonics Week*, February 17, 1994, p. 16; George Vidor, "Jet Nozzle Uranium Enrichment Project Cancelled," *O Globo*, March 19, 1994, in *FBIS-LAT-94-056*, March 23, 1994, p. 48; "Brazil: Angra-1 Restart Readied," *Nucleonics Week*, April 21, 1994, p. 14; Armin Schmid, "Angra-1 Readied for Restart After Emergency Plan Approved," *Nucleonics Week*, October 27, 1994, p. 2. **1995:** Armin Schmid, "After 21 Months Off Line Angra-1 Restarts with New Emergency Plan," *Nucleonics Week*, January 5, 1995, p. 4.

10
SOUTH AFRICA

South Africa

On March 24, 1993, President F.W. de Klerk, in an address to parliament, revealed that during the 1970s and 1980s, South Africa had pursued a secret nuclear weapons program that had included the manufacture of a total of six nuclear devices before the program was halted in late 1989.[1]

South Africa's first nuclear efforts are believed to have started in the early 1970s under the auspices of a peaceful nuclear explosions (PNE) program to bolster South Africa's mining industry. However, former President de Klerk stated in his 1993 speech to the parliament that in 1974 the government secretly decided to develop nuclear weapons. The project soon expanded with the construction and operation of a pilot-scale uranium enrichment plant (the "Y-Plant") at Valindaba (now Pelindaba East) and the construction of a nuclear test site in the Kalahari Desert. South Africa completed two nuclear test shafts in 1976 and 1977.[2]

In mid-1977, a Soviet observation satellite discovered that South Africa was making significant preparations for an underground nuclear test at the Kalahari site. In response, Washington and Moscow applied substantial diplomatic pressure on Pretoria, which soon abandoned the site and sealed up the bore holes. South Africa did not abandon its nuclear weapons program, however, and continued its efforts to enrich uranium to weapons-grade and to perfect the design of a nuclear explosive.[3]

South Africa produced its first dummy nuclear device (without a core of weapons-grade uranium) and used it to conduct a "cold test" in August 1977. The country's first operational nuclear device was then completed in November 1979.[4]

South African officials insist they had never intended to use nuclear weapons in a conflict. Pretoria's intent, they state, was to use nuclear weapons as part of a "three-phase nuclear strategy" to deter potential adversaries—especially Soviet-backed forces from neighboring states—and to compel Western involvement in a military crisis with such

forces, should deterrence fail. Phase I involved neither confirming nor denying the nation's nuclear capability in order to keep adversaries wary. During Phase II, if an attack were imminent, Pretoria would reveal its capability to Western leaders in the hopes that they would intervene. If Western nations did not respond, then Phase III involved conducting an overt nuclear test to demonstrate South Africa's possession of nuclear weapons to potential enemies.[5] South Africa's weapons designers, however, took steps to permit the weapons to be delivered by aircraft and went to great lengths to ensure their reliability, suggesting that military use had not been entirely ruled out.

The election of F.W. de Klerk as South Africa's president in September 1989 marked the end of the nuclear weapons program. On February 26, 1990, de Klerk issued internal orders to terminate the effort and dismantle all existing weapons. Beginning in July 1990, the uranium enrichment plant at Pelindaba East was decommissioned, the six devices were dismantled, the hardware and technical documents were destroyed, the highly enriched uranium (HEU) was recast and sent back to the Atomic Energy Commission for permanent storage, and Advena, the weapons manufacturing site, was neutralized and sealed. The entire dismantlement process was completed in early July 1991. (De Klerk did not reveal the program's existence publicly, however, until his March 1993 address to parliament.)[6]

South Africa subsequently acceded to the Nuclear Non-Proliferation Treaty (NPT) on July 10, 1991. It then concluded a full-scope safeguards agreement with the International Atomic Energy Agency (IAEA) on September 16, 1991, placing all its nuclear plants and all previously produced enriched uranium under IAEA safeguards. On August 19, 1994, the IAEA confirmed de Klerk's statement that all nuclear devices had been dismantled.[7]

De Klerk, in a historic reform of South Africa's politics, ended the country's decades-long policy of racial separation (apartheid) and brought an end to white minority rule. Following nationwide elections open to all races in April 1994, Nelson Mandela became South Africa's president. The Mandela government remains committed to the country's status as a non-nuclear-weapon state under the NPT. The weapons-grade uranium produced during the 1970s and 1980s remains in South Africa, controlled by the Atomic Energy Corporation and under IAEA inspection. The HEU may be used to fuel the SAFARI research reactor.

NOTES

[1]"De Klerk Tells World South Africa Built and Dismantled Six Nuclear Weapons," *Nuclear Fuel*, March 29, 1993, p. 6; Helmoed-Romer Heitman, "South Africa Built Six Nuclear Weapons," *Jane's Defence Weekly*, April 10, 1993, p. 14.

[2]See Mark Hibbs, "South Africa's Secret Nuclear Program: From a PNE to a Deterrent," *Nuclear Fuel*, May 10, 1993, p. 3; Mark Hibbs, "South Africa's Secret Nuclear Program: The Dismantling," *Nuclear Fuel*, May 24, 1993, p. 9; Mark Hibbs, "Pretoria Replicated Hiroshima Bomb in Seven Years, Then Froze Design," *Nucleonics Week*, May 6, 1993, p. 16; David Albright, "South Africa and the Affordable Bomb," *Bulletin of the Atomic Scientists*, July/August 1994, p. 37; Dr. Waldo Stumpf, "South Africa's Limited Nuclear Deterrent Programme and the Dismantling Thereof Prior to South Africa's Accession to the Nuclear Non-Proliferation Treaty," speech at the South African Embassy, Washington, DC, July 23, 1993.

[3]Mark Hibbs, "South Africa's Secret Nuclear Program: From a PNE to a Deterrent," *op. cit.*, p. 3; David Albright, "South Africa and the Affordable Bomb," *op. cit.*

[4]See note 3.

[5]See David Albright, "South Africa and the Affordable Bomb," *op. cit.*; Roger Jardine, J.W. de Villers, and Mitchell Reiss, "Why South Africa Gave up the Bomb," *Foreign Affairs*, November/December 1993; Daryl Howlett and John Simpson, "Nuclearization and Denuclearization in South Africa," *Survival*, Autumn 1993.

[6]Mark Hibbs, "South Africa's Secret Nuclear Program: The Dismantling," *op. cit*, p. 9; David Albright, "South Africa and the Affordable Bomb," *op. cit.*; David Albright, "A Curious Conversion," *Bulletin of the Atomic Scientists*, June 1993, p. 6; Roger Jardine, J.W. de Villers and Mitchell Reiss, "Why South Africa Gave up the Bomb," *op. cit.*; Mark Stansfield, "Kalahari Test Site Explored," *Sunday Star*, March 28, 1993, in *JPRS-TND-93-010*, April 16, 1993, p. 7.

[7]"IAEA Confirms All South African Warheads Destroyed," *Reuters*, August 19, 1994; Michael Knapik, "South African AEC Head Says Stockpile of HEU Will Be Maintained for SAFARI," *Nuclear Fuel*, August 16, 1993, p. 5.

South Africa:
Map and Chart

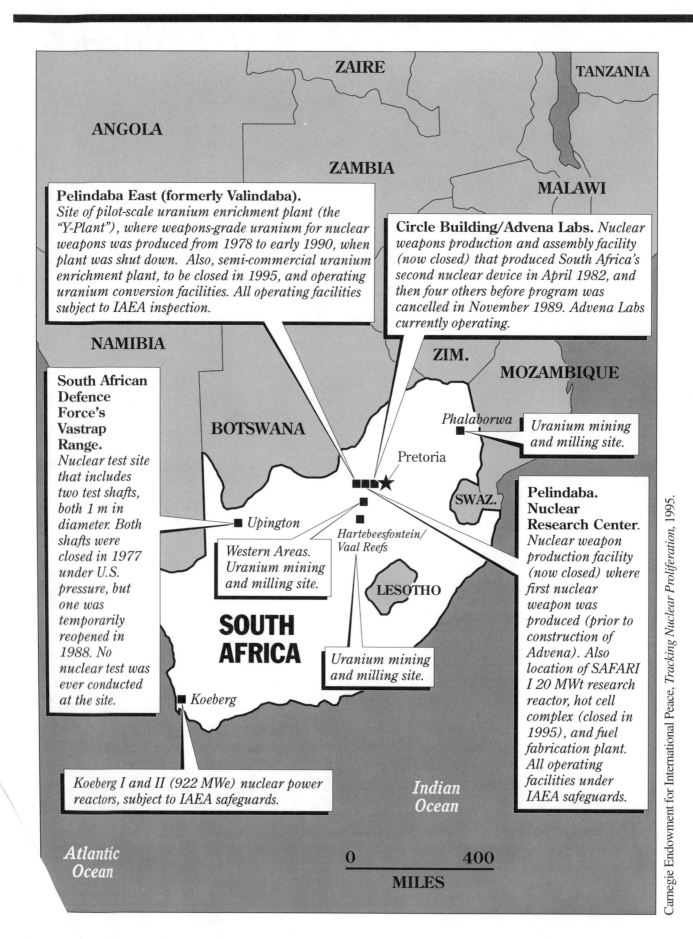

ZAIRE

TANZANIA

ANGOLA

ZAMBIA

MALAWI

Pelindaba East (formerly Valindaba). *Site of pilot-scale uranium enrichment plant (the "Y-Plant"), where weapons-grade uranium for nuclear weapons was produced from 1978 to early 1990, when plant was shut down. Also, semi-commercial uranium enrichment plant, to be closed in 1995, and operating uranium conversion facilities. All operating facilities subject to IAEA inspection.*

Circle Building/Advena Labs. *Nuclear weapons production and assembly facility (now closed) that produced South Africa's second nuclear device in April 1982, and then four others before program was cancelled in November 1989. Advena Labs currently operating.*

NAMIBIA

ZIM.

MOZAMBIQUE

South African Defence Force's Vastrap Range. *Nuclear test site that includes two test shafts, both 1 m in diameter. Both shafts were closed in 1977 under U.S. pressure, but one was temporarily reopened in 1988. No nuclear test was ever conducted at the site.*

BOTSWANA

Phalaborwa

Uranium mining and milling site.

Pretoria

■■■★

■

■

■ *Upington*

SWAZ.

Pelindaba. Nuclear Research Center. *Nuclear weapon production facility (now closed) where first nuclear weapon was produced (prior to construction of Advena). Also location of SAFARI I 20 MWt research reactor, hot cell complex (closed in 1995), and fuel fabrication plant. All operating facilities under IAEA safeguards.*

Western Areas. Uranium mining and milling site.

Hartebeesfontein/ Vaal Reefs

LESOTHO

SOUTH AFRICA

Uranium mining and milling site.

■ *Koeberg*

Koeberg I and II (922 MWe) nuclear power reactors, subject to IAEA safeguards.

Indian Ocean

Atlantic Ocean

0   400

MILES

Carnegie Endowment for International Peace, *Tracking Nuclear Proliferation*, 1995.

SOUTH AFRICA: Nuclear Infrastructure

NAME/LOCATION OF FACILITY	TYPE/STATUS	IAEA SAFEGUARDS
FORMER NUCLEAR-WEAPONS (R&D) COMPLEX		
Pelindaba Nuclear Research Center	Nuclear weapons production and assembly facility; closed.[1]	IAEA visited and verified dismantlement.
Building 5000 (isolated building at Pelindaba)	Dedicated to development and assembly of nuclear explosives; closed.[2]	IAEA visited and verified dismantlement.
Pelindaba East (''Y-Plant'')	Pilot-scale facility for producing weapons-grade uranium; closed.[3]	IAEA visited and verified dismantlement.
Circle Building/Advena Central Labs	Two generations of buildings involoved in nuclear weapons production and assembly; closed.[4]	IAEA visited and verified dismantlement.
Upington (Vastrap Range)	Nuclear test site; closed.[5]	IAEA visited and verified dismantlement.
POWER REACTORS		
Koeberg I	Light water, LEU, 922 MWe; operating.	Yes
Koeberg II	Light water, LEU, 922 MWe; operating.	Yes
RESEARCH REACTORS		
SAFARI I, Pelindaba	Light water, 45 percent enriched, 20 MWt; operating.	Yes
URANIUM ENRICHMENT		
Pelindaba East (Formerly Valindaba)	Semi-commercial plant able to produce low-enriched uranium, jet-nozzle (''helikon'') method; scheduled to be closed (March 1995).[6]	Yes
	Pilot-scale molecular laser isotope separation (MLIS) uranium enrichment plant; not yet enriching uranium, but nuclear materials present.	MLIS pilot plant under IAEA safeguards
REPROCESSING/PLUTONIUM EXTRACTION		
Pelindaba	Hot cell complex; operating.	Yes
URANIUM PROCESSING		
Phalaborwa	Uranium mining; operating.	N/A (Not applicable)
Buffelsfontein	Uranium milling; closed.	N/A
Hartebeesfontein	Uranium milling; operating.	N/A
Vaal Reefs	Uranium milling(3 mills); operating.	N/A
Western Areas	Uranium milling; operating.	N/A
Phalaborwa	Uranium milling; operating.	N/A
Pelindaba East	Pilot-scale uranium conversion plant (UF_6); operating.	Yes
Pelindaba East	Semi-commercial-scale uranium conversion plant (UF_6); operating.	Yes
Pelindaba	MTR fuel fabrication plant; operating.	Yes
Pelindaba	LEU fuel fabrication plant; closed (March 1995).	Yes

Abbreviations:

LEU	= low-enriched uranium
MWe	= millions of watts of electrical output
MWt	= millions of watts of thermal output

NOTES (South Africa Chart)

1. South Africa's first nuclear device was produced at this facility.

2. One criticality experiment was conducted at this facility; it is also the site where the first nuclear weapon was produced.

3. According to South Africa's declaration to the IAEA, the plant generated about 1,500 kg of enriched uranium while active, ranging from low-enriched uranium to weapons-grade HEU. Out of this inventory, 350 kg had been enriched to 90 percent U-235 and above. Each South African nuclear weapon required an estimated 55 kg of weapon-grade uranium.

South African officials have indicated that they would like to keep at least a portion of the weapons-grade HEU to fuel the SAFARI-1 research reactor.

4. Five additional nuclear devices were manufactured at the Circle building between April 1982 and November 1989. When then-President De Klerk cancelled the nuclear weapons program, construction of Advena Central Labs had just been completed and equipment was being moved into the facilities. The labs continue to conduct non-nuclear research.

5. The test site, which was never used, comprised a 385 m shaft and a 216 m one, both 1 m in diameter.

6. Michael Knapik and Wilson Dizard III, ''South Africa Will Shut Enrichment Plant in March,'' *Nuclear Fuel*, January 30, 1995, p. 20. Research and development on laser isotope separation expected to continue.

Additional References

1990: Leonard S. Spector with Jacqueline R. Smith, *Nuclear Ambitions* (Boulder, CO: Westview Press, 1990). **1992:** Datafile: ''South Africa,'' *Nuclear Engineering International*, January 1992, pp. 12-17; ''South Africa,'' *1992 NUEXCO Review*, 35. **1993:** IAEA, *The Annual Report for 1992* (Vienna: IAEA, July 1993), 152-64. **1994:** Brendan Boyle, ''South Africa Testing Laser-Uranium Process,'' *Reuters*, August 24, 1994; Ann MacLachlan, ''South Africa AEC Looking for Partners to Help Fund Laser Enrichment Facility,'' *Nuclear Fuel*, August 29, 1994, p. 1; Mark Hibbs, ''South Africa Reinstatement Ends 18-Year Ban From IAEA Board,'' *Nucleonics Week*, September 29, 1994, p. 6.

11

APPENDICES

Appendix A
NUCLEAR WEAPONS—A PRIMER

A nuclear weapon is a device in which most or all of the explosive energy is derived from either fission, fusion, or a combination of the two nuclear processes. Nuclear fission is the splitting of the nucleus of an atom into two (or more) parts. Highly enriched uranium and plutonium, when bombarded by neutrons, will release energy and emit additional neutrons while splitting into lighter atoms. In nuclear fusion, light isotopes of hydrogen, usually deuterium and tritium, join at high temperatures and similarly liberate energy and neutrons.

Fission Weapons

Many heavy atomic nuclei are capable of being fissioned; but only a fraction of these are fissile, which means fissionable by neutrons with a wide range of velocities. It is this property of fissile material, principally U^{235} and Pu^{239}, that allows a chain reaction to be achieved in weapons employing the fission process. In a chain reaction, fissile nuclei that have been bombarded by neutrons split and emit two or more neutrons, which in turn induce proximate nuclei to fission and sustain the process. With each successive fission "generation" additional energy is released, and, if the fission of one nucleus induces an average of more than one fission in the following generation, the energy yield of each generation is multiplied. A fission explosion in the range of 1 to 100 Kt for example, would occur over a few microseconds and involve over fifty generations, with 99.9 percent of the energy released coming in the last seven. The minimum mass of material necessary to sustain a chain reaction is called the critical mass. This value may be lowered by increasing the material's density through compression or by surrounding it with "reflectors" to minimize the escape of neutrons; this makes it difficult to pin down the precise amount of uranium or plutonium required for a bomb.

Two basic nuclear-weapon-design approaches that are used to achieve a supercritical mass (i.e., exceeding the critical level) are the implosion technique and the gun assembly technique. In the implosion technique, a peripheral charge of chemical high explosive is uniformly detonated to compress a subcritical mass of plutonium or highly enriched uranium into a supercritical configuration. In the gun assembly technique, two (or more) subcritical masses of highly enriched uranium (plutonium cannot be used) are propelled together by a conventional explosion, resulting in a supercritical mass. In both cases, a tamper may be used to keep the material from exploding before enough generations of a chain reaction have occurred, and this tamper often doubles as a reflector to reduce the escape of neutrons.

Fusion Weapons

Fusion of light atomic nuclei requires a high density of fusion material and extraordinary heat, both of which are provided by a fission explosion in a "thermonuclear" or "hydrogen" bomb. Lithium-6 deuteride is the most widely used thermonuclear material, serving as a source of both deuterium and tritium, the atoms whose nuclei merge, in a fusion weapon.

In a "boosted" weapon, fusion material is introduced directly into (or next to) the core of fissile material, improving the efficiency of a fission weapon and thus increasing the yield of a given quantity of highly enriched uranium or plutonium. Although energy is released in the fusion reaction of a boosted weapon, the primary contribution of the fusion material to the explosion is that it provides additional neutrons for the fission process and therefore allows a more rapidly multiplying chain reaction to occur.

Other thermonuclear weapons are designed to capitalize on the energy released in a "secondary" fusion reaction triggered by a "primary" fission explosion. In such devices, fusion material is kept physically separate from a fissile or boosted fissile core that compresses and ignites it. Additional "stages" of fusion or fission material may be included to augment the weapon's yield, with each layer being triggered by ones closer to the core. For example, the hydrogen bomb includes a third stage or "blanket" of natural uranium, a widely available fissionable but not fissile material, that is fissioned by fast neutrons from the primary and secondary fission and fusion reactions. Hence, the energy released in the explosion of such a device stems from three sources—a fission chain reaction, the first stage; "burning" of the thermonuclear fuel, the second stage; and the fission of the U^{238} blanket, the third stage—with, very roughly, half the total energy stemming from fission and the other half from fusion.

Notes

This Appendix is adapted from Thomas B. Cochran, William M. Arkin, and Milton M. Hoenig, *U.S. Nuclear Forces and Capabilities* (Cambridge, MA: Ballinger Publishing Company, 1984), Chapter 2.

Additional References

1992: Robert Serber, Richard Rhodes, *The Los Alamos Primer* (Berkeley, CA: University of California Press, 1992).

1993: U.S. Congress, Office of Technology Assessment, *Technologies Underlying Weapons of Mass Destruction* (Washington, DC: Government Printing Office, December 1993); David Albright, Frans Berkhout, and William Walker, *World Inventory of Plutonium and Highly Enriched Uranium—1992* (New York, NY: Oxford University Press, 1993). **1994:** Gary T. Gardner, *Nuclear Nonproliferation: A Primer* (Boulder CO: Lynne Rienner Publishers, 1994).

Appendix B
MANUFACTURING NUCLEAR WEAPONS

Overview

A nation seeking to manufacture nuclear arms must complete a number of essential, often extremely demanding steps.

- It must develop a design for its nuclear device or obtain such a design from another state;

- It must produce the fissile material for the core of the device or obtain it from an external source and must then machine the fissile material to fabricate the nuclear parts of the weapon;

- It must fabricate, or obtain from outside, the non-nuclear parts of the device, including the high-explosive elements and triggering components that will detonate the nuclear core;

- It must verify the reliability of these various elements individually and as a system; and

- It must assemble all of these elements into a deliverable nuclear armament.

Design

It is generally accepted today that designing an atomic bomb—drawing the blueprint—is within the capabilities of most nations. Indeed, a number of American college students have come up with workable designs based on unclassified information.

Several states are believed to have received nuclear weapons design information or assistance from other states. France and Israel, for example, are believed to have collaborated on the design of French nuclear weapons in the late 1950s and early 1960s, after which France is thought to have provided Israel with information from a number of its nuclear tests. China, similarly, is believed to have provided Pakistan with the design of the nuclear device that it detonated in its fourth nuclear test, which involved the firing of a nuclear-armed missile. India, however, apparently designed the plutonium-based, implosion device that it detonated in 1974 without outside assistance, and South Africa also apparently designed its uranium-based "gun-type" nuclear weapons without foreign aid.

Acquiring Fissile Materials

The major technical barrier to making a nuclear device is obtaining the necessary fissile material, i.e., weapons-grade uranium or plutonium, for the weapon's core.

Amounts Required. How much would be needed for a nuclear weapon depends on the technical capabilities of the country involved and the size of the weapon it sought to produce. International Atomic Energy Agency (IAEA) regulations assume that 25 kg of weapons-grade uranium or 8 kg of plutonium are the minimum amounts needed to manufacture a nuclear device with a yield of about 20 Kt (equivalent to the explosive force of 20,000 tons of TNT), roughly the size of the Nagasaki bomb. However, by utilizing more sophisticated designs that rely on high compression of the core material, neutron reflecting "tampers," or both, a state could build such a weapon with considerably less material. According to one recent estimate, a country possessing a "low technical capability" could build a 20-Kt device with only 6 kg of plutonium or 16 kg of weapons-grade uranium. A state with a "high technological capability" could potentially build such a device with as little as 5 kg of weapons-grade uranium or 3 kg of plutonium; a 1-Kt device, which would require considerable sophistication to manufacture, might need only about half these amounts.[1]

Highly Enriched Uranium. To make a weapon from uranium, the unstable "isotope" of uranium, U^{235}, having a total of 235 protons and neutrons in its nucleus, is used. Since natural uranium consists of less than 1 percent U^{235}, while nuclear weapons use material that is made up of 90 percent or more U^{235}, natural uranium must be upgraded or "enriched" at an enrichment plant to achieve this concentration.[2] Uranium enrichment is a highly complex process and requires considerable investment. For this reason, the uranium enrichment route was generally considered a less likely path to proliferation than the plutonium option. However, Argentina, Brazil, Iraq, South Africa, and (with extensive outside aid obtained mostly by clandestine means) Pakistan all selected uranium enrichment as their preferred route for acquiring nuclear arms or the potential to manufacture them, and all developed independent uranium enrichment capabilities.[3] India and Israel, although they have relied on the production of plutonium for their nuclear weapons capabilities, have also conducted research on uranium enrichment. India is known to have two experimental enrichment plants. The status of Israel's enrichment program is not publicly known.

Enriched uranium can also be used as a fuel in nuclear power reactors, research reactors, or naval propulsion reactors. The power reactors used in the United States and most other countries (called "light-water reactors") use low-enriched uranium fuel, i.e., uranium that has been enriched from 3 percent to 5 percent U^{235}.[4] Thus a country can have entirely legitimate, non-weapons-related reasons for developing uranium enrichment technology even though the same technology can be used to upgrade uranium to the high enrichment level useful for nuclear weapons. On the other hand, developing a sizable independent uranium-enrichment capability is economically justifiable only for nations with large domestic nuclear power programs or significant potential export markets.

Because highly enriched uranium is sometimes used to fuel research reactors, a nation can have legitimate reasons for obtaining quantities of this material, despite its usefulness in nuclear explosives. In recent years the United States and France have developed lower enriched uranium fuels that can be used in lieu of highly enriched material in most of these reactors, considerably reducing the proliferation risks posed by fuel from these research facilities.[5]

Several methods have been developed for enriching uranium. All ultimately rely on differentiating among the isotopes of uranium and isolating material with increased concentrations U^{235}. Two principal techniques are in use today: the gaseous diffusion method, in which uranium hexafluoride gas is forced through a selectively porous barrier, and the ultra-centrifuge or gas centrifuge method, in which uranium hexafluoride gas is swirled in a cylinder rotating at extremely high speeds. Electromagnetic isotope separation (EMIS) using uranium tetrachloride is an inefficient, but less complex method, that was abandoned in the 1950s. Iraq, however, unexpectedly revived this option in the 1980s as part of its nuclear weapons program. Considerable research and development has been conducted on two additional enrichment techniques, the chemical method and laser isotope separation, but neither is used in commercial production of enriched uranium or for weapons-manufacturing purposes.

Producing highly enriched uranium entails many steps apart from the enrichment process itself, and many other installations and capabilities are necessary. Nations wishing to obtain highly enriched uranium, without international restrictions prohibiting its use for nuclear explosives, would have to develop enrichment technology independently, or obtain it illegally, since virtually all nuclear exporter states are unwilling to sell nuclear equipment and materials unless recipients pledge not to use them for nuclear explosives and agree to place them under the inspection system of the International Atomic Energy Agency. (See Appendix C.)

For illustrative purposes, the basic nuclear resources and facilities that would be needed to produce weapons-grade uranium indigenously include:

- uranium deposits;
- a uranium mine;
- a uranium mill (for processing uranium ore usually containing less than 1 percent uranium into uranium oxide concentrate, or yellow-cake);
- a conversion plant (for purifying yellowcake and converting it into uranium hexafluoride (UF_6), or uranium tetrachloride (UCl_4) the material processed in the enrichment plant);
- an enrichment plant (for enriching the uranium hexafluoride gas or uranium tetrachloride in the isotope U^{235}); and
- a capability for converting the enriched uranium hexafluoride gas or uranium tetrachloride into solid uranium oxide or metal.[6]

Plutonium. To obtain plutonium a country needs a nuclear reactor. This can be one designed specifically to maximize plutonium production (a "production reactor"), a large research reactor, or a power reactor for producing electricity. Uranium fuel, usually in the form of uranium-filled tubes (fuel rods) made of zirconium alloy (zircaloy) or aluminum, is placed in the reactor. For most production and power reactors and many large research reactors, the fuel itself is either natural or low-enriched uranium, which is not usable for nuclear weapons at this point. As the reactor operates, the uranium fuel is partly transformed into plutonium. This is amalgamated in the fuel rods with unused uranium and highly radioactive waste products, however, and must then be extracted.

To do this, "spent" fuel rods are taken to a reprocessing plant where they are dissolved in nitric acid and the plutonium is separated from the solution in a series of chemical processing steps. Since the spent fuel rods are highly radioactive, heavy lead casks must be used to transport them. In addition, the rooms at the reprocessing plant where the chemical extraction of the plutonium occurs must have thick walls, lead shielding, and special ventilation to prevent radiation hazards.

Although detailed information about reprocessing was declassified by the United States and France in the 1950s and is generally available, it is still a complex procedure from an engineering point of view. Indeed, almost every nation that tried to develop nuclear-weapons via the plutonium route—

India, Iraq, Israel, and Pakistan—has sought outside help from the advanced nuclear-supplier countries, although North Korea apparently succeeded in constructing a reprocessing facility at Yongbyon without such foreign assistance.

Like enrichment facilities, however, reprocessing plants can also be used for legitimate civilian purposes, because plutonium can be used as fuel in nuclear power reactors. Indeed, through the 1970s it was generally assumed that as the use of nuclear power grew and worldwide uranium resources were depleted, plutonium extracted from spent fuel would have to be ''recycled'' as a substitute fuel in conventional power reactors.

In addition, research and development is under way in a number of nations on a new generation of reactors known as breeder reactors, most notably in France, Japan, and Russia. Breeder reactors use mixed plutonium-uranium fuel surrounded with a ''blanket'' of natural uranium; as the reactor operates, slightly more plutonium is created in the core and the blanket together than is consumed in the core, thereby ''breeding'' new fuel.

Like plutonium recycling, the economic advantages of breeders depends on natural uranium's becoming scarce and expensive. However, over the past two decades new uranium reserves have been discovered; nuclear power has reached only a fraction of its expected growth levels; and reprocessing spent fuel to extract plutonium (a critical step in the manufacture of plutonium-based fuels) has proven far more expensive and complex than anticipated. Moreover, concern over the proliferation risks of wide scale-use of plutonium as a fuel has grown. These factors led the United States in the late 1970s to abandon its plans to recycle plutonium in light-water reactors and, in the early 1980s, to abandon its breeder reactor development program. Germany has abandoned its breeder reactor program and is phasing out its recycling of plutonium. Great Britain, too, has frozen its development of breeder reactors, although it is continuing to reprocess spent fuel on a commercial basis for itself and several advanced nations.

The principal proponents of the use of plutonium for civilian purposes are France, Japan, and Russia, which are all continuing to develop the breeder reactor option and are moving forward with sizable plutonium recycling programs. Belgium and Switzerland, although they do not have breeder reactor programs, are using increasing amounts of recycled plutonium in light-water reactors. Broadly speaking, the proponents of nuclear energy in these countries have maintained support for the civil use of plutonium by arguing that, although it may not be economical, it represents an advanced technology that will pay off in the future and reduce dependence on foreign sources of energy.

A new factor that will affect the economics of civil plutonium use is that many hundreds of tons of low-enriched uranium produced by blending down weapons-grade uranium from dismantled Russian warheads will soon be added to the international power-reactor fuel market. This will keep prices of this material low and should reduce the attractiveness of high-cost plutonium fuel cycles.

Whatever the thrust of their domestic nuclear programs, the advanced nuclear-supplier countries are strongly discouraging plutonium's use by nations of proliferation concern.

The longstanding view that plutonium is a legitimate and anticipated part of civilian nuclear programs, however, has allowed India and North Korea to justify their reprocessing programs—even though such efforts provided these nations with a nuclear-weapons capability.

Like the production of enriched uranium, the production of plutonium entails many steps, and many installations and capabilities besides the reactor and reprocessing plant are needed. For illustrative purposes, the following facilities and resources would be required for an independent plutonium production capability assuming that a research or power reactor, moderated by either heavy-water or graphite, and employing natural uranium fuel, were used:

- uranium deposits;
- a uranium mine;
- a uranium mill (for processing uranium ore containing less than 1 percent uranium into uranium oxide concentrate, or yellowcake);
- a uranium purification plant (to further improve the yellowcake into reactor-grade uranium dioxide);
- a fuel fabrication plant (to manufacture the fuel elements placed in the reactor), including a capability to fabricate zircaloy or aluminum tubing;
- a research or power reactor moderated by heavy-water or graphite;
- a heavy-water production plant or a reactor-grade graphite production plant; and
- a reprocessing plant.

In contrast to heavy-water and graphite moderated reactors, which use natural uranium as fuel, a light-water moderated reactor would necessitate use of low-enriched uranium, implying that an enrichment capability may be available. If so, highly enriched uranium could, in theory, be produced, obviating the need for plutonium as a weapons material. (It is also possible that a state might import fuel for a light-water reactor under IAEA inspection and, after using the material to produce electricity, reprocess it to extract plutonium. Although IAEA rules would require the country involved to place any such plutonium under IAEA monitoring, the state might one day abrogate its IAEA obligations and seize that material for use in nuclear arms.)

Acquisition of Fissile Material from Abroad. Although, historically, every state that has developed nuclear weapons has also built an indigenous capability to produce fissile material for this purpose, the weakening of controls over such material in the former Soviet Union has increased the possibility of its becoming available on an international black market. As discussed in the body of this report in "Russia," during 1994, the smuggling of plutonium and weapons-usable enriched uranium, apparently of Russian origin, was observed for the first time. The widespread availability of clandestine supplies of weapons-usable nuclear materials could greatly accelerate the pace at which emerging nuclear powers could develop nuclear arms and could simultaneously undermine the inspection and auditing system of the International Atomic Energy Agency.

Testing

It is generally assumed that by rigorously testing the non-nuclear elements of a nuclear device and performing computer simulations, a state could build a reliable first-generation fission weapon without having to conduct a full-scale nuclear test.

The greatest confidence could be achieved with a uranium-based, gun-type weapon (plutonium cannot be used in this design). The United States, for example, was so confident that the gun-type Hiroshima bomb would work as designed that it did not need to conduct a test of the device before it was used against Japan. (The Trinity test was of the more complex implosion-type bomb, the type that was later used against Nagasaki). As noted above, South Africa employed the gun-type design and is not known to have conducted a nuclear test. Although a full-scale nuclear detonation may not be essential to develop a reliable nuclear weapon, of the three current de facto nuclear powers, India conducted such a test, while Israel and Pakistan received assistance from more advanced countries, which may be deemed the equivalent of such experimental proof of design.

Since Israel is thought to have "boosted" fission weapons but is not known to have conducted a nuclear test, building reliable versions of such weapons without testing appears possible. To build multi-stage hydrogen bombs, which are far more complex, nuclear testing would be required.

There has been speculation that an ambiguous signal detected on September 22, 1979, by a U.S. satellite overflying the South Atlantic may have been the flash from a nuclear test and, if the event was indeed a test, that it was conducted by Israel or South Africa. Uncertainties about the event have never been resolved, however, and, in addition to the five declared nuclear powers, India remains the only country that is known to have detonated a nuclear device.

Non-Nuclear Components, Assembly, Delivery

Finally, the manufacture of nuclear weapons requires the design and fabrication of: specially designed high-explosive components to compress the fissile-material core of the device; high-speed electronic firing circuits, or "triggering packages" to set off the high explosives uniformly at precisely the correct instant; and, in most designs, an "iniatior"—an intense source of neutrons to initiate the nuclear chain reaction in the core. Developing all of these components necessitates considerable technical skill and, though less demanding than producing fissile material, can nonetheless be quite challenging. Iraq's effort to develop these elements of nuclear weapons, for example, is known to have suffered considerable setbacks and had not succeeded prior to the 1991 Gulf War, despite several years of effort.

Assembly of the completed components of nuclear weapons and delivery by aircraft are relatively less demanding. To produce nuclear warheads for ballistic missiles, however, additional steps are necessary, such as the development of reentry vehicles, the miniaturization and/or reconfiguration of nuclear weapons to fit into missile nose cones, and certifying the weapons to withstand the rigors of blast-off, extremely high altitudes, and reentry.

Notes

[1] Thomas B. Cochran and Christopher E. Paine, *The Amount of Plutonium and Highly-Enriched Uranium Needed for Pure Fission Nuclear Weapons* (Washington, DC: Natural Resources Defense Council), August 22, 1994.

[2] Technically, a weapon could be made of uranium enriched to more than 20 percent. As a practical matter material enriched to more than 90 percent is preferred. The Hiroshima bomb used uranium enriched to 80-85 percent, however, and South Africa's first nuclear device used material enriched to 80 percent for the first device and 90 percent for the remaining 5 nuclear weapons.

[3] For details and the current status of these efforts, some of which have been terminated, see the individual country sections in the main body of this volume.

[4] Technically, low-enriched uranium is defined as uranium enriched to less than 20 percent in the isotope U^{235}. Such material cannot be used in the core of a nuclear device.

[5] Large research reactors can, however, be used to produce plutonium. See discussion below.

[6] The conversion of uranium hexafluoride into uranium oxide or metal is often associated with a yellowcake-to-hexafluoride conversion plant.

Appendix C
INTERNATIONAL ATOMIC ENERGY AGENCY (IAEA) SAFEGUARDS

The International Atomic Energy Agency (IAEA) is an independent UN-affiliated body, based in Vienna, with 122 member states. The Agency was founded in 1957 to promote the peaceful uses of nuclear energy and to administer a program of on-site inspections, audits, and inventory controls (collectively known as "safeguards") to ensure that nuclear materials subject to its oversight are not used for weapons. Today, the IAEA monitors more than 800 installations in more than 110 nations and is widely regarded as a principal bulwark against the spread of nuclear arms.

The IAEA has a 35-member Board of Governors, which meets five times a year and is the organization's main policy formulation organ. It reports to the General Conference of all members, which meets annually in September. The IAEA has a staff of more than 2,000. Hans Blix, the Director General (DG), was reappointed to his fourth four-year term in September 1993.[1]

The basic purpose of IAEA safeguards is to deter the diversion of nuclear materials from peaceful uses to military purposes through the risk of timely detection. In simplified terms, the Agency monitors the flow of nuclear materials at nuclear installations by auditing plant records and conducting physical inventories. Seals and cameras are used to ensure materials are not diverted while IAEA inspectors are not present.

In recent years the IAEA has had to cope with several challenges to its credibility, principally from Iraq and North Korea, both parties to the Nuclear Non-Proliferation Treaty (NPT). The Agency has also had to address a series of less controversial but nonetheless difficult challenges, including the verification of South Africa's elimination of its six-weapon nuclear arsenal, the establishment of comprehensive inspection regimes in Argentina and Brazil in cooperation with the Argentine-Brazil Accounting and Control Commission, and the conducting of special visits to Iran to examine a number of sites where it was alleged that undeclared nuclear activities were being conducted. Each of these efforts is described in detail in the body of this book in the sections dealing with each of these states. In addition, the Agency will soon undertake the difficult task of applying safeguards comprehensively in Belarus, Kazakhstan, and Ukraine.

Finance remains a problem for the Agency. In the late 1980s and early 1990s it endured a seven-year period of zero real growth in its budget. This was followed by the dissolution of the Soviet Union and Russia's subsequent inability to pay its contribution in 1991. This resulted in a 13 percent budget cut across the range of the Agency's activities in 1992. This state of affairs has coincided with a large increase in the number of facilities requiring safeguarding following the conclusion of new agreements. The amount of material under IAEA safeguards has more than doubled in the last ten years while there has been only a small increase in the number of inspectors. In 1993, the safeguards budget was increased by 0.8 percent (to $65 million), and another small increase was accepted for 1994. The overall IAEA budget for 1994 was approximately $200 million.

The IAEA is currently evaluating changes to the safeguards system to minimize costs and improve effectiveness. (As an example of the scale of the Agency's activities, approximately 2,000 inspections were made at roughly 500 installations during 1993.) This includes persuading national nuclear accounting bodies to provide more data than strictly required in safeguards agreements and to provide more practical help in the conduct of inspections. The possibility of using new environmental monitoring techniques to detect the presence of undeclared facilities is also being evaluated in the context of improving the Agency's effectiveness. In addition, consideration is being given to a reorientation of safeguards priorities to increase the level of inspections in areas of proliferation concern and reduce them in areas of lower concern, but political realities currently militate against the acceptance of such a move.

The current IAEA safeguards system has some well-recognized limitations that would not, however, be addressed by these proposed reforms. First, and most important, key installations in countries of proliferation concern, including a number of enrichment and reprocessing facilities, are not under the IAEA system. Thus, India, Israel, and Pakistan all remain free to use unsafeguarded installations to manufacture material for nuclear weapons. (In each of these countries, however, at least some installations are subject to the IAEA system, and nuclear materials produced in them cannot, therefore, be used for this purpose.) Nations that have ratified the Non-Proliferation Treaty (NPT) or for which the Treaty of Tlatelolco is in force have accepted safeguards on all their nuclear facilities.

Second, certain types of facilities, such as fuel fabrication, reprocessing, and enrichment installations, handle nuclear materials in bulk form, i.e., as powders, liquids, or gasses. Such materials are particularly difficult to safeguard, since measurement techniques are not accurate enough to keep track of 100 percent of these substances as they move through the facilities processing them. This makes it theoretically possible to divert a certain small percentage of material for military purposes without detection since this could appear to be a normal operating discrepancy. The problem is especially dangerous at fuel-fabrication plants handling plutonium or weapons-grade uranium in powdered form, at reprocessing plants where plutonium is dissolved in various liquids for processing, and at enrichment plants, which use uranium hexafluoride gas as feed. The NPT permits parties to produce weapons-usable materials provided that they are placed under IAEA monitoring.

Finally, even assuming that IAEA safeguards functioned perfectly, their usefulness may be limited when applied to weapons-grade uranium and plutonium, materials directly usable for nuclear arms. Here, even if the IAEA system reacted instantaneously to diversion, it might still be possible for the nation appropriating such materials to manufacture nuclear weapons within a matter of weeks if all the non-nuclear components had been prepared in advance, presenting the world community with a *fait accompli*. In such a setting, safeguards would not be able to provide "timely warning" sufficient to allow the international community to react before the nation diverting the material had achieved its objective.

For these reasons, the United States has worked actively to curtail commerce with nations of proliferation concern involving plutonium, highly enriched uranium, or enrichment and reprocessing facilities—whether or not safeguards would be applied. Virtually all other nuclear supplier nations have adopted the cautious approach of the United States in transfering such items.

It must be stressed, however, that even if safeguards as applied are imperfect, their deterrent value remains strong, since would-be diverters could not have confidence that their misuse of nuclear materials would go undetected or unpunished.

Indeed, in the event of a safeguards violation, the Agency's Board of Governors has the authority to notify the United Nations Security Council. UNSC members could then pass a resolution imposing economic, political, or military sanctions on the violator, as happened with Iraq in 1991 and almost occurred with North Korea in June 1994.

Notes

This Appendix is adapted from Ewen Buchanan, "The Non-Proliferation Regime" (Washington, DC: Carnegie Endowment for International Peace, unpublished consultant's report, 1994).

[1]For further details of the structure and work of the IAEA see "Against the Spread of Nuclear Weapons: IAEA Safeguards in the 1990s," (Vienna: IAEA Division of Public Information, December 1993).

Appendix D
NUCLEAR SUPPLIER ORGANIZATIONS:
The Non-Proliferation Treaty Exporters Committee and the Nuclear Suppliers Group

Non-Proliferation Treaty Exporters Committee (Zangger Committee)

(Note: The Nuclear Non-Proliferation Treaty (NPT) is discussed in detail on pp. 13–15 of this volume.)

Formation. Shortly after the Nuclear Non-Proliferation Treaty (NPT) came into force in 1970, a number of countries began consultations about the procedures and standards they would apply to nuclear fuel and equipment exports to non-nuclear-weapon states. These consultations were necessary to implement the NPT requirement that such exports and any enriched uranium or plutonium produced through their use be subject to International Atomic Energy Agency (IAEA) safeguards in the recipient state. The supplier countries engaged in those consultations, which were chaired by the Swiss expert, Claude Zangger, were parties to the Non-Proliferation Treaty (or have since become parties) and were also exporters or potential exporters of material and equipment for peaceful uses of nuclear energy.

In August 1974, the governments of Australia, Denmark, Canada, Finland, West Germany, the Netherlands, Norway, the Soviet Union, the United Kingdom, and the United States each informed the Director General of the IAEA, by individual letters, of their intentions to require IAEA safeguards on their nuclear exports in accordance with certain procedures described in memoranda enclosed with their letters. Those memoranda were identical and included a ''Trigger List'' of special nuclear materials (enriched uranium and plutonium) and items of equipment ''especially designed or prepared'' (EDP) for the production of these materials. The memoranda declared that these items would be exported only if the recipient agreed to place them under IAEA safeguards, agreed that they would be used only for peaceful purposes, and agreed not to retransfer such items unless under the same conditions. (The individual letters and the identical memoranda were published by the IAEA in September 1974 in document INFCIRC/209).[1]

Soon afterward, Austria, Czechoslovakia, East Germany, Ireland, Japan, Luxembourg, Poland, and Sweden sent individual letters to the Director General, referring to and enclosing memoranda identical to those transmitted by the initial groups of governments.

The agreed procedures and Trigger List represented the first major agreement on uniform regulation of nuclear exports by actual and potential nuclear suppliers. It had great significance for several reasons. It was an attempt to enforce strictly and uniformly the obligations of Article III, paragraph 2, of the Non-Proliferation Treaty requiring safeguards on nuclear exports. It was intended to reduce the likelihood that states would be tempted to cut corners on safeguards requirements because of competition in the sale of nuclear equipment and fuel-cycle services. In addition, and very important in light of subsequent events, it established the principle that nuclear-supplier nations should consult and agree among themselves on procedures to regulate the international market for nuclear materials and equipment in the interest of non-proliferation. Notably absent from the list of actual participants or potential suppliers, as from the list of parties to the Non-Proliferation Treaty, were France, India, and the People's Republic of China. (The current members of the Zangger Committee are listed below.)

Subsequent Developments. Due to advances in technology, the parameters of some of the items on the Zangger Committee trigger list (principally enrichment, reprocessing, and heavy water production equipment) were subject to substantial clarifications and upgrades during the 1980s. (The Zangger Committee has also been responsible for almost all of the clarification and upgrade work later taken up by the Nuclear Suppliers Group). Prompted by the discovery that Iraq was pursuing a number of enrichment technologies, the important changes agreed by the Zangger Committee in 1993 have added new forms of enrichment technology to the trigger list (including electro-magnetic isotope separation (EMIS) and chemical or ion exchange techniques) not previously covered in the enrichment category.

Changes to the trigger list are adopted into controls on a national basis; implementation dates for member states can therefore vary depending on the bureaucratic measures required by each member. Unlike the NSG, the Zangger Committee has controls only on EDP items; it does not control dual-use equipment or technology, nor does it call on participants to exercise particular restraint in the supply of equipment to nuclear facilities deemed sensitive (i.e., reprocessing and enrichment facilities). Nor do the Zangger Committee guidelines require comprehensive IAEA safeguards as a condition of supply; single facility arrangements are sufficient.

The Zangger Committee meets in Vienna twice a year (usually May and October with the former being considered the main Plenary meeting). The Committee is currently chaired by Fritz Schmidt (Austria) who has long been associated with the work of the Zangger Committee. The United Kingdom provides Secretariat services. The Committee's detailed deliberations are kept confidential, as are the criteria for membership and attendance at policy-making meetings (although NPT adherence, adoption of the Committee's guidelines, and adherence to "non-proliferation" norms are among the requirements for membership).

With the 1992 agreement to harmonize the specifications of the items and equipment on the Zangger trigger list with those of the NSG (see below), some have questioned the relevance of the Committee. Member governments recognize some duplication of effort and the overlap with the NSG. But the different memberships and the fact that the Committee is a child of the NPT, mean that none are (yet) willing to suggest that the group be disbanded and its work be folded into the NSG.

As of March 1995, the members of the Zangger Committee were : Australia, Austria, Belgium, Bulgaria, Canada, the Czech Republic, Denmark, France, Finland, Germany, Greece, Hungary, Ireland, Italy, Japan, Luxembourg, Netherlands, Norway, Poland, Portugal, Romania, Russia, Slovakia, South Africa, Spain, Sweden, Switzerland, United Kingdom, and the United States. Argentina was expected to become a member of the Zangger Committee in the near future.

The Nuclear Suppliers Group (NSG)

Formation. In November 1974, within a year of the delivery of the Zangger Committee memoranda to the IAEA, a second series of supplier negotiations was initiated. This round, convened largely at the initiative of the United States, was a response to three developments: (1) the Indian nuclear test of May 1974, (2) mounting evidence that the pricing actions of the Organization of Oil Exporting Countries were stimulating Third World and other non-nuclear states to initiate or accelerate their nuclear power programs, and (3) recent contracts or continuing negotiations on the part of France and West Germany for the supply of enrichment or reprocessing facilities to Third World states, facilities that could provide access to weapons-usable fissile material.

The initial participants in these discussions, conducted in London, were Canada, the Federal Republic of Germany, France, Japan, the Soviet Union, the United Kingdom, and the United States. One of the group's chief accomplishments was to induce France to join in such efforts, since France (which had not joined the Non-Proliferation Treaty or the Zangger Committee) could have undercut reforms of nuclear supply. The French, hesitant about becoming involved and uncertain as to where the effort might lead, insisted that any meetings be kept confidential—which was also the preference of some other participants. Thus the meetings in London were held in secret. It soon became known, however, that such meetings were taking place, and this led to suspicion and exaggerated fears of what they were about. The group was inaccurately referred to as a "cartel." Instead, one of its purposes was to foster genuine commercial competition based on quality and prices, untainted by bargaining away of proliferation controls.

Two major controversies arose in the series of meetings that led to a new agreement in late 1975. The first concerned whether, and under what conditions, technology and equipment for enrichment and reprocessing, the most sensitive parts of the nuclear fuel cycle from a weapons proliferation perspective, should be transfered to non-nuclear states. The United States, with support from several other participants, was reported to argue in favor of both a prohibition on such transfer and a commitment to reprocessing in multinational facilities (rather than in installations under the control of individual states). France had already signed contracts to sell reprocessing plants to Pakistan and South Korea, and West Germany had agreed to sell technology and facilities for the full fuel cycle (including enrichment and reprocessing) to Brazil. They successfully resisted the prohibition proposed by others.

The second controversy that emerged during the formation of the Nuclear Suppliers Group concerned whether transfers should be made to states unwilling to submit all of their nuclear facilities to IAEA safeguards, or whether such "full-scope" safeguards should be made a condition of all sales. The NSG came close to reaching consensus on requiring full-scope safeguards in recipient countries as a condition of future supply commitments but was unable to persuade the French and the West Germans, although they did not rule out later reconsideration of the issue and possible changes by unanimous consent. At the time, Argentina, Brazil, India, Israel, Pakistan, and South Africa would have been barred from receiving NSG-controlled exports if the full-scope safeguards rule had been adopted, since each of these developing countries possessed or was developing nuclear installations not subject to IAEA monitoring. While not making full-scope safeguards a condition of nuclear supply, the NSG did act to expand safeguards coverage by adopting a "Trigger List" of nuclear exports, similar to that of the Zangger Committee, that would be permitted only if they were, themselves, covered by IAEA safeguards in the recipient state.

On January 27, 1976, the seven participants in the negotiations exchanged letters endorsing a uniform code for conducting international nuclear sales. The major provisions of the agreement require that before nuclear materials, equipment, or technology are transfered the recipient state must:

(1) Pledge not to use the transfered materials, equipment, or technology in the manufacture of nuclear explosives of any kind;

(2) Accept, with no provision for termination, international safeguards on all transfered materials and facilities employing transfered equipment or technology, including any enrichment, reprocessing, or heavy-water production facility that replicates or otherwise employs transfered technology;

(3) Provide adequate physical security for transfered nuclear facilities and materials to prevent theft and sabotage;

(4) Agree not to retransfer the materials, equipment, or technology to third countries unless they, too, accepted the constraints on use, replication, security, and transfer, and unless the original supplier nation concurred in the transactions;

(5) Employ "restraint" regarding the possible export of "sensitive" items (relating to uranium enrichment, spent fuel reprocessing, and heavy-water production); and

(6) Encourage the concept of multilateral (in lieu of national) regional facilities for reprocessing and enrichment.[2]

The industrialized states of Eastern Europe soon joined the NSG, so that it included virtually all of the advanced supplier countries.

The Nuclear Suppliers Guidelines extended the Zangger Committee's requirements in several respects. First, France (which had not participated in the Zangger group) agreed to key points adopted by that Committee, such as the requirement that nuclear export recipients pledge not to use transfered items for nuclear explosives of any kind and that safeguards on transfered items would continue indefinitely. Second, the Suppliers Group went beyond the Non-Proliferation Treaty and the Zang-

ger Committee requirements by imposing safeguards not only on the export of nuclear materials and equipment but also on nuclear technology exports. India had demonstrated the existence of this serious loophole by building its own unsafeguarded replica of a safeguarded power reactor imported from Canada. The Suppliers Group was unable to reach agreement on the application of this reform to reactor technology, however, and so confined its recommended application to "sensitive" facilities—i.e., reprocessing, enrichment, and heavy-water production plants built with the use of exported technology. The group's acceptance of this limited reform was facilitated by the fact that such a condition was incorporated by West Germany in its safeguards agreements for sale of enrichment and reprocessing facilities to Brazil and by France in its safeguards agreements covering their proposed sales of reprocessing plants to the Republic of Korea and Pakistan. (France subsequently canceled both contracts.)

Third, the Suppliers Guidelines, while not prohibiting the export of these sensitive facilities, embodied the participants' agreement to "exercise restraint" in transfering them. Wherever transfers of enrichment plants are involved, the participants agreed to seek recipient-country commitments that such facilities will be designed and operated to produce only low-enriched uranium, not suitable for weapons.

Subsequent Developments. The Nuclear Suppliers Group was largely dormant during the 1980s in terms of new policy making. In March 1991, however, in the wake of the 1991 Gulf War, the group convened after a ten-year hiatus in The Hague and decided to adopt the clarified and upgraded specifications on the Zangger Committee trigger list. The exercise, which became known as "harmonization," was completed in 1992. During 1993, the NSG added another category to its trigger list, uranium conversion plants and equipment, items that are not covered by the Zangger Committee, which has a more limited scope.

At the urging of the United States, the NSG Plenary meeting in Warsaw in March/April of 1992 took a major step and agreed that as a condition of supply, all members would insist that all contracts of EDP trigger list items drawn up after April 1992 would require recipient states to agree to full-scope safeguards on all of their nuclear facilities and any future facilities. (Previously, some NSG members, including the United States, had required full-scope safeguards as a condition of supply but the definition of what was covered and the effective date of this requirement were not uniform). Member states adopted this new full-scope safeguards requirement into national legislation during the first half of 1993. The new updated guidelines reflecting the changes were issued by the IAEA in July 1993.[3] In 1993 the NSG also agreed to add to its trigger list additional equipment used in new forms of enrichment that had been worked out in the Zangger Committee. The Group set a target date of March 1, 1993, for the implementation of these new category controls.

In a new departure for the NSG, the Hague meeting of March 1991 also agreed on the need to expand controls to cover dual-use items that have legitimate non-nuclear uses. (The original NSG and Zangger Committee rules apply only to ''nuclear-unique'' equipment and material). The working group established by NSG met under U.S. stewardship in Brussels in June 1991, Annapolis in October 1991, and Interlaken in January 1992 and produced agreement on a list of sixty-five dual-use items with detailed definitions and a series of guidelines on conditions of transfer. These were formally endorsed by the full Plenary meeting of the Group in Warsaw in April 1992. The NSG members set a target implementation date of the end of 1992 for the Part 2 Guidelines, but administrative and national legislative delays have prevented some members from meeting it.

The dual-use Guidelines (known as INFCIRC/254/Rev.1/Part 2 and published by the IAEA in July 1992) require exporting states not to ship items on the list if they are for use in non-nuclear-weapon states for unsafeguarded nuclear fuel cycle facilities or in nuclear explosive activity: in other words, for facilities such as enrichment or reprocessing plants not subject to IAEA monitoring or for other activities that can aid in the production of nuclear explosives. In addition, the dual-use Guidelines require states not to transfer items on the list ''when there is an unacceptable risk of diversion to such an activity, or when the transfers are contrary to the objective of averting the proliferation of nuclear weapons.'' Suppliers must obtain a statement from the recipient as to the use to which the item will be put and as to its location, as well as an assurance that it will not be put to proscribed uses and that no retransfer will take place without the consent of the supplier. Decisions on whether a transfer should proceed are also to be guided by additional criteria, such as the recipient's non-proliferation credentials. Although decisions on whether to grant export licenses are left to national discretion, there is a system of consultation among members to ensure uniformity in the implementation of the dual-use Guidelines and to guard against commercial disadvantage to a particular state if it denies a transfer request. Members are also encouraged to consult and exchange information on proliferation developments that might be relevant to licensing decisions.[4]

The Japanese (through their mission in Vienna) have taken on the role of administrative secretariat (Point of Contact) for the trigger list ''Part 2'' dual-use mechanism. They are responsible for the circulation of denial notices, documents, and information to members as well as for arranging meetings. The United States has proposed the establishment of a computer network between member states and the point of contact to speed up the communication process. This is still under consideration.

Any state can adhere to either part of the NSG Guidelines by notifying the IAEA that it has adopted the necessary legislation to control items on the NSG lists. This does not, however, confer immediate membership in the Group or the right to attend its policy-making meetings. There are no strict criteria for membership, but potential members must satisfy the existing membership that they have the proper credentials. These include a commitment to other non-proliferation norms (e.g., through membership in other agreements, such as the NPT and the Chemical Weapons Convention), the adoption of the necessary legislation to bring the NSG controls into national law, and effective enforcement capabilities. Membership decisions are taken by consensus. The chairmanship of the group rotates. Spain currently holds the position, which will be transferred to Finland when the group meets in Helsinki in 1995.

As of March 1995, the thirty members of the NSG were : Argentina, Australia, Austria, Belgium, Bulgaria, Canada, the Czech Republic, Denmark, France, Finland, Germany, Greece, Hungary, Ireland, Italy, Japan, Luxembourg, Netherlands, New Zealand, Norway, Poland, Portugal, Romania, Russia, Slovakia, Spain, Sweden, Switzerland, the United Kingdom, and the United States. South Africa was expected to become a member in the near future.

As of March 1995, Belarus, China, Kazakhstan, South Korea, Taiwan, and Ukraine were not yet members of either of the nuclear supplier groups, although South Korea was expected to join the NSG.[5]

Notes

This Appendix is adapted from Charles N. Van Doren, "Nuclear Supply and Non-Proliferation: The IAEA Committee on Assurances of Supply," A Report for the Congressional Research Service (Rep. No. 83-202-8), October 1983, pp. 61–64; and Ewen Buchanan, "The Non-Proliferation Regime" (Washington, DC: Carnegie Endowment for International Peace unpublished consultant's report, March 1994).

[1] INFCIRC is the IAEA shorthand for the series of Information Circulars distributed to IAEA members.

[2] See INFCIRC/254.

[3] See INFCIRC/254/Rev.1/Part 1.

[4] For further details of the development of the dual-use arrangement and the adoption of full scope safeguards as a condition of supply, see Carlton E. Thorne, "The Nuclear Suppliers Group: A Major Success Story Gone Unnoticed," *Directors Series on Proliferation* (Lawrence Livermore Laboratory), January 5, 1994, p .29.

[5] "Government Plans on Participating in NSG," Seoul, *Maeil Kyongje Sinmun*, March 8, 1995, in *FBIS-EAS-95-045*, March 8, 1995, p. 30.

Additional References

1979: U.S. Congress, Office of Technology Assessment, *Nuclear Proliferation and Safeguards* (Washington, DC: OTA, 1977), pp. 220–21; U.S. Department of State, "Report to the Congress Pursuant to Section 601 of the Nuclear Non-Proliferation Act of 1978" (January 1979), pp. 25–27. **1993:** U.S. Congress, Office of Technology Assessment, *Proliferation of Weapons of Mass Destruction: Assessing the Risks* (Washington, DC.: Government Printing Office, August 1993), pp. 85, 88; Zachary S. Davis, "Non-Proliferation Regimes: Policies to Control the Spread of Nuclear, Chemical and Biological Weapons and Missiles" (Washington, DC: Library of Congress, Congressional Research Service), February 8, 1993. **1994**: Gary T. Gardner, *Nuclear Nonproliferation: A Primer* (Boulder CO: Lynne Rienner Publishers, 1994), p. 58. **1994, 1995:** Roland Timerbaev and Lisa Moskowitz, *Inventory of International Nonproliferation Organizations and Regimes* (Monterey, CA: Monterey Institute of International Studies, 1994, 1995).

Appendix E
THE MISSILE TECHNOLOGY CONTROL REGIME

The Missile Technology Control Regime (MTCR) was established in April 1987 by Canada, France, the Federal Republic of Germany, Italy, Japan, the United Kingdom, and United States to reduce the risk of nuclear proliferation by placing controls on equipment that could contribute to the development of unmanned nuclear-weapons delivery systems, including cruise and ballistic missiles. It is an informal arrangement (not a treaty), with no enforcement or compliance mechanism.

The aim of the regime (later amended) was to prevent the spread of missiles capable of delivering a basic nuclear warhead (assumed to weigh about 500 kg) to a range of 300 km or more. The original members of the regime also agreed that in seeking to control missile technology, their actions would not impede legitimate space programs. This provision later led to significant disputes within the regime on the supply of space launch technology to India and Brazil.

The original members acknowledged that the regime would, at best, only slow missile development programs in countries of concern. But the growing effectiveness of the regime has been evidenced from statements by countries that have been its targets. Officials of both Brazil and India, for example, have stated that the MTCR controls have seriously hampered their space launch vehicle programs[1]. Argentina's decision to scrap its Condor missile can also, in part, be attributed to the MTCR.

Under the original MTCR Guidelines, member states agree to require export licenses for a list of systems, equipment, and technology relevant to the development of 500 kg/300 km-capable missiles. The list of items (the "Equipment and Technology Annex") is divided into two categories according to the importance of particular items for missile development. The more significant items (Category I) include complete missile systems, major subsystems, rocket engines, guidance systems, and missile production facilities. Smaller components, machinery, and equipment, such as electronics and other dual-use items, comprise the second list (Category II).

The Guidelines apply to all destinations and set out basic criteria to help judge whether a transfer should go ahead. Beyond that, however, the regime's members have agreed to a strong presumption of denial for exports of items in Category I of the Annex. Members who wish to transfer such items must consult other regime partners before doing so, although the final decision on whether to go ahead with the transfer remains a national prerogative; thus no member possesses the right to veto an export by another. The transfer of complete missile production facilities is prohibited. The items in Category II may be exported only after receipt of "end-use" assurances from the recipient, as well assurances against re-transfer to third countries or entities. Transfers between regime members are permitted but are also subject to license and end-use assurances (except within the European Union).

Membership

All states are encouraged to adopt and observe the policy guidelines of the regime, but full membership (including attendance at the policy-making Plenary meetings, information exchanges on programs of concern, and involvement in the future direction of the Regime) remains at the discretion of the current membership. Several states listed below have declared their adherence to the Guidelines but are not full MTCR members.

The original seven members sought at first to involve only "like-minded" states that were also significant producers of missiles or components. Nonetheless, the MTCR was soon expanded to include countries that produced little in the missile technology field but shared the same non-proliferation goals as the original seven and wanted to avoid the risk that, in the absence of MTCR-style export controls, they might be used as intermediate transshipment points by states seeking to purchase missile technology by circumventing the Regime's controls.

The Regime has no formal membership criteria, and decisions on new members are made case by case. In practice, however, aspirants must adopt what have been termed "non-proliferation norms." This includes, adherence to other non-proliferation instruments and the adoption of effective export controls on the full list of items in the Annex. In some cases, applicants for membership in the Regime may also be required to renounce any existing ballistic missile program or ambitions. In addition, potential members are required to demonstrate a credible record of export control enforcement. The Regime members have undertaken a series of outreach seminars to explain the basic aims of the MTCR, encourage wider adherence to its Guidelines, and promote the adoption of credible controls to reduce the risk of missile proliferation.

Prior to the 1993 MTCR Plenary meeting, membership was limited to Western states, but at this session the group agreed to admit Argentina and Hungary. Argentina's membership was a new departure for the Regime as hitherto the Condor missile program had been one of its main targets. Argentina's undertakings to halt the Condor program and destroy or render harmless components and production facilities resulted in its membership being approved. The group has also taken steps to encourage full membership by Brazil, Russia, the Republic of Korea, South Africa, Turkey, and Ukraine. Russia restated its intention to join during President Bill Clinton's visit to Moscow in January 1994.[2]

By March 1995 the members of the MTCR were: Argentina, Australia, Austria, Belgium, Canada, Denmark, Finland, France, Germany, Greece, Hungary, Iceland, Ireland, Italy, Japan, Luxembourg, the Netherlands, New Zealand, Norway, Portugal, Spain, Sweden, Switzerland, the United Kingdom, and the United States. Brazil, the Czech Republic, Israel, Romania, South Africa, and Ukraine control missile exports according to the current standards of the MTCR and are considered to be unilateral adherents to the regime. China controls missile exports according to the original MTCR standards. (The distinction between the old and new MTCR rules is described below.)

Meetings

Plenary policy-making meetings are held roughly every nine months, the most recent having been held in Sweden, in October 1994. The sessions operate by consensus. Meetings of technical experts from the member countries who administer the regulations on a national basis (mainly export licensing officials) take place semi-annually. These meetings (known as TEMs) discuss problems arising from technical specifications and examine ways to establish conformity in the interpretation and implementation of the Guidelines. They are directed by the Plenary meeting of all MTCR members and report to it.

As membership has grown, the Regime has had to establish a central point of contact for administrative and procedural issues. This function is provided by France, with representatives from the Paris embassies of the member countries meeting about every six weeks.

Update of Guidelines and Annex

The first revision of the Annex took place in November 1991 and added two new items to the existing list of sixteen. The revision also included new, more detailed, definitions of some equipment and further defined technical parameters. At the sixth Plenary meeting in Oslo in June/July of 1992, the membership agreed on the desirability of expanding the terms of the Guidelines to include all missiles intended to carry weapons of mass destruction (WMD) to a range of 300 km. This was done so that the Regime would be able to control missiles capable of carrying smaller WMD payloads, such as chemical or biological weapons (CBW). This resulted in the creation of two new items in the Annex. By January 7, 1993, all MTCR members had adopted the revised Guidelines into their national export control policies.[3] Further revisions of the Annex are likely as the result of new technological developments.[4]

Missile Export Sanctions Legislation

In 1990 the U.S. Congress enacted legislation to enable the administration to punish U.S. and foreign entities that trade in MTCR equipment and technology that can contribute to the production of Category I missiles in a non-MTCR member. The legislation, which was contained in the National Defense Authorization Act for Fiscal Year 1991, amended the Arms Export Control Act and the Export Administration Act, to add the new missile-related restrictions.[5] In the case of companies in the United States and other MTCR member states, the sanctions are applied only if a transfer is illegal and takes place without the required export license. In the case of companies or entities in non-MTCR member states, the sanctions are imposed regardless of whether the transfer violated any national controls.[6] The United States is the only MTCR member with such sanctions provisions in its national law.

The extent of the sanctions to be imposed on both seller and buyer is determined by the nature and sensitivity of the items transferred. For transfers involving items in Category I of the Technical Annex (complete missiles and major sub-systems), the sanctions are a minimum two-year ban on access to *any* equipment that requires a U.S. dual-use or munitions list export license. The entity is also banned from competing for *any* U.S. government business or procurement contract for the same term. For transfers of Category II items (less sensitive components and dual-use items) the sanctions are a two-year ban on U.S. export license approvals for *all MTCR Annex items* and denial of the right to bid for U.S. government procurement contracts for *MTCR Annex items*. (The law provides waivers of these sanctions if the entity in question is a sole supplier of an item needed for U.S. defense purposes.)

If the Administration determines that a particular transfer has "substantially" contributed to a missile program, the additional sanction of a two-year U.S. import ban on all products produced by that company may be imposed.

The Helms Amendment (part of the FY 1992–93 Foreign Relations Authorization Act) added a provision for countries with non-market economies (principally China and North Korea) to ensure that not only government trading entities would be affected but that wider sectors of the economy would be injured by any missile-export sanctions that the United States might impose. It broadens the sanctions so that they apply to all government activities relating to missile equipment and technology and to all activities of the sanctioned government in the development or production of electronics, space systems or equipment, and military aircraft. (Thus a ban on U.S. export licenses, for example, would apply not only to a particular trading company but to all agencies of the government at issue that were engaged in aerospace activities.)

In the case of companies and in countries that are regime members, sanctions are invoked only if the transfers are illegal and the foreign government is not thought to be taking strong enough action against the offending company. States that are not full members of the MTCR can be exempted from the sanctions and treated as adherents of the Regime if they have entered into a bilateral understanding with the United States which recognizes that they control MTCR equipment and technology in accordance with the criteria and standards of the Regime. Russia, South Africa, Ukraine, and apparently Israel have entered into such agreements.

Russia obtained MTCR-adherent status for the purposes of U.S. law in July 1993 following agreement to limit the sale of rocket technology to India and an undertaking to enforce the MTCR provisions by November of that year. Israel is believed to have obtained similar status, but the agreement has not been made public.

Despite its stated adherence to the MTCR Guidelines, China has been the subject of U.S. missile sanctions because of its transfers of M-11 missile components to Pakistan. Entities in India, Iran, North Korea, Pakistan, Russia, South Africa, and Syria have also been sanctioned under the legislation. The sanctions imposed on South Africa pre-date its adherence to the Guidelines. Sanctions on Russian and (some) Chinese entities have been lifted in response to measures they have taken to adopt the Guidelines or halt contracts that breach their provisions.

Catch-All Provisions

The U.S. Enhanced Proliferation Control Initiative (EPCI), promulgated by the Bush Administration in the form of a series of Executive Orders in August of 1991, included new provisions designed to make U.S. exporters look more carefully at the proliferation risk associated with overseas orders for missile items and components. Potential exporters are now required to seek an export license if they have reason to know or are informed by the U.S. government that their export is destined for certain missile projects in countries of concern. The regions/countries named in the regulations are the Middle East, Brazil, India, South Africa, North Korea, Pakistan, China, and Iran. Companies are advised to scrutinize potential orders carefully and to take steps themselves to verify that their products are not likely to be used in targeted missile programs. Companies are encouraged to seek expert government advice and advisory opinions in cases where there are doubts. In addition to the United States, a number of other members of the MTCR have adopted similar controls.

Notes

[1]U.S. Arms Control and Disarmament Agency, Office of Public Affairs, ''Report Submitted to Congress by the President Pursuant to Section 1704 of the National Defense Authorization Act for FY 1991,'' October 2, 1991.

[2]See ''Joint Statement by Presidents Clinton and Yeltsin on Non-Proliferation,'' ACDA Office of Public Information Fact Sheet, January 14, 1994.

[3]The text of the revised MTCR Guidelines is set out in ''The Missile Technology Control Regime,'' ACDA Fact Sheet, May 17 1993.

[4]For a fuller account of MTCR developments, see Deborah A. Ozga ''A Chronology of the Missile Technology Control Regime,'' *The Nonproliferation Review*, Winter 1994, p. 66.

[5]See Arms Export Control Act, Chapter 7, and Export Administration Act, Section 11B.

[6]In other words, the exporter in such cases is subject to sanctions if the export transgresses the MTCR Guidelines, even if the exporter has a valid export license from its national government. The theory behind this stricture is that if the government involved is not prepared to discipline the exporter, the United States will.

Additional References

1994: Ewen Buchanan, ''The Nuclear Non-Proliferation Regime'' (Washington, DC: Carnegie Endowment for International Peace, unpublished consultant's report, March 1994). **1995**: Interviews with U.S. officials, February 1995.

Appendix F
GLOSSARY

atomic bomb A bomb whose energy comes from the fission of uranium or plutonium.

beryllium A highly toxic steel-gray metal, possessing a low neutron absorption cross-section and high melting point, which can be used in nuclear reactors as a moderator, reflector, or cladding material. In nuclear weapons, beryllium surrounds the fissile material and reflects neutrons back into the nuclear reaction, considerably reducing the amount of fissile material required. Beryllium is also used in guidance systems and other parts for aircraft, missiles or space vehicles.

blanket A layer of fertile material, such as uranium-238 or thorium-232, placed around the core of a reactor. During operation of the reactor, additional fissionable material is produced in the blanket.

breeder reactor A nuclear reactor that produces somewhat more fissile material than it consumes. The fissile material is produced both in the reactor's core and when neutrons are captured in fertile material placed around the core (blanket). This process is known as breeding. Breeder reactors have not yet reached commercialization, although active research and development programs are being pursued by a number of countries.

CANDU (Canadian deuterium-uranium reactor.) The most widely used type of heavy-water reactor. The CANDU reactor uses natural uranium as a fuel and heavy water as a moderator and a coolant.

centrifuge See ultracentrifuge.

chain reaction The continuing process of nuclear fissioning in which the neutrons released from a fission trigger at least one other nuclear fission. In a nuclear weapon, an extremely rapid, multiplying chain reaction causes the explosive release of energy. In a reactor, the pace of the chain reaction is controlled to produce heat (in a power reactor) or large quantities of neutrons (in a research or production reactor).

chemical processing Chemical treatment of materials to separate specific usable constituents.

coolant A substance circulated through a nuclear reactor to remove or transfer heat. The most common coolants are water and heavy water.

core The central portion of a nuclear reactor containing the fuel elements and, usually, the moderator.

Also the central portion of nuclear weapon containing highly enriched uranium or plutonium.

critical mass The minimum amount of fissionable material required to sustain a chain reaction. The exact mass varies with many factors such as the particular fissionable isotope present, its concentration and chemical form, the geometrical arrangement of the material, and its density. When fissionable materials are compressed by high explosives in implosion-type atomic weapons, the critical mass needed for a nuclear explosion is reduced.

depleted uranium Uranium having a smaller percentage of uranium-235 than the 0.7 percent found in natural uranium. It is a by-product of the uranium enrichment process, during which uranium-235 is culled from one batch of uranium, thereby depleting it, and then added to another batch to increase its concentration of uranium-235.

enrichment The process of increasing the concentration of one isotope of a given element (in the case of uranium, increasing the concentration of uranium-235).

feed stock Material introduced into a facility for processing.

fertile material Material composed of atoms which readily absorb neutrons to produce fissionable materials. One such element is uranium-238, which becomes plutonium-239 after it absorbs a neutron. Fertile material alone cannot sustain a chain reaction.

fission The process by which a neutron strikes a nucleus and splits it into fragments. During the process of nuclear fission, several neutrons are emitted at high speed, and heat and radiation are released.

fissile material Material composed of atoms which readily fission when struck by a neutron. Uranium-235 and plutonium-239 are examples of fissile materials.

fusion The formation of a heavier nucleus from two lighter ones (such as hydrogen isotopes), with the attendant release of energy (as in a hydrogen bomb).

gas centrifuge process A method of isotope separation in which heavy gaseous atoms or molecules are separated from light ones by centrifugal force. See ultracentrifuge.

gaseous diffusion A method of isotope separation based on the fact that gas atoms or molecules with different masses will diffuse through a porous barrier (or membrane) at different rates. The method is used to separate uranium-235 from uranium-238. It requires large gaseous diffusion plants and significant amounts of electric power.

gas-graphite reactor A nuclear reactor in which a gas is the coolant and graphite is the moderator.

heavy water Water containing significantly more than the natural proportion (1 in 6,500) of heavy hydrogen (deuterium) atoms to ordinary hydrogen atoms. (Hydrogen atoms have one proton, deuterium atoms have one proton and one neutron.) Heavy water is used as a moderator in some reactors because it slows down neutrons effectively and does not absorb them (unlike light, or normal, water) making it possible to fission natural uranium and sustain a chain reaction.

heavy-water reactor A reactor that uses heavy water as its moderator and natural uranium as fuel. See CANDU.

highly enriched uranium Uranium in which the percentage of uranium-235 nuclei has been increased from the natural level of 0.7 percent to some level greater than 20 percent, usually around 90 percent.

hot cells Lead-shielded rooms with remote handling equipment for examining and processing radioactive materials. In particular, hot cells are used for reprocessing spent reactor fuel.

hydrogen bomb A nuclear weapon that derives its energy largely from fusion. Also known as a thermonuclear bomb.

kilogram (kg) A metric weight equivalent to 2.2 pounds.

kiloton (Kt) The energy of a nuclear explosion that is equivalent to an explosion of 1,000 tons of TNT.

laser enrichment method A still experimental process of uranium enrichment in which a finely tuned, high-power carbon dioxide laser is used to differentially excite molecules of various atomic weights. This differential excitation makes it possible to separate uranium-235 from uranium-238.

light water Ordinary water (H_2O), as distinguished from heavy water (D_2O).

light-water reactor A reactor that uses ordinary water as moderator and coolant and low-enriched uranium as fuel.

low-enriched uranium Uranium in which the percentage of uranium-235 nuclei has been increased from the natural level of 0.7 percent to less than 20

percent, usually 3 to 6 percent. With the increased level of fissile material, low-enriched uranium can sustain a chain reaction when immersed in lightwater and is used as fuel in lightwater reactors.

medium-enriched uranium Uranium in which the percentage of uranium-235 nuclei has been increased from the natural level of 0.7 percent to between 20 and 50 percent. (Potentially usable for nuclear weapons, but very large quantities are needed.)

megawatt (Mw) One million watts. Used in reference to a nuclear power plant, one million watts of electricity (Mwe); used in reference to a research or production reactor, one million watts of thermal energy (MWt).

metric tonne One thousand kg. A metric weight equivalent to 2,200 pounds or 1.1 tons.

milling A process in the uranium fuel cycle by which ore containing only a very small percentage of uranium oxide (U_3O_8) is converted into material containing a high percentage (80 percent) of U_3O_8, often referred to as yellowcake.

moderator A component (usually water, heavy water, or graphite) of some nuclear reactors that slows neutrons, thereby increasing their chances of fissioning fertile material.

natural uranium Uranium as found in nature, containing 0.7 percent of uranium-235, 99.3 percent of uranium-238, and a trace of uranium-234.

neutron An uncharged elementary particle, with a mass slightly greater than that of a proton, found in the nucleus of every atom heavier than hydrogen.

nuclear energy The energy liberated by a nuclear reaction (fission or fusion) or by spontaneous radioactivity.

nuclear fuel Basic chain-reacting material, including both fissile and fertile materials. Commonly used nuclear fuels are natural uranium, and low-enriched uranium; high-enriched uranium and plutonium are used in some reactors.

nuclear fuel cycle The set of chemical and physical operations needed to prepare nuclear material for use in reactors and to dispose of or recycle the material after its removal from the reactor. Existing fuel cycles begin with uranium as the natural resource and create plutonium as a by-product. Some future fuel cycles may rely on thorium and produce the fissionable isotope uranium-233.

nuclear fuel element A rod, tube, plate, or other mechanical shape or form into which nuclear fuel is fabricated for use in a reactor.

nuclear fuel fabrication plant A facility where the nuclear material (e.g., enriched or natural uranium) is fabricated into fuel elements to be inserted into a reactor.

nuclear power plant Any device or assembly that converts nuclear energy into useful power. In a nuclear electric power plant, heat produced by a reactor is used to produce steam to drive a turbine that in turn drives an electricity generator.

nuclear reactor A mechanism fueled by fissionable materials that give off neutrons, thereby inducing heat. Reactors are of three general types: power reactors, production reactors, and research reactors.

nuclear waste The radioactive by-products formed by fission and other nuclear processes in a reactor. Most nuclear waste is initially contained spent fuel. If this material is reprocessed, new categories of waste result.

nuclear weapons A collective term for atomic bombs and hydrogen bombs. Weapons based on a nuclear explosion. Generally used throughout the text to mean atomic bombs, only, unless used with reference to nuclear-weapon states, (all five of which have both atomic and hydrogen weapons).

plutonium-239 (Pu^{239}) A fissile isotope occurring naturally in only minute quantities, which is manufactured artificially when uranium-238, through irradiation, captures an extra neutron. It is one of the two materials that have been used for the core of nuclear weapons, the other being highly enriched uranium.

plutonium-240 (Pu^{240}) A fissile isotope produced in reactors when a plutonium-239 atom absorbs a neutron instead of fissioning. Its presence complicates the construction of nuclear explosives because of its high rate of spontaneous fission.

power reactor A reactor designed to produce electricity as distinguished from reactors used primarily for research or for producing radiation or fissionable materials.

production reactor A reactor designed primarily for large-scale production of plutonium-239 by neutron irradiation of uranium-238.

radioactivity The spontaneous disintegration of an unstable atomic nucleus, resulting in the emission of subatomic particles.

radioisotope A radioactive isotope.

recycle To reuse the remaining uranium and plutonium found in spent fuel after they have been separated at a reprocessing plant from unwanted radioactive waste products also in the spent fuel.

reprocessing Chemical treatment of spent reactor fuel to separate the plutonium and uranium from the unwanted radioactive waste by-products and (under present plans) from each other.

research reactor A reactor primarily designed to supply neutrons for experimental purposes. It may also be used for training, materials testing, and production of radioisotopes.

spent fuel Fuel elements that have been removed from the reactor after use because they contain too little fissile and fertile material and too high a concentration of unwanted radioactive by-products to sustain reactor operation. Spent fuel is both thermally and radioactively hot.

thermonuclear bomb A hydrogen bomb.

thorium-232 A fertile material.

tritium The heaviest hydrogen isotope, containing one proton and two neutrons in the nucleus, produced most effectively by bombarding lithium-6 with neutrons. In a fission weapon, tritium produces excess neutrons, which set off additional reactions in the weapon's fissile material. In this way, tritium can either reduce the amount of fissile material required, or multiply (i.e., boost) the weapon's destructive power as much as five times. In fusion reactions, tritium and deuterium, another hydrogen isotope, bond at very high temperatures, releasing approximately 14 million electron-volts of energy per set of neutrons.

ultracentrifuge A rotating vessel that can be used for enrichment of uranium. The heavier isotopes of uranium hexafluoride gas concentrate at the walls of the rotating centrifuge and are drawn off.

uranium A radioactive element with the atomic number 92 and, as found in natural ores, an average atomic weight of 238. The two principal natural isotopes are uranium-235 (0.7 percent of natural uranium), which is fissionable, and uranium-238 (99.3 percent of natural uranium), which is fertile.

uranium-233 (U^{233}) A fissionable isotope bred in fertile thorium-232. Like plutonium-239 it is theoretically an excellent material for nuclear weapons, but is not known to have been used for this purpose. Can be used as reactor fuel.

uranium-235 (U^{235}) The only naturally occurring fissionable isotope. Natural uranium contains 0.7 percent U^{235}; light-water reactors use about 3 percent and weapons grade, highly enriched uranium normally consists of 93 percent of this isotope.

uranium-238 (U^{238}) A fertile material. Natural uranium is composed of approximately 99.3 percent U^{238}.

uranium dioxide (UO₂) Purified uranium. The form of natural uranium used in heavy water reactors. Also the form of uranium that remains after the fluorine is removed from enriched uranium hexafluoride (UF_6). Produced as a powder, uranium dioxide is, in turn, fabricated into fuel elements.

uranium oxide (U₃O₈) The most common oxide of uranium found in typical ores. U_3O_8 is extracted from the ore during the milling process. The ore typically contains only 0.1 percent U_3O_8; yellowcake, the product of the milling process, contains about 80 percent U_3O_8.

uranium hexafluoride (UF₆) A volatile compound of uranium and fluorine. UF_6 is a solid at atmospheric pressure and room temperature, but can be transformed into gas by heating. UF_6 gas (alone, or in combination with hydrogen or helium) is the feed stock in all uranium enrichment processes and is sometimes produced as an intermediate product in the process of purifying yellowcake to produce uranium oxide.

vessel The part of a reactor that contains the nuclear fuel.

weapons-grade Nuclear material of the type most suitable for nuclear weapons, i.e., uranium enriched to 93 percent U^{235} or plutonium that is primarily Pu^{239}.

weapons-usable Fissionable material that is weapons-grade or, though less than ideal for weapons, can still be used to make a nuclear explosive.

yellowcake A concentrate produced during the milling process that contains about 80 percent uranium oxide (U_3O_8). In preparation for uranium enrichment, the yellowcake is converted to uranium hexafluoride gas (UF_6). In the preparation of natural uranium reactor fuel, yellowcake is processed into purified uranium dioxide. Sometimes uranium hexafluoride is produced as an intermediate step in the purification process.

yield The total energy released in a nuclear explosion. It is usually expressed in equivalent tons of TNT (the quantity of TNT required to produce a corresponding amount of energy).

zirconium A grayish-white lustrous metal which is commonly used in an alloy form (i.e., zircaloy) to encase fuel rods in nuclear reactors.

References

1979: Anthony V. Nero, Jr., *A Guidebook to Nuclear Reactors* (Berkeley: University of California Press, 1979). **1984:** Thomas B.Cochran, William Arkin, Robert S. Norris, and Milton Hoenig, *Nuclear Weapons Databook, Volume 2: U.S. Nuclear Warhead Production* (Cambridge, MA: Ballinger Publishing Co, 1984); *Nuclear Power in an Age of Uncertainty* (Washington, DC: Office of Technology Assessment, 1984). **1993:** U.S. Congress, Office of Technology Assessment. *Technologies Underlying Weapons of Mass Destruction* (Washington, D.C.: U.S. Government Printing Office, December 1993); David Albright, Frans Berkhout, and William Walker, *World Inventory of Plutonium and Highly Enriched Uranium, 1992* (Oxford, England: Oxford University Press, 1993).

CARNEGIE ENDOWMENT FOR INTERNATIONAL PEACE

The Carnegie Endowment for International Peace was established in 1910 in Washington, D.C., with a gift from Andrew Carnegie. As a tax-exempt operating (not grant-making) foundation, the Endowment conducts programs of research, discussion, publication, and education in international affairs and U.S. foreign policy. The Endowment publishes the quarterly magazine, *Foreign Policy*. It also publishes policy studies written by its associates and from time to time issues reports of commissions or study groups convened under its auspices.

Carnegie's Senior and resident associates—whose backgrounds include government, journalism, law, academia, and public affairs—bring to their work substantial first-hand experience in foreign policy through writing, public and media appearances, study groups, and conferences. Carnegie associates seek to invigorate and extend both expert and public discussion on a wide range of international issues, including worldwide migration, non-proliferation, regional conflicts, multilateralism, democracy-building, and the use of force. The Endowment also engages in and encourages projects designed to foster innovative contributions in international affairs.

In 1993, the Carnegie Endowment opened the Center for Russian and Eurasian Studies in Moscow. Through joint projects on issues of common interest, Carnegie associates and researchers at the Moscow Center are working with Washington-based Carnegie associates to enrich intellectual and policy debate in the United States as well as in Russia and other post-Soviet states.

The Endowment normally does not take institutional positions on public policy issues. It supports its activities principally from its own resources, supplemented by nongovernmental, philanthropic grants.

About the Authors and Contributors

Tracking Nuclear Proliferation: A Guide in Maps and Charts, 1995, was prepared by the Nuclear Non-Proliferation Project of the Carnegie Endowment for International Peace.

The report was produced under the direction of Leonard S. Spector, the Director of the Nuclear Non-Proliferation Project. A specialist on the spread of nuclear weapons for more than fifteen years and the author of five books on the subject, Mr. Spector served as a Special Counsel at the U.S. Nuclear Regulatory Commission and as Chief Counsel of the Senate Energy and Nuclear Proliferation Subcommittee before joining the Carnegie Endowment in 1984.

Mark G. McDonough was Senior Managing Editor of *Tracking Nuclear Proliferation*. He prepared substantial portions of the report and managed the research and drafting of the manuscript. A consultant to the Nuclear Non-Proliferation Project, Mr. McDonough has worked on defense and proliferation issues since the mid-1980s, providing support to the U.S. Departments of Energy and Defense and contributing to numerous publications.

Evan S. Medeiros, Project Associate with the Nuclear Non-Proliferation Project, has been with the Endowment since mid-1993. He prepared the report's sections on China, Algeria, Libya, and South Africa and made significant contributions in the research, editing, and preparation of materials for other sections.

Tessie Topol, a Carnegie Junior Fellow during the latter half of 1994, assisted in the preparation of the charts for the former Soviet Union and other segments of the report.

Noah Sachs, a Carnegie Junior Fellow during the first half of 1994, drafted the initial versions of the Russia charts and map and contributed to the preparation of the Belarus, Kazakhstan, and Ukraine maps.

The global proliferation map, the maps of Non-Proliferation Treaty members, and the maps for the traditional states of proliferation concern were drawn by Brad Wye.

The maps for Belarus, China, Kazakhstan, Russia, Ukraine, and Romania were drawn by David Merrill.

Carnegie Endowment for International Peace
2400 N Street, N.W.
Washington, D.C. 20037
Tel.: (202) 862-7900
Fax: (202) 862-2610